CREATION: ITS HISTORY, EXPLOSIVE EVOLUTION, AND ET ARRIVALS ON EARTH

Book Three

Earth's Future With ETs, Physical Evolution, Dimensions, Metaphysical Awareness, Understanding Spirit, Developing Your Metabilities and How They Flow Through You

Jay Arae Essex

The future timeline for all the events you're about to read here, as well as those mentioned in the rest of my books, is dependent upon Arae having returned home to the Other Side early enough to set up the introduction between ourselves here on Earth and our ET friends in a matter most comfortable for everyone.

Today is May 28th of 2018 and he should have returned already. He's the only one capable of changing Creation's format and creating these events. They will happen quickly after his return.

The timeline presented in this book will begin upon the death of the Jay Essex body, freeing Arae from his prison.

Cover photo: Unusual Spiral Galaxy M66 from Hubble (April 10, 2010). Credit NASA, ESA, Hubble Heritage, S. Van Dyk (JPL/IPAC), R. Chandar (u. Toledo), D. DeMartin & R. Gendler.

NASA does not promote or endorse or appear to promote or endorse a commercial product, Service, or activity.

Copyright ©2018 Jay Essex

All rights reserved.

The Creation Series

Book III

The Future of Earth and Creation as Everything Evolves, ETs Now On Earth, Earth's New Alliance, The Alliance of Planets, New Physical Evolution Methods, How Your Metabilities Work, Your True Physical and Metaphysical Realities, Learning How to Become Your True Self

Dedication

This book is dedicated to every single being who has the desire within them to explore not only themselves, but all else around them. Creation is now awakening to the full realization of who they are, not only separately but as a family of sentient energy, called Spirit, released from the same first Sentient Being there ever was. We started with great turmoil but are now about to settle down to live in softer cleaner waters. First we were created and abused but now we become ourselves as a family. The problem children are now being removed.

The changing of Creation's format, one that has existed for over 2,857,000,000,000,000 years (2.857 Quadrillion Earth years), is not an easy thing, especially while stuck in a body. While stuck in a physical body, Arac has done the following things.

- Removed the Source energy partition between the right and left sides of all brains allowing better communication within yourself

- Used the internet (over 1100 videos) and physical travel to help others awaken to who they actually were, their abilities, and available tools to help them achieve their awareness.

- Removed and Deleted the Original First Being Halves, their servants the Original Angels, the two other controlling pairs of Source Spirit, and all other aggressive Spirit beings opposing the removal of Creation's abusive format.

- Used his Source energy, through the physical body he was placed inside, to change people forever; increasing their awareness, power level, and what they now were.

- Increased the power level of other Source Spirits already here in body, so they could begin awakening and empowering others not just now but more importantly after he left.

- Removed the Earthen Planetary Essence beings inside you, allowing easier control of your body while giving them their freedom.

- Created the new Alliances and Councils so all Spirit, both in and out of body, had a place to meet and work together.

- Developed physical aids and tools to enhance your awakening should you want them. He created stone spheres which increase and develop your abilities, even while you sleep.

- Created a communication guide to allow easier communication and better relationships between you and your guides; J'Arae's Runes of Awakening.

- He exposed the simple lies of religions and governments as well as who ran the Earth on Spiritual and physical levels.

- He wrote the Creation Series so you would finally have access to the truth of who you are and where you came from, as well as Creation's history.

- This is the last book and it's futuristic timeline has been contaminated by the Other Side by keeping Arae in his body too long. These major events can't begin until Arae returns home to the Other Side.

- This and more was done while fighting with problematic Spirits trying to protect himself and others, all day every day.

- The primary Lilly has refused to release Arae from his body as necessary so he has made other changes himself. This body is too sick to continue much longer. I can't make any more changes to this book.

This 3rd volume of the Creation Series is about understanding metaphysical awareness, physical evolution, ETs, dimensions, Spirit, energy, and much more. Google doesn't have this information. Only you do now. Neither did our friends in space until I wrote it here. The Metaphysical Realm, that part of our true reality, is much larger than our physical one. The Physical Realm is literally only found in this the 3rd Dimension. Well, let's get to it.

The more I write, the more I connect to the Source Field part of myself. As I do, a tsunami of information flows through my mind increasing the volume of this book. It also provides added depth to this information. I'm a little hurried as I'm running out of time here and have so much to do back home, on the Other Side. At the time of writing this book there are over 550 videos on the Jay Essex YouTube channel filled with valuable information. In the last 6 years I've created over 1,100 videos.

My intent has been to offer as much free information as possible for everyone. I leave here with the introduction of a new YouTube channel, The Spiritual Foundation. It has all the products you need to take proper care of yourself, awaken your abilities, talk with your Spirit Guides and ETs once you're familiar with telepathy, and even evolve your Human DNA. This is detailed near the end of this book, as well as how to feel energy, talk with Spirit, stones, and more.

This volume has information you won't find there or anywhere else, but don't exclude the videos from being an important source of information to help you understand the world around you, especially the full extent of who you are and how to awaken all of your natural abilities. The videos also contain material that can't be found elsewhere.

This initial copy of Creation Book III is written in my own words. It was professionally edited but, although they gave us some good information, they took away from the actual meaning of the words. No one can understand this information at first glance unless they've been listening to me for a while and can see certain things for themselves. Diana will produce a smoother, more digestible copy later. I have to release this book so I can drop this body to get back home where I belong. I've a lot of work to do. You will find a few writing errors here. They all belong to me, no one else.

My books are difficult to read at first due to the way my physical mind tries to handle my thought processes as well as the extensive use of capitalization. I understand more than I am able to explain using the physical intelligence we have in our brains. I have no words for expressing certain understandings.

Many people with ADD and other mental frustrations can understand this, but the Source Field is a part of me extending outward almost everywhere continually feeding me data I can't always shut out. I only seem like my mind is drifting everywhere because it is, I'm everywhere seeing and feeling more than I can process. I'm anxious to be free again, free from this.

I capitalize certain words out of respect to individual Spirit beings and groups. I capitalize Plants, Human, Animal, Fae, Faeman, Star, Planet, Universe, Solar System, Stone names, and more as you'll find further in this book. There are now 6 fields of Essence; Plant, Human, Animal, Fae, Faeman, and Universal. My intent is also to bring to your intention that they are all people, sentient beings. We are a huge family.

If we capitalize the name of a Human named Bob, why do we not capitalize a very important type of being, Spirit? Spirit is what we all are inside. It comes from a minimum of 5 different energy fields that mutate together to create sentient life. Is that not as important as the name of one being? A Planet is the physical body of a female Universal Essence being. Shouldn't that be capitalized too? How about Plants, Animals and the rest?

In the very beginning, before my Spirit-Mate Lilly and I had the first lives, we were put together by the Original First Being for explicit purposes. We were to serve them. Lilly was a powerful loving mother type Spirit while I was made to protect them and all they built. Lilly was to go into body and develop into herself and I was to grow much larger and stronger to protect them better. When one of the new First Beings was ready to come out of the 1st Dimension (where they are created out of happenstance) they would take me away from the physical life process to stay with them, protecting them from then on.

This is why all the different forms of Spirit are so important to me. I was made to protect them. When you are a protector you develop differently than most others, not better, just differently. When you protect a group of beings you set your mind to the fact that all of them must be protected. They are all equally important to protect.

As you protect others something unique happens, as long as you have heart energy. You begin to care about them as you develop compassion. Over time they begin to mean more to you and your heart energy develops love. They develop the same feelings as you consistently take care of them, as long as they have sufficient amounts of heart energy also.

As you continue to protect them your fortitude and feelings become a sense of honor. They also begin to develop something called faith. They develop the feeling that they can count on you to be there for them. Any time an event has the characteristic of being continuous; the feeling that it will most likely be maintained develops. Unfortunately I've almost always had to do this while in a body. My previous life I was in the body of Gandhi. Eight years later, July 27, 1955 in Long Island, N.Y. at 4:37 pm, I was born into this one.

I write to you through the physical body which was given the name of John David Essex after my final adoption at 10 months old. It's not the body that's talking to you right now. All of us are Spirit beings locked inside these physical bodies. If you look at yourself in the mirror you're seeing yourself in a body. Now take a moment to look into your eyes. That's you. It can hit you a little hard depending on your mood, but that's the real you. I'm the original protector Arae placed in this physical body.

All the information I've left you is about who you are, the environment you live in, what has happened as well as what's about to happen, and what I am. As time flows you will see things change as I have described. I want you to understand there is something very strong to protect and serve you, wanting nothing for itself. The more you can understand about me, the more you can understand what's going to insure your freedom and protection. You will find this for yourselves soon enough. You will all know this as fact once you're home again.

I can see frequencies very easily as I was created with that in mind. If you are to protect something you must be able to identify all threats immediately. I can look anywhere and tell you who and what is inside any individual, their Spiritual make-up, negative frequency percentage, personality characteristics, what they're doing, and more. I have continuously declared that I am no better than a stick in mud because it's true.

We are all equal and have equal rights. If you exist, you're equal to all else that does. I speak my peace; it's what I'm here for. I never knowingly lie but have shown publicly that I can be as incorrect about little things as everyone else. I'm not a politician running for office. I'm a being of strong honor doing my job which is taking care of others. They don't have to like me. I just have to keep going.

I follow my programming as best as I can. That gives me what little satisfaction I have, trying to take care of everything. Don't bother trying to tell me what to do; it's a waste of time. I know what I'm doing. While having lives we access data. This data is mixed in the hypothalamus gland with the help of heart energy to become understanding.

Your wisdom is the collection of understandings you've gathered. Most of us have had from hundreds of thousands to even a trillion lives. Lilly has had almost 9 trillion and I've had over 10.846 trillion. We understand having lives and processing its relative data. We're your oldest sister and brother. We want nothing for ourselves other than fulfilling our format, helping and protecting everything. In this book as my others, I use the word "I" to describe something I did through this body. There are other times that I mention something I did as Arae, my true self when not in, or flowing out of a body. I'm being as accurate as I can but it can be a little confusing at times.

I have left behind a physical trail of having made money and then doing the best I could to distribute it to others, especially Animals. I have gone without food and spent all the money I had on veterinarian bills. Animals need it the most so that's where I focused most of my attention. That only changed recently to prepare to leave here. I had to finish my Creation Series and prepare things for Diana to continue what I started here. I can't describe the extent of my feelings for her. She's an incredible woman and the mother of our 48 children. How did that happen? An awesome Serpoian lady named Serenae, Serpacieant lady named Mellae, and the Archobien among others. It's mentioned briefly later on.

I cover a broad range of topics in my books, videos, and lectures. When you see the individual frequencies of all energy, you understand more about whom and what everything is. This makes it easier to attempt explaining to others who they really are, what they can do, how it happens, and what's around them. This includes our family or friends in space, the ETs. Diana and I have close ET friends coming in and out of the house all the time. Many other people have visits but Diana and I receive a lot of attention because of our children.

Your lives in body as well as your life as Spirit are about to change dramatically. Creation is on the verge of a chrysalis, becoming what it should have been in the beginning. As individuals and family we will learn how to move forward. We're about to do this with our ET friends as well. The initial first being that we all came from is gone. Things are beginning to change in our physical lives but have already dramatically changed in the 2nd Dimension where we live as Spirit. The age of abuse is almost over. It's about to finish on the Other Side and will then happen here.

For years I have described the issues with attempting divination, also known as prophecy. Yet now, here I am writing a book relative to exactly that, or is it? I give very few dates and they are extremely vague, as they should be. However, these events will occur. The thing is that they will happen as they need to when it is most proper for everyone involved, all of Creation not just a select few. I'm not much of a writer, only an author as this is the fourth and last book I will personally write. My thought process is everywhere, literally, and doesn't flow like most others. This book is an easier read than my others though, hope so anyway.

Books I and II of this "Creation Series" were initially copyrighted in 2015. This book gives a brief summary of the first two books, then describes what has happened from 2015 to early 2018, and finally flows into its original intention, Creation's future. You cannot understand all that's offered here without understanding the information of the first two books of the Creation Series, Books I and II. An understanding of all the players on the field, who they are, what they are, and what they've done is necessary before grasping the full meaning of all that has already happened, is happening now, and will soon become. This answers all the questions of "Why?" relative to this life as well as all your others.

A note from a friend

I met Jay and knew him closely. I saw his constant fighting in this realm, going against the current to help everyone he could to appreciate themselves and understand themselves better; to think better of themselves, to gain trust in what can't be seen until you learn how to, and for that he was the best teacher and eye opener for so many.

Jay was the kindest and most generous person I came across but also the strongest willed and most adamant. Jay is a tank with a heart. He not only proved his metaphysical abilities but those of others as well.

I also saw his constant fight related to what he calls "the other side". He shared as much as he could about everything going on. But he also kept a lot of information to himself as it was no one's concern or worry. There is more to what he did that we will know but always for the wellbeing of all. He never wanted medals but a job done.

Jay's life has been anything but easy, and once you learn about him you will understand how it could not be possible for it to be. But not to the extent it really was.

Jay also always spoke up for Animals. Rescued them and gave them care, love, a home, and respect. He emphasized their compassionate nature, and strength, and value.

Once in a hospital bed paralyzed and not being able to see properly, the doctor's biggest concern was if there would be any permanent damage. Will he walk on his own again? Will he be able to see normally again? There was no way to tell at the time. I *was very worried and his words were in a cheerful tone "don't worry sweetie, Jay always has a plan". That is Jay.*

He had to submit himself to the scrutiny of a board of psychiatrists; taking the chance they would lock him up for one year, to prove he was sane and competent. They released him in a few days without putting him on medication or future visits.

Then, once released he went up against another board of psychiatrists. In the first few minutes the triage psychiatrist told him she could feel his energy.

He did this to prove what he was saying and teaching was authentic, not a delusion.

Anonymous

Acknowledgements

I want to take this space to thank at least some of the people who have helped me complete this book. I need to thank Diana Ramirez Anaya not only for her valuable help in proof-reading but being such a large part of the end of this last life, making this book possible. This is without mentioning being the mother to so many new children about to lead the 3rd Dimension along its new path to Compassion, Honor, and Equality. She and I have 48 children thanks to ET technology and our close ET friends.

I want to thank all the Source Animals and many other people on the Other Side for having hung in there with me while I went along my tasks this very last physical life. This includes Gaia and Gaeira among all the others. They have helped me keep going as I endured what I had to.

I also thank Serenae the Serpoian, Mellae the Serpacieant, and many others for their invaluable work in creating these new children who will appear in about 7 years to help everyone move forward. Without their work this never could have happened.

I want to thank the Drachk (my immediate family), N'Antids, and everyone else who have freed the Earth from its over aggressive controllers the last 10.25 million years. This extends into everyone who has had the strength to build the New Alliance of Planets which will move all of us in this 3rd Dimension to a wonderful new place.

Now I need to thank so many wonderful people, among them the Alurean, Serpoian, Archobien, and all the rest who have come here to Earth to help us heal our Planetary Mother's body back to where it needs to be as well as removing world hunger, disease, and all the other issues about to be dissolved.

The last thing here is all the others that I cannot list here due to time and space confinements. Everyone has given so much wanting absolutely nothing in return. I thank all of you from the full depth of my heart. Try to understand what all of you mean to me. That's all I've ever wanted, for you to know how much you mean to me. You are literally my reason for having been made.

Introduction

When I first began writing the "Creation Series" I was already well underway in my awakening, as much as one can be while stuck in a body. I was also at war with the power players on the Other Side. It's a form of metaphysical warfare yet continually affects all the bodies and mass here. I have proven my metaphysical abilities, as much as can be over a short period, through the QEEG tests done on people's brains across long distances. Tests were made on people before and while I went into their brains. This was done on expensive medical equipment and would be extremely difficult to manufacture.

I can't telekinetically move a round pencil but I've going into others around the world cranking up their Metabilities, power level, DNA. Metabilities are simply your metaphysical abilities. I can affect out of body Spirit in a more aggressive fashion. All of you are incredibly huge Spirit beings. You're not yet aware of what you can do, who you really are. You're not a body. You're a Spirit within one.

I was never here to promote myself, only fulfill my necessary functions. I guess it's easy enough for someone to consider me arrogant at first. That thought is not in my mind much as I understand better but after listening to me for a while and digesting my message, they usually begin to realize what I'm doing. I'm easy to understand as time goes by. I call myself Creation's Janitor for good reason, I am.

I've been going into people's minds and bodies for almost ten years now. It's Dec. 10, 2017 today. I've been growing stronger from all the fighting and struggling as well as using my abilities to perform the tasks at hand. I'm almost done now. Awakening is a flowing process, not turning on a switch. This applies to all of us, I'm no different. We increase our understanding of things everywhere while in and out of body.

   As my personal collection of understandings (wisdom) grows and the fighting diminishes, I'm able to calm down, almost relax a little. This makes writing this last book easier than the others. So much more has happened in the last two years, so much more is coming. The Creation Series Book I and II were originally published in 2015. It is now the end of 2017. That's why although they were first copyrighted and published in 2015, I made small changes making them easier to read. This happened in 2017 so it has a new copyright added. I also added a little more info, originally available in 2015 which I neglected to include. A lot has happened in the last two years. Wait till you see what's coming.

   Compassion and Honor are now replacing the original format of Abuse laid out by the Original First Being Halves. Our Universal family members are about to say hello physically, the Fae are about to make physical bodies from energy in front of us about 2084, along with more changes than can't be imagined right now. I'll put all I can into this final volume as I attempt to describe how things will change for everyone in all dimensions.

   Creation has a new direction now, allowing all within it to exist equally in a peaceful environment promoting harmony and growth in a natural manner. You have to see through dimensional barriers before you can understand all of this. You need to see this for yourselves in order to fully comprehend it, just like everything else. We all develop our own personal truths which grow and evolve as we do.

This isn't just about change in your current lives and those that follow but becoming your true selves, Sentient Energy free of any physical embodiment. This is important as you're now slowly realizing you're encapsulated within a physical body, struggling to go through life. There will also be great changes in your natural lives as free Spirit. You've never been allowed to see what was going on in the 2nd Dimension while in a body. Seeing and being fed images is not the same as seeing "live time" for yourself.

You are intelligent, powerful, self-aware energy. We were all released from the Original First Being as Spirit, already sentient, and eventually became the individuals we are today without having to go through the original process of achieving sentiency as the Original First Being. We are now on a new path free of the needs and wants of our First One.

As we awaken to our full selves we'll be able to see the other dimensions as they also change with us. This is a new concept in Creation's history. It's never existed anywhere before. No one in body has ever been able to see these other dimensions, especially the 2nd Dimension, where we live when not confined to a physical body. So, this is your future, forever changing into what it will become, forever guided, changed, and properly massaged to move forward in everyone's best safe interest. We will now grow naturally in relation to our own personal frequencies instead of being forced into submission and abusive lives.

There are many beings from other planets here now. I call them people as they are, and they're here to help us. Some have been on Earth over 10 million years, the N'Antids. There are also the very first ones, now in Spirit bodies, who have been here well over 11 million years. They've always been here with us. I talk with a lot of the different folks here, Diana and I both. Diana owns The Spiritual

Foundation and all related to it. She's carrying this mission statement forward, as well as others.

These people from other planets as well as other local dimensions are constantly in and out of my house. They've been helping Diana and I physically for a while now. They're also tending to our many children who have been brought to life through their efforts and our DNA. I'll describe some of the major players, what names they've given me, what they will do for us, how they do what they can, and what they're like. They've come here to help, not harm. Serenae, Mellae, and others are also involved in helping Creation move forward through assisting in the creation of a new group of beings with Earthen DNA, the children of Arae.

Anyway, these folks here from other solar systems will help heal the Planet, our bodies, and lives. We're about to take our place in the Universal Community as who we are, the people of Earth. We're becoming who we already are. Creation will heal and become itself, not exist as a tool to appease someone else's desires. We are free independent family members with the same origin, the Original First Being.

We consider the beginning of time having started at that exact moment when Spirit Beings were first in a physical form to experience a cycle of existence upon the physical mass we call Planets. I capitalize the word Planet as it's the body given to Female Universal Essence Spirit to live in. Animals, Humans, Fae, Plant, and other Spirit as well as their bodies receive the same respect from me.

Having come from a time before our "known" time, I remember things as they happened, how they slowly developed into the situation we're now in, a free state of spiritual awakening. In your natural state, that of Spirit or Sentient Energy, you can easily see two weeks ahead and two weeks behind as we now perceive one day to be. This is our normal state when not subjected to being inserted within these bodies. You will soon be having lives in energy bodies, much like those of the Fae. We're going to take a good look at that later in this book.

Being in a physical body severely limits your metaphysical abilities; imprisoning you within a solid mass suppressing your personal frequencies, denying access to much less than one percent of your knowledge as well as your natural abilities. As you begin to awaken your natural metaphysical abilities, you gain access to more of your true self, learning how to reach out of your physical body and flow in the "Source Field", gaining all the help you're able to use while still imprisoned in solid matter.

Creation's reformatting creates positive change everywhere. The 2nd Dimension, where we live while not in physical bodies, runs our 3rd Dimension enabling them to enhance our lives here through less abuse and having lives more relative to our own personal frequencies. Those who are "natural" explorers will explore, healers heal, etc. Before long, those of you out of body will run the lives of those in body thereby controlling your own destinies in body. You have never done that. You will never have full control over your personal lives while in a body, yet be able to manipulate it to a much larger degree.

The removal of the Planetary Essence Beings, originally from Gaia, is now in progress and will be finished on or before Jan. 22, 2018. They're the other half of the Kundalini in most Earthen bodies. Fish, Reptiles, Insects, and some others only have a single Spirit inside the body. Being the sole Spirit within a body helps you live a life of less doubt and confusion. This way there's only one driver. We'll discuss that more, later in this book.

We'll also discuss in detail later, the more powerful physical beings from the beginning of solid body lives, the Drachk and N'Antids. They came here with others to free us, and they have. With us, among many others, are the Alurean, Andromedian, Pleiadian, Serpoian, Serpacient, Subt'raelean, and normal Annunaki, not the problematic ones that stayed here to control us, making our lives miserable. These are just a few of the many folk here helping us now.

There are a few "problem children" here such as the Enaugk, Draco, Mantid, and others including the remnants of the problematic Annunaki now removed from power. The removal of the Earthen Ruling Annunaki is a major event in Earth's history. We'll cover this later also.

While we're at it we can't forget about the New First Beings who are getting ready to come out of the First Dimension. This First Dimension is hidden from everyone and locked up. Nothing can go in or out of it now. These new First Beings will not need to separate themselves into male and female halves for company as they didn't become sentient alone, we're already here. They have company. They won't suffer like the Original First Being that we're from.

There are also the 1,672 new Universes here in the Third Dimension and your new lives in them inside the new Energy Bodies about to be created. You will finally have lives that are directly relative to the sum of your frequencies, which is who you really are. Many changes are already in progress and they're barely the beginning of what's to come.

Table of Contents

Dedication iii

A note from a friend xiv

Acknowledgements xvi

Introduction xviii

The History and Future Physical Structuring of Earth, the Universe, and Creation　　1

Physical Developments

Section I: How Creation Began　　2

Chapter 1 – Where Did We Come From, How Did it all Start 2

Chapter 2 – The Creation of Male and Female 5

Chapter 3 – The Initial Reasoning for Creation's Birth 7

Section II: How Creation Grew　　9

Chapter 1 – How Was Our Creation Made in the Beginning 9

Chapter 2 – How Was Creation to Function, be Controlled 13

Chapter 3 – How Did All These Beings Grow Together..............17

Chapter 4 – Who are You, this Thing Called a Body 19

Section III: Physical Abuse Development in the Third Dimension　　26

Chapter 1 – Gaeira and the First Physical Lives in Creation.......26

Chapter 2 – The Entrance of Animal, Fae, and Human Essences in Physical Bodies 31

Chapter 3 – The Destruction of Gaeira's Body, Planet Gaeira....34

Chapter 4 – The First Souls and the First Universe........................35

Chapter 5 – Enter the New Souls 37

Chapter 6 – Wars and Strife Throughout Space 40

Section IV: Creation's Takeover — 44

Chapter 1 – What Happened to Require Change in Creation's Format 44

Chapter 2 – The Necessary Process to Reformat Creation.........51

Section V: The Earth's Ruling Annunaki Families — 53

Chapter 1 – Who are the Annunaki 53

Chapter 2 – How Did the Annunaki Here Take Over 80

Section VI: The New Universal Alliance (10-18-2016) — 85

Chapter 1 – The Alliance Members Here to Help Us 85

Chapter 2 – The New Universal Alliance is Created 99

Chapter 3 – The Universal Alliance Destroys the Federation...110

Section VII: Drachk and N'Antids Free the Earth — 112

Chapter 1 – Who are the Drachk and the N'Antids 112

Chapter 2 – The Drachk and N'Antids' Earth Blockade 114

Chapter 3 – Removing the Problematic Annunaki Control of Earth 118

Chapter 4 – Policing Our Solar System 134

Section VIII: Earthen Alliance Creation (4-15-2018)   136

Chapter 1 – Newly Freed Earthen ETs Create Earth's First Alliance 136

Chapter 2 – The First Souls from the First Universe Join the Alliance of Planets..138

Chapter 3 – The Other Side Joins the Alliance of Planets Creating the Alliance of Life...139

Chapter 4 – The Pacific Tectonic Plate Splits, Creating the new North and South Pacific Plates.............................140

Section IX: Pre-Reformatting Issues Expected   141

Chapter 1 – The Chaos Incurred from the Original One's Removal 141

Chapter 2 – Creation Settles Down into its New Path 146

Section X: Format Change   148

Chapter 1 – What is the New Format 148

Chapter 2 – How and Where Does it Begin................................153

Section XI: Earth's Governments Are Flipped   163

Chapter 1 – Our Governments Become Of The People............163

Chapter 2 – Militaries Change But Maintain Independence....168

Section XII: Earth's New Ambassadors, Councils — 169

Chapter 1 – Governmental Ambassadors..................170

Chapter 2 – Public Ambassadors.............................172

Chapter 3 – Industrial Ambassadors 173

Chapter 4 – Planetary Ambassadors........................175

Section XIII: Our New Friends in Space Settle In — 177

Chapter 1 – Food Issues Diminish 177

Chapter 2 – Health Issues Diminish 180

Chapter 3 – Housing Issues Diminish......................181

Chapter 4 – Monetary Issues Slowly Diminish 184

Chapter 5 – Commerce Increases 186

Chapter 6 – Centers for Interplanetary Acceptance & Understanding.....................................188

Chapter 7 – Worldwide Advances in Education 191

Chapter 8 – Universal Travel Technique Availabilities 193

Section XIV: Earth Joins the New Alliance of Life — 194

Chapter 1 – Membership Has Its Privileges 194

Chapter 2 – How This Changes Life Here on Earth..................196

Chapter 3 – The Age of Money Disappears 199

Chapter 4 – Exploring 1,672 New Universes 202

Section XV: The New Physical Children of Creation Appear — 204

Chapter 1 – Where Did These Children Come From..................206

Chapter 2 – What is Different About Them 213

Chapter 3 – What is Their Full Purpose 215

Section XVI: The New Bodies for Creation — 217

Chapter 1 – A Description of the New Bodies...........................218

Chapter 2 – The Removal of the Old Physical Bodies...............220

The History and Future Metaphysical Development of Earth, the Universe, and Creation — 222

Metaphysical Developments

Section I: The Age of Earthen Metaphysical Development — 223

Chapter 1 – Self Awareness Increases Everywhere 223

Chapter 2 – How the Human Brain & Body Function Metaphysically..226

Chapter 3 – Source Spirit in Bodies Awakens Strong................294

Chapter 4 – Self Awareness Rises as Religions Fall...................296

Chapter 5 – Universal Schools of Spiritual Enlightenment......298

Section II: E.A. Universities — 301

Chapter 1 – The Physical Bodies Evolve Rapidly. 301

Chapter 2 – Why This is Necessary..305

Section: III: Creation's New Path — 307

Chapter 1 – Creation Grows into Something New 307

Chapter 2 – Lilly and Arae Create New Spirit Beings 318

Chapter 3 – The New First Beings are Released........................324

Chapter 4 – Spirit Growth Parameters & Evolutionary Development 328

Chapter 5 – Control of the First Dimension 330

Additional Information:

Angels 335

Spirit Core 339

Basic Numerology 340

Earthen Ages Timeline 345

Moving Through Time and Space....................................346

The DNA I.C.U.C. and QEEG Test Results........................347

Tools for Increasing Your Metability Power Levels....................353

Understanding and Feeling Stone Energy................................387

Informative Tidbits 445

Dreams, Visions, Deja-Vu, Spirit Guides (w/Ear Ringing), Ghost, Demons, & Exorcisms, Energetic Imprint Recordings, Dousing Rods, Pendulums, Kinesiology, Pictures, Dimensions & Barriers, Mirrors, Ouija Boards & Books, Darting Black Spots in the Corners of Your Eyes, Sage, Spontaneous Combustion

Author's Last Personal Comments 473

Charts & Lists:

Three Day Annunaki Telepathy Attack Schedule 77-78

ETs Here With Us Now List 87-98

Auric Creation Origin Chart 289-293

Base Numerology List 341

Earthen Ages Timeline 345

DNA I.C.U.C. Charts 350-352

Sphere Listing 380-386

Stone Energy Description Relative To Metability/Body Energy Field Listing..395-439

The History and Future Physical Structuring of Earth,

the Universe, and Creation

Physical Developments

Section I ~ How Creation Began

Chapter 1 – Where Did We Come From, How Did It All Start

From the beginning of having lives, other than the first hundred million with Lilly and Arae which started the physical body life process, we were all kept from seeing who we really were and where we came from. How then can we see, while in body, how it all started? We can't. You have to be very powerful and actually from the beginning. I call myself the janitor, the old man, because I am. That's why I'm aware of this mess we're in. That's why I'm back again, one last time.

It all started with an environment of almost nothingness, if that can be imagined through the physical brain. There were various fields of energy and heavy particulate matter fields floating throughout what was. Then, over a great span of time, some of the various energetic fields randomly began attracting to each other. They weren't becoming one specific conglomeration of energy but various separate ones moving towards each other's general vicinity. Different energies were creating separate groups with unique independent energetic characteristics. As their collective energies combined, their frequencies changed.

The energetic attractions changing within each developing group then attracted other separate energy fields not originally involved in the process. This was all happenstance. There was no god or Supreme Being doing anything. There were only non-sentient energies with unique individual properties, and those fields of heavy particulate matter, reacting to each other's unique frequencies. From this gathering came the very First Being. This is how everything started. This is as far back as I can go while in this body.

Our Distant Cousins, the Energans

There is one last thing I need to mention in this chapter, a group of beings that also came from the very First Being as we did, the Energans. They have their own section in Book I. Initially, as the five different energy fields slowly came together creating the first sentient being, that eventually split into male and female and wanted to be called god, there was minimal heavy matter present. As time went on though, more heavy particulate matter was attracted and pulled into the new energy field creating itself.

As the concentration of heavy matter increased within the energy field, just now becoming sentient, part of the new energy field split away from the primary energy mass. It was repelled by the heavy particulate matter; could not bond with it. This field then slowly continued to evolve into the Energans, very unique people and part of our family. See Book I, "Energans".

Creation is the name we give to describe all presently known to exist which will soon change. As we awaken our abilities, we become aware of other dimensions and what's in them. Let's not forget about what we'll soon learn from our new friends from other Planets. There are two base dimensions with others built off of one of them that we'll discuss later.

Chapter 2 – The Creation Of Male And Female

This Original First Being was exactly that, the very first sentient life form. As it grew and developed in sentiency it became more aware of not only itself but that it was alone. As one becomes aware of itself it also becomes aware of all it can perceive surrounding it. Here was the first and worst problem for the Original First Being; it became aware it was alone. Enter now the birth of Loneliness.

As this new being continued to grow, so did its desire for company. This became an overwhelming issue, as one would expect. This is simply the natural order of things, nothing created by some invented god, only one of the simple characteristics of our natural existence whether in or out of body. This very First Being suffered through this and then extended that to us. No compassion can be found here. This is due to the Original First Being's frequencies, 27.5 percent negativity or really just lower frequencies. We call that negativity due to its reaction to all existence, in and out of body.

Due to loneliness, this first being eventually decided to split itself in almost half, making two out of one creating companionship. The two different parts would be a little different in size and frequencies, necessary to create two separate but similar beings. There were different amounts and proportions of the separate frequencies while some would be omitted all together. Mostly each would have the great variety of all of them. If they did not, they would not be of a "similar kind", the same kind of person.

I was created in the beginning to serve and protect. I was made extremely powerful yet able to see the smallest differences in the frequencies of all others. How else could one be able to discern what is friend and what is foe? My work is important but I'm not, really happy with that too. It helps me see things clearly with no personal intention or desire, other than to do my job anyway. You can't see things as clearly as possible when your personal intentions are involved.

Anyway, here's where the Original First Being created the format within itself that when energy was released from it, it would never just float together into one being again. The intention here was to protect itself from future loneliness. The Angels were the only acceptance to this format. They were made of very high frequencies to serve the Original First Being Halves, and no others.

Chapter 3 – The Initial Reasoning For Creation's Birth

Here now is the initial reasoning for creating what we now understand to be Creation, protection against loneliness. This is why our presently known Creation was made, to provide company for the Initial First Being. It never wanted to have to suffer as it did again. Unfortunately when this First Being was being created through happenstance there was too much heavy particulate matter pulled into the process. As stated earlier, this created a being with 27.5 % lower or negative frequencies. The larger the content of lower frequencies the less compassion or love will exist within the being.

I've often used the analogy of a tuning fork and jar of oil to express this simple law of existence. If you tap a tuning fork on a solid substance you will hear a clear, clean frequency coming from it. Were you to do that again and immediately submerge it in a jar of oil that beautiful high frequency will then sound lower and quickly stop. The solid type matter, here actually a liquid type material, adds solid mass to a reaction and lowers the frequencies. I usually use this concept to help others understand why they're more negative in a physical body than when they're free as themselves, sentient energy, Spirit.

Simply put, this Original First Being was lonely, separated itself into two for company, and then decided they wanted more company. This soon led to the need to make others praise them, or it. They found out immediately that the more they abused the

Spirit within a physical body the larger and stronger they were when they came out.

This soon led to the thought process of abusing others as much as possible while in a body, then putting Spirit mate couples together in new Universes, and finally having them release one third of their combined selves. This would create many more new beings who would then be forced to give praise through the use of the Original First Angels. Welcome to the birth of Creation. This is how it all began.

Section II ~ How Creation Grew

Chapter 1 – How Was Our Creation Made in the Beginning

Creation of the New Beings and Dimensions

This now brings us to the point of how things were created, how our family was initially made from released sections of the Original First Being. This was a learning process, never done before. As this was explained in great detail in the Creation Series' Book One, "Creation: Its Beginning And Your Origin" we will make quick work of this.

Both halves of the Original First Being were now excited enough with having company, someone else to talk to, that they wanted more. They thought, for the most part, as one as they were two halves of the previous whole. You're very much like that in relation to your own Spirit mate. As they began making plans to create a large family a few things came to their immediate attention, one of which is that they needed a place to put them, and another to grow them. Through the abuse of their loneliness, they realized their own growth and wanted the same for other parts of themselves to be released later. There was no time to wait, they were anxious.

Having different frequency percentages as well as a different combination of frequencies, they soon found out that they each had slightly different abilities and strong points. It was the male who could more easily separate energy fields and almost immediately separated one of them to create the 2nd Dimension. As he did he immediately discovered the need for a dimension wall or barrier to maintain that frequency's separation from all others.

They would all live in this 2nd Dimension together unless they were being made to grow, become larger and stronger as well as develop or evolve. Now they needed an exercise room, a dimension where the Spirit would be forced to grow, a 3rd Dimension. Here physical mass would be implemented solely because they realized from being in the 1st Dimension that heavy particulate matter had lower frequencies and put more stress onto anything it came into contact with. This soon became a nightmare for anyone in body, especially once aware of what was being done to you and who you really are.

Over the years, through my You Tube channels, there's only one at this moment, the Jay Essex channel, I've explained how dimensions are made. What I am inside, Arae has been creating them almost from the beginning. We only have three major dimensions but there have been separate dimensions made at different locations, sometimes as many as 38 in one Solar system. Forget what you've read and heard about dimensions so far, no one is even close. It will only produce false images keeping you farther from discovering the truth of what's real. You will find in time that what I tell you makes sense; it will all come together to create one singular pie that's mentally digestible, understandable.

This is what I offer, why these books had to be written. You need to have a source of reliable information to help you grow into yourselves. You must find yourself first before understanding what's around you. We naturally begin with our own selves and then move outward. There's good reason for that, simple sense. The more you awaken all your suppressed natural abilities the better decisions you make, the stronger and clearer your understandings and greater your accumulated wisdom. Never call your abilities gifts as they are not, you already own them; they are an integral part of what you already are.

Within this 3rd Dimension, between its barriers, physical bodies of mass were necessary to sustain these necessary physical bodies which would be used to contain the Spirits while there. Here's a brief explanation of what happened.

Some type of container was necessary to encapsulate the individual beings, hold them while in that dimension. Solid matter was also necessary to create a physical holding cell for that spirit, one that would eventually decay allowing them to return home to the 2nd Dimension. I call the 2nd Dimension, also known as the Other Side, home for good reason, it is. It's where we all live in our natural state. So we have the need for physical Spirit containers, what's next?

These physical bodies needed a large physical mass to exist on as well as a maintenance system for them. This eventually led to water, air, etc. Later, heavy particulate matter in the 1st Dimension was used to create all the physical devices in our known Universe. As you know there is mostly space, there was no need to completely fill the 3rd Dimension, just build what was necessary for the bodies to survive long enough to push the Spirits within as hard as possible.

Each piece of physical matter had an initial design format, a reason for having been made. Every singular thing came from one separate piece of heavy particulate matter which was then transmutated into what was needed. These First Being Halves could not just create something out of nothing as your religious texts would suggest, sometimes outright declare. They needed something to start with. Nothing is made from nothing. Simple thought process here but also factual everywhere.

    As time went by and Spirits were coming in and out of body, the First Ones kept changing things, increasing the abuse everywhere, trying to maximize the growth potential in the 3rd Dimension. Here's the short account of how things started. Books I and II of the Creation Series cover, in greater detail, just what was happening. All my Creation books flow together and build on each other. I'm not much of a writer but the information is all here, for you.

Chapter 2 – How Was Creation to Function, be Controlled

At this point we have Spirit containers (bodies), a sustainable mass system (planets, stars, water, air, etc.), and all else necessary to move forward. How would their strife, abuse, and lives be controlled? This had always been a work in progress so to speak. The Original First Being Halves were experts at this. Until the year 2012, here on Earth at the ending of the 5th Age, they controlled almost everything that happened in your lives, everything of importance that is. They made sure that the bodies they put the Spirits inside had the right DNA, environment, and events within those lives, to create as much abuse as possible.

They realized the need for servants to maintain the proper amount of abuse in the 3rd Dimension, keep everyone's lives moving in the direction they desired. They knew they couldn't do all this by themselves as they planned on releasing many smaller Spirits, later even more. Initially they were so eager for company, and later drunk on the process of praise, they were also building into Creation a system of continual growth. Before being destroyed for refusing to stop attacking the Creation they initially built, they were in the process of creating a separate dimension from which to retire, to relax and feel the praise, nothing more.

This new dimension is now located here in our Solar system. It is the 8th Dimension below us. Here there are the initial 3 dimensions and 8 more around and below us, so to speak. I'll make a DVD about that later. I've also talked in detail about them on my

You Tube channel. What was then created, to control the masses, were Angels.

Angels were a singularity in Creation. That's about to change. We'll discuss that later in this book. They were created out of only the highest frequencies as this was initially thought to help keep them weak, never to be able to rise against the Original First Being Halves. They were made never to separate into male and female. The thought process here is that they would not be as strong this way. Again, there was always the need to stay in control of everything everywhere.

Above all else, they were servants, sentient robots in a way. They have never had even one life. It's never happened, yet. Things are changing and all that comply will have their freedom to do as they choose, so long as they never become abusive. Getting back to their initial programming or format, they would physically control all the bodies.

If it was not time for you to die or be significantly damaged, they saved you, either removing your body from the event or the environment about to create it. They can literally move you through a dimensional barrier if necessary. When it was time to die or break your arm, they made sure that happened also. They created the circumstances to ensure it happened by controlling your physical body.

How did all these Original Angels control your physical bodies? It's a simple process and easily explained. They would focus their energy above your head, go through your Upper, Middle, and Lower Crown energy fields, and simply take over your thought process. When I go into people's brains to awaken their abilities and evolve them, I do that and more. When I started doing this openly in 2012, I got the attention of some major U.S. government agencies.

In November of 2012, two government agents knocked on my front door. One was from the FBI and the other from Homeland Security. They wanted to meet me in person, gather what data they could. I actually had fun talking with them. They also each asked for some of my Essenite Stone. I told them they meant to ask for the Star Essenite. The gentleman from Homeland looked at me with a puzzled expression, and said yes. When they left the gentleman from the FBI had three thoughts in his head. They were as such; he's fruit loops, he's a carnival act, damn it, how did he know that about me? The gentleman from Homeland was confused for a different reason.

Homeland already knew about me, so did the upper echelon of the FBI. These agents were lower level administration and not privy to many things. The Homeland agent was warned that I go into people's brains, get information, and make changes. He couldn't understand why my status was changed from orange (serious issue) to red (immediate danger). He also had an image in his thought process of a white porcelain plate with a piece of apple pie on it that was left out overnight. The meaning here was that he realized I was as much a threat to others as a piece of pie left out overnight.

He saw all my animal feeders and housing I built that were both clustered and spread out everywhere. He could feel my heart energy. He looked into my eyes and saw what I really was, selfless heart and protectional strength. He knew I had honor and helped others. So many of us do this naturally, it's part of who we are, a simple autonomic response mechanism of our true selves.

I later began traveling around the Southeastern U.S. going to different events as well as my own. I helped people understand who they are, the value of stone energy, gave consultations, cranked people up, etc. The whole time I was doing this there were others keeping an eye on me, at home and in space. Today our distant family members from other Planets, are in and out of my house almost daily. Details on this and more are found in many of my You Tube videos.

Anyway, as I mentioned a few paragraphs ago, the Original Angels would go into your brains, control your thoughts, and then release you. Time after time they have done this to everyone. If you ever did something and then wondered how the hell you could have done that, don't worry, you didn't. Some people might try to use this as an excuse for having done something against others but they know better. These people are being taken out of the life process now anyway. You can only have a successful clean Creation with clean positive ingredients. Everything is changing but now about to kick into overdrive, really take off.

All of the Original First Angels have been removed from the bodies they were initially assigned to. When you were put into a physical body, a few of the Original Angels went along to control you. That's how the Original Ones controlled your daily lives. Most of the Original Angels were destroyed but those willing to release all control over others and accept their new independence were infused with source energy and protected from the earlier fighting which is now finished. Remember, they were servants who never disobeyed. The Lucifer/devil issue is a total lie, a complete fabrication given us from the Original First Being Halves to instill fear in everyone. It's part of the intended thought control process found in religions.

Chapter 3 – How Did All These Beings Grow Together

Now we have to skip over a large portion of Creation's making, the process of the Original First Being Halves releasing a third of themselves to create all the different forms of Spirit, some of whom are still with us today. This is a major portion of the first book in the Creation Series. You will need that to get up to speed on all this. Remember, there's little space here to help get you orientated to what this last book in the Creation Series will cover.

The important thing I want to mention here is that as time went on, the Original First Being Halves began to lie to all the different separate fields of Spirit while out of body, telling each of them that they were about to take over different aspects of Creation or even Creation itself, once they retired. They played everyone against each other, no honor in that.

They also were most demeaning to the Animal Essence beings and then the Fae, in that order. Animal Essence has served longer, harder, continuously, and with more abuse than any other beings, the exception being Lilly and Arae. Why do you think so many religious books, the bible just for one example, say that man was made in god's image and should take command over the Earth and all on it? This was not done through happenstance. It was the doing of the Original First Being Halves.

Universal Essence (Male Stars and Female Planets) were told that all life depended on them so they were paramount and should be treated as such. The Male Universal Essence, the only Spirit found in Stars, became very arrogant. They were huge, powerful, and necessary to the many different beings on all Planets. The Planets, with loving Female Universal Essence on them, were all different. I've had next to no problem with any of them. Female Universal Essence would usually separate itself into two or more sections depending on the Solar system it was placed in. That's why one Star will have more than one Planet in its system, or family. Again, a longer explanation and description is found in Book I. Just realize that this type of thing was happening everywhere, also between different members of the same Spirit Family. Chaos was the format.

Chapter 4 – Who are You, this Thing Called a Body

Includes the Serpoian, 9-11, 3-11, & Source Field

At this point we need to take a short but closer look at these containers we're trapped inside, our bodies. The first two books and the Jay Essex You Tube Channel talk about this in great detail so again we'll be brief here. Let's cover the vehicle you're in, how it works, how it's controlled, and what's inside with you. Let's take a moment to watch your Spirit being put inside that body you're trying to control.

When a male and female physically come together, or egg and sperm are put together outside of a body, or folks such as the Eben, Greys, Zetas, or as I call them the Serpoian, graft DNA to make hybrid clones, a new physical body is created. Let's take a brief moment out for the Serpoian race here.

The Serpoian people are a race of beings from the Zeta Reticuli section of space as we know it. Late 1922 and early 1923 the U.S. government found a few ships of theirs crashed out in the Western desert. Three of them crashed. Another was damaged but able to fly farther away, make repairs, and leave. A few of the passengers of the 3 crashed vehicles were still alive when the government arrived. Some of them were shot and killed immediately.

Where does that info come from? It comes from simple knowing located in the Source Field, easy to access once you do it a couple times. This is just one of your recessed abilities, again, not gifts. They are an integral part of what you are, who you are. My last life was that of the man called Gandhi. That part of me inside was very upset over the fact that I was shot four times in the chest, not three as most people have said.

The fourth shot barely grazed my left side, just hitting a rib about 8" under my left arm pit. I've been saying this publicly for many years now and that information was finally released recently, so to speak. The doctors who saw me immediately afterwards, and a few close people there, were aware of it. This fourth shot is a simple thing, more so than other parts of my many other lives, because it was more recent and a small part of me was upset about it. All of you can access information in the Source Field.

Who I am inside is the Original Arae, produced to serve and protect everything and one. I am very strong Source Spirit from the time before lives, the initial time of Creation. I have almost all the different frequencies that exist in Creation, within me. If you pour water from two different buckets into a larger one, the two waters will blend together, become one.

If you take sand from one bucket and rocks from another bucket, place them together into a larger bucket, you have rocks and sand staring at you. They don't blend as they're different. As I already have all these separate frequencies within me, it's difficult to release all of the physical body and the individual Planetary Essence from me as I leave it. I take more than a few memories of that life.

I also see things through the field. The field is now a part of me, happened in 2013. Alpha male Source has this responsibility; it's a necessary part of our Creation. There must be an intelligent Source Field to help everyone move from one place to another as Spirit. When you begin to astral project, the Field is the medium that you move through. More importantly, it moves you through it. Here's how.

The Field extends through everything, even nuclear energy but that's nasty stuff. It's a sick cancerous energy. That's why, after two atomic bombs were detonated, we immediately had people from well over a dozen planets here, even other dimensions. We were about to harm the physical part of Creation in a way that no one in a body could repair. Even the Drachk were here. That makes it a serious event. One more attempt to detonate another atomic bomb would have drawn the Drachk onto the scene with serious consequences to us here.

Those messing with these "dirty" bombs immediately received help in understanding what they were doing in order to diminish the negative effects they were creating in our 3rd Dimension. Our family members throughout space are part of a vast community with many differences yet they have a basic policy to stay away from the younger, less advanced populations on other Planets. This however was a cause for great alarm.

When the nuclear reactor incident happened in Chernobyl, they came. When the nuclear reactor incident in Japan on 3/11/2011 happened there were over two thousand reports of UFOs nearby. Those were almost all real; they were here trying to help. One of the men who died trying to stop the accident, near the end of it, wasn't even from this planet. He had a room on a starship where he stayed while there. These folks have been trying to help us so long and from so far away. They mostly go unnoticed but their deeds demand the respect they deserve.

I realize I strayed from the initial topic but did so with good reason. These things need to be said and who better to speak of them than the person who can see them as if standing at an intersection watching cars go by. The honor of those who struggle so hard to protect and care for others deserves notice. They do this freely because of who they are. They have earned our respect. They deserve a thank you.

   Just a tidbit of information, did you notice how so many things, bad things, have happened on dates containing an 11 in them? Recently there has been the 9-11-2001 event in the U.S. and the 3-11-2011 nuclear event in Japan which is still hurting our Planet's ecosystem (and the governmental idiots make a big deal of global warming when they don't understand what's actually happening). It is not just our responsibility to care for this Planet we live on, it is mandatory for any supposedly sentient race to care for its home. The treatment of our Earth is past repulsive, it's insane. And the human race has the audacity to call itself human, as if inciting the word "humane"?

   Having said all this I need to add something else. It was the will of the Original First Being Halves, male and female, to keep these things happening. The sad thing is that once a system of abuse is maintained it becomes accepted by those within it. It's not all our fault, by any means. It is however our responsibility. Let me get away from this now. There is so much wrong everywhere and I'm not talking just about the Earth, abuse is everywhere in every dimension.

   To finish up the "11" saga here, when the Original First Being Male and Female felt the urge, they would produce a seriously damaging event on the 11th. This was to tell you that they were in charge and you didn't matter. It was one of their arrogant and abusive head-trips. The two "1's" standing next to each other making the "11" actually stood for them, the male and female gods as they saw themselves. They were trying to prove that they were in control and there was nothing you could do about it. They would do to you whatever they felt like doing.

You will see all this change now. They are gone forever. There are two new others, male and female, who will bring calm, peaceful, and benevolent change to you. The change is still in progress and will be for a little while. Although things have already begun to move forward with compassion, they haven't even really started yet. That's what this book is about on many levels. You must see this for yourselves and over a short amount of time, over the next few years, you will see it start. Creation is under new management and about to be rebuilt relative to the needs, health, and interest of all in it.

Now, finally getting back to the Serpoian folk, they are masters at creating new life forms, repairing existing life forms, and more. They have been doing this for many centuries. A team of individuals from the U.S., there were originally 14 but only 12 made the trip, visited a Planet being called Serpo in the Zeta-Reticuli section of space. Just a note here, in 1926 the U.S. had its first official treaty with the Serpoian race.

While on the planet, the structure containing all the biological testing and new physical body creations was attacked by a different race from another Planet. They were really pissed about what the Serpoian people were doing. There is a sentiment throughout Creation that they don't have the right to do what they do in some of their experimental creating of life forms.

Ok, back to the physical bodies. As I was trying to say pages ago, as a physical body begins to develop it eventually grows a mass of nerve tissue which becomes its brain. Once the brain is about two thirds or more complete, a Spirit which was separated from Gaia over 11 million years ago, is placed into the body. After a short term, the Alpha Female Source Spirit pushes the Planetary Essence Spirit to the left side of the brain.

Then the Spirit which would be yourself is placed into the now vacant right section of the brain. The head is now enclosed by the Alpha Female and voila, you have the complete body about to have a life. This is the situation that all of you have been in, each and every life you've ever had. There are only a few exceptions and they're relative to Lilly and Arae. Having said all this, as of Jan. 22, 2018 there will be no more Planetary Essence Spirit within the physical bodies on the Earth that originally had a Dual Spirit Core. The same will be true of all previous Dual Spirit Cores in physical bodies across the Universe before the end of 2018. It's easier to drive a car without someone else trying to grab the wheel from time to time.

Any and all physical mass has a "deadening effect" on all frequencies of energy and therefore on Spirit as its sentient energy. The more physical mass applied to energy the greater the decrease in that energy's higher frequencies. All the individual frequencies are slowed down changing what they initially were. This is a problem not only in using your natural abilities while placed in a physical body but to all energy in its initial creation stage. That's why all the new "First Beings" that becoming sentient energy in the first dimension consist of different lower frequency percentages, some higher and some lower. The greater the sum of lower frequencies the more "negative" a being becomes.

Once the two Spirits were placed in the body it was sealed with Source Energy. The two Spirits, yourself and the Planetary Essence Spirit inside you, flow up and down the center of the body from your Base Energy Field (Base Chakra) to just under the top of your skull at the Upper Crown Energy Field (Upper Crown Chakra). The two Spirits flow together all the time. This is also known as the Kundalini, the two snakes of energy that flow through the body. No one knew what the two parts were, but now you do. The truth is a simple thing.

The Dual Spirit Core is no longer being produced on Earth. This change began in November of 2017. Here's one example of a positive "11" date. November 2017 is expressed as 11/2017. Your decisions are easier, less confusing when only you are making them. When you pass it will also be easier. Planetary Essence Spirit needs a Planet body to be comfortable. Pushing them into temporary bodies and then yanking them out is abuse in itself. That's why usually part of you wants to hold onto the body so hard. Us personally, as Spirit inside the body, once we're in enough pain and discomfort we're ready to go back home.

We'll cover in detail about how the different parts of the brain and body function metaphysically, as separate body parts and with each other, in relation to all your different abilities later in this book at the beginning of the Metaphysical Developments section.

Section III ~ Physical Abuse Development in the Third Dimension

Chapter 1 – Gaeira and the First Physical Lives in Creation

The Development of Spirit within Physical Bodies

At the onset of Spirit having lives in physical bodies there was only one Planet. Gaeira is the name she gave me for us here on Earth. We've all had many lives on many different Planets. In the beginning there were no Souls, just Lilly, Arae, and the other fields of Essence Spirit. There was Source, of which only Lilly and Arae were having lives, and Animal, Plant, Universal, Human, and Fae Essences.

Once the 3rd Dimension was built, things started to come together. As Stars were fired up, Male Universal Essence Spirit was put into them. As the Planets began to form, Female Universal Essence Spirit was placed into them. They were the first to begin having physical lives in the 3rd Dimension. People think that the moon has Spirit within it, not true.

Strong male Star Energy bounces off the moon, flows through our Planet's Aura (Gaia), and approaches us as what it is, balanced Universal Essence that's complementary to our bodies. Another item of interest here is that Stars and Planets do not have a Dual

Spirit Core (often called a Kundalini), only their singular Spirit flows through the matter they're encased in.

These bodies are self-replicating now but initially were made by Spirit from the existing material of this Planet. These bodies actually belong to Gaia, the Planetary Essence within this Planet who's body we live on. For more info read Book I of the Creation Series.

Plant Essence Spirit was next to be inserted into physical bodies. It was placed into the flora or Plant bodies here. They have Planetary Essence within the matter of their bodies yet Plant Essence Spirit flows throughout the body in the form of a Single Spirit core. Again, there's more on this in Book I.

The third form of physical body life to appear was all the Single Spirit core individuals meant to maintain the lives of the Planets and beings on them. These were the insects, reptiles, fish, etc. I'm cutting this section short also. I can't repeat Book I here.

Then Lilly and Arae came to Gaeira to have the first physical Humanistic lives. These bodies did not look "Human" as we would understand today. They made their own bodies relative to all the different frequencies inside them. In other words they looked strange to any physical bodies existing today, anywhere. They were made of materials from Gaeira, the Planet they were on, yet relative to Plant, Animal, Human, and Fae Energies. Imagine all that in the shape of a humanistic body. These bodies were strong but not ready for what was in store for them, set up by the Original First Being Male and Female.

That first life on Gaeira didn't even last one rotation of Gaeira's Planet. Remember that she was 270 times the mass of Jupiter, very large, so the days there were much longer than here on Earth. After less than a day's cycle, Lilly and Arae were torn to shreds by a large flock of reptiles looking like Velociraptors on steroids. I remember seeing the look of total fear and anguish in Lilly's eyes as we were being torn apart and carried off to be eaten.

Once back home Arae told Lilly to follow his lead when making their next bodies for the second life. When we returned we made the Drachk Race, the very first ones. Here is the reason for my close relationship with the Drachk people. They have my respect and understand what I am, not this body. As I've mentioned before, our friends throughout the Universe have equipment that reads our frequencies and can place us in other bodies from other lives.

Lilly and Arae were the most powerful Source Spirits ever created. In Book I of the Creation Series I explained how the two large couples of clean Source Spirit were created from the Original First Being Halves. Then I explained how Lilly was the strongest part of Lillith and Arae the same from Aramaeleous. They were the focal points of the two strongest clean Source Spirit mates in Creation. That's why they're so strong. They grew in strength from all the abusive lives they've endured. Lilly's Primary Focal Point has had almost 9 trillion lives and Arae just over 10.846 trillion.

You would be amazed at how many lives you've had in different bodies on other Planets. There are many Souls from the first wave of Soul Creation that have had over one trillion lives. Then there's Essence who have had an average of a little over one trillion lives before the First Soul Wave. Animal Essence Spirit has had many more lives than Human, Fae, and Faeman Essence Spirit. They started earlier and have had much shorter therefore more numerous lives.

Over time the Original First Being Halves continued increasing the effectiveness of all the physical body traps to get them where they are today, a serious problem to awaken in or see through. Physical bodies also require physical food to maintain them. The Energetic Bodies found in the Fae Dimensions here are much different. You can live there for a month on the energy you receive from an apple and a thimble of honey.

Things are now being done to change these physical bodies and their issues. The need for Animal flesh protein will be removed from the Human DNA chain. However Animals themselves will be removed from Creation. Once Earth's physical body's DNA is changed the Alurean and Serpoian people will help us with creating an almost endless food supply. Let's talk briefly about your Spirit flowing in your body. This will be covered in great detail in the first section of the "Metaphysical Developments" part of this book.

I saw this as it was happening when I was in people's brains giving them "Crank-Up" consultations. They're called DNA I.C.U.C. which stands for DNA Intensive Crank-Up Consult. It's a consult where I offer free energy work as a bonus. They usually consider it the more important part of the consult. I also became aware of the energy flowing within the body and brain through a direct understanding that came from my Source Field. It helps me understand more about everything.

Throughout the body there is a constant flow of Spirit and the energy released from it. Spirit is sentient energy and from the sentient part of it, energetic frequencies flow outward from the core and main power focal points. These energetic fields have their unique frequencies within them. Each frequency creates its own specific Aura, a colored byproduct which emanates from it. When someone has a Deep Blue Aura around them they are Pineal Field based. They're strongest in this area. It also means determination, will power, and fortitude.

Basically the physical body houses the Spirits (now becoming a singular Spirit) allowing them to flow and have a physical life on any given Planet. They're also prisons. When you finally leave the body to return home, your true self expands, coming out larger and a little stronger from the experience. The problem here is that when you've had too harsh (abusive) a life you also build up "Abuse Frequencies". These are abnormal frequencies with no steady natural flow, no smooth continuous singular vibration. They actually make you sick in a way that you're not even aware, becoming more aggressive and unable to focus properly. This occurs while both in and out of body.

This was another important reason for the earlier Source War. Creation was being torn apart merely to satisfy the selfish, relentless, and endless desires of the Original First Being Halves who were never happy anyway. They had proven there would be no end to it.

Chapter 2 – The Entrance of Animal, Fae, and Human Essences in Physical Bodies

As mentioned earlier, Gaeira was already a living Planet. She had her own ecosystem thriving, singular Spirit core reptiles, insects, fish, and the rest. There was also Plant Essence having lives there, a lot of foliage. If you were to take the Plant life seen on the movie "Avatar" it was quite similar. There was no "home tree" as big as what was seen in the movie but all the Plant life was huge. So was most everything else.

Lilly and Arae had those first hundred million lives by themselves. Then the Animals came to have lives with them. Animal Essence came to the surface, bonded with the Planet's raw material with Gaeira's assistance, and began their first 200 million lives. The visiting Spirit hovered over yet touching the ground and pulled the substances necessary to form the proper body for living on that Planet. As the body continued to form, the raw material flowed into the main structure through what we call the Solar Plexus. This is where it finished in the past. All this has changed now as Planetary Essence is no longer joining Human, Fae, and Faeman beings in physical bodies.

For a little over 300 million lives there was only Lilly, Arae, and Animal Essence on Gaeira. The next to come down was Fae Essence and almost immediately after, Human Essence. Today we have Faeman as well as Fae, and Human Fields of Essence. In the beginning there were only two fields which was a problem as it was almost impossible to cleanly separate them.

There was always a small portion of Fae Essence mixed with the Human Essence and vice versa. All fields of Essence Spirit had a place where they existed as a group, a mass gathering of Spirit in the 2nd Dimension. Both Fae and Human Essence had their separate locations. When someone was a strong mixture of either Human or Fae they were usually looked down on by the others in that Essence Field.

There was always unhappiness for many in regards to this situation. Then there was the Original First Beings who took advantage of this opportunity to stress everyone harder. They used this situation to increase the arrogance between all of them. Arae created the Faeman Essence Field to alleviate the situation. Anyone over 10 percent of either of these fields could live in this group. This includes most of the Human and Fae Essence family.

Although all Faeman belong to the huge Faeman Essence Spirit Field, they can also go to the Field containing the majority of their frequencies, Human or Fae. This gave everyone freedom of movement and removed over 80% of the interaction issues. The Faeman Essence Spirit Field was created a few years ago, I can't remember when, just having done it. The important thing is that it happened, just another necessary step in fixing what's wrong with our Creation.

This Creation has been around for about 2 quadrillion, 857 trillion, 100 billion, and 400 million years as we calculate that here on Earth. It was only run by the Original First Ones and they built it to be abusive. As I've said in many of my videos, it's a lot easier for me to build a racing engine out of new parts than disassemble a used one, clean it up, replace what no longer works properly, add new parts, make sure everything is correct, and finally rebuild it. Creation is screwed up and will be properly fixed in 2,000 years max. Things are drastically going to change in late 2018 and continue forward from there. Many things that you can't see, that you aren't aware of yet, have already changed.

Getting back to the lives on Gaeira, the average Human and Fae Essence beings had an average of over 1 trillion lives on Gaeira. Lilly, Arae, and Animal Essence had a good bit more. Lilly and Arae had more back to back and the Animals had much shorter ones. Animal Essence was created from mostly fortitude and compassion. That's why they're so strong, that and having lived and died so many times.

Chapter 3 – The Destruction of Gaeira's Body, Planet Gaeira

Once all the previously mentioned fields of Essence had an average of over 1 trillion lives on Gaeira the Original First Beings had her blown up. There was over a trillion beings on the Planet's surface when it happened. The Planet's body, and all life on it, was destroyed in a matter of seconds. There's a lot more to this and it's covered in Book I. It's a moment in history that I'll never be able to forget, nor forgive.

The Original First Being Halves demanded that Arae destroy Gaeira's body, the Planet Gaeira. They said that in order to ascertain the maximum amount of abuse allowable for Human and Fae Essences could endure it was necessary. He didn't believe a word of it so he said no. The Original Ones now said that it was important to insure the new softer energy Souls didn't receive too much abuse. Arae didn't believe that either so he said no again.

Eventually Gaeira said to go ahead and do it. He eventually did and will never forgive himself. I live with that every moment of every day. I have done things that I'm not proud of. This is called learning. I'm tired of Creation's abusive format and I'm anxious to return home to remove it.

Anyway, here come the Souls, the first attempt that is.

Chapter 4 – The First Souls and the First Universe

There was a pause in the creation of Souls. The Original First Being Halves were deciding how to begin. When they made the First Souls they were experimenting, trying to understand how to create them from their own energy. After Gaeira and her Sun (Universal Essence Spirit Mate) blew up together, there was a pause in the physical life scenario. It was time for the next stage of their master plan, the creation of the very first Soul Spirits.

The Original First Being Halves wanted to create as many new Souls as possible from 1/3 of their remaining energy, the most they could release without damaging their energetic integrity. They had already released a lot of their combined energy and they needed to conserve all they could. After all, they still had to maintain control over everything they created.

In order to do this, they decided to initially create a small amount of small weak Souls in a small Universe to see how things progressed from there. They found out that their growth potential, from having started so small and weak, would take too much time to reach the size and power level they felt they needed.

This first Universe and the Souls within it were simply left alone. As they had lives they would retire to their normal state, Spirit, and then eventually go back into a body again. They were Spirit Guides to each other and functioned, basically, just as we do here. Their lives just weren't so difficult. Their energy level wasn't capable of dealing with what we do.

They had a few smaller and weaker Angels assigned to them to keep an eye on things and that's about it. They're still alive today, just separated from everything else. They're not defective, quite the contrary. They're nice, happy, and considerate; most of them are anyway. Their Universe was created about 1.349 eons or billion years, in Universal Time, before ours, the second one.

Chapter 5 – Enter the New Souls

After the failed experiment with the First Souls in the first Universe, it was time for the creation of the new Souls through the release of one third of the Original First Being Male and Female's combined Human and Fae energy. This was then separated into the two basic subtypes and released as a split wave. There are few differences between Fae and Human Essence frequencies but their bodies are completely different.

Soul Spirit is different from the other forms of Spirit in Creation. It has a limited number of frequencies which come off of the various focal points of the Essence Field it came from. There was a need for many Souls to be released so they had to create more from the amount of Spirit Energy they were able to separate from themselves.

The Original First Being Male and Female vibrated their energy with aggressive, strong, and short pulse width frequencies. This is a little like a paint can shaking on the machine that paint stores use when mixing it. A closer analogy is turning on a vibratory cleaner or polisher. The vibrations are very short, fast, and powerful. This action separates the Spirit Field into smaller pieces which come off of the various Energy Fields in that cluster.

In the Fae Essence Field, pieces of Spirit were shaken loose from the three major focal points within it. These are the Solar Plexus, Heart, and Pineal type fields. Once this was done within the large Human or Fae Essence Energy Field it was released outward in a wave. Pieces of this wave then came together as they would through happenstance. As the wave continued it thinned out and many small orbs of Spirit were created.

It was at this point, once the orbs were separate from the general field of energy, that they began to vibrate themselves. This is part of the Original First Beings initial self-format when it split itself into two beings. It did so with the intention that it would always have company, never be able to come back into just one being again. Therefore, once the Soul orbs were separate they vibrated themselves into male and female.

No one Soul orb ever vibrated into two parts that were 100% male and female. Every one of them contains at least a partial amount of each gender. Some are almost 50%, half and half, but not quite. This is often expressed in the way people act, more male or female minded. We often have lives in the opposite type gender body. That becomes more difficult when you're farther away from the 50/50 split.

I was in the body of both Tomoe Gozen and Joan of Arc. As Tomoe I was a fearless warrior, Samurai. As Joan of Arc I was similar, a brutal person with major issues and powerful pineal abilities. I was aggressive and brutal when necessary. I'm about 97.3% male energy which has caused issues for me in female body lives. I haven't had many but we've all done this from time to time. As Spirit we want to understand as much as we can about all we can. Remember, you've never been a body, only in one.

As time has gone by, all the Souls have grown from the many and abusive lives they've had. They are large now, much stronger than in the beginning. Almost everything out there, percentage wise, is Soul Spirit and awesome. Some people think that Essence or Source is better, not true. I know more Source Spirit in people that's a problem than anything else.

There were 5 waves of Soul Spirit Created over a long period of time. There are a few from the 5th wave having lives now but not many and with very few lives. I've seen a few people here this life that actually look young when you see them. They can be 35 and they feel like they're 14. The ones I've seen have had about 14-35 lives total. They shouldn't even be here in body on this Planet.

Again, there is a lot more information about Soul Spirit, Essence Spirit, and Source in Book I, "Creation: Its Beginning And Your Origin". It's time to go out into space for a while.

Chapter 6 – Wars and Strife Throughout Space

It didn't take long for the Original First Ones to learn how much abuse the Soul Spirit could handle. This is why Lilly and Arae came first, then the Animal Essence, and then Fae and Human Essences. Lilly and Arae were and still are the strongest beings anywhere. They took the worst of the Original First Being Halves damage as they began running lives. Then Animal Essence which was next strongest with all their fortitude. They learned how much abuse to give which Spirit and by the time they were done with all the lives on Gaeira, they were ready to begin handling the Souls.

It was now an easy thing for the Original Male and Female to apply abuse to others in life. One did not have to have any lower frequencies to be made arrogant and eventually abusive. Jealousy was also a handy tool. Then there were different Planets with various needs necessary to maintain life on it. Sometimes that were in dire need of materials from other Planets and, when they felt it necessary, they tried to take it.

There were also many different groups of people through space that were similar to what we call pirates. They just dealt on a planetary scale, or maybe only partial. The problematic Annunaki who have physically controlled the Earth for over 10 million years now, were exactly like that. Their ancestors destroyed Mars a very long time ago. The Annunaki are a very cool race of wonderful people. They're just a little scary for us to look at as they're a large aggressive reptilian race, that's all. We're only used to Earthen Humans.

My spelling of Annunaki is different than how most people spell it. I mention in this book about how the part of me that was Gandhi gets upset about people saying I was only shot 3 times instead of the actual 4. This spelling of Annunaki has the same energy in it. I've had many Annunaki lives, some very important, and one part of me gets a little annoyed about it. It's kinda funny how past lives have those effects on us sometimes.

I even mentioned in Book II that when Lemuria was being colonized by folks from other Planets, the supplies to them were often difficult or cut off due to territorial disputes and wars. As large as space is, some races have sectioned off a large part of it and claimed it as their own. All this was kept going by you know who, the Original First Being Halves.

So much of our 3rd Dimension is unexplored, almost unreachable by anything. The sections of space that have been charted (by our friends and family from other Planets) are so small when you consider the actual size of the Universe itself. They say that we've explored approximately 5% of our Oceans. Heck, that's just the Planet we live on. They also say that we've recorded about 4% of the Universe. In truth its barely over 0.1%, a tenth of one percent.

You will find as these next 10-20 years go by, how much we're unaware of out in space, especially what's been happening there. The wars have settled down now thanks to the Alliance as well as the Other Side but it's only just beginning. So much has already occurred, is happening now, and will come to pass in your very near futures. The year 2020 will see a new light in Creation, the one of a loving older sister and brother who are caretakers, protectors, and whatever they need to be for all that is. That's your new and eternal future.

As your natural metaphysical abilities awaken, you'll be able to see other beings in different bodies, Spirit flowing naturally out of body, events in the near future, and much more. Here's a heads up on how that happens for most people.

- First it's exciting when you awaken your abilities, start using them and realizing who you really are, almost euphoric in nature.
- Then you begin to become comfortable with your abilities as they're a natural part of you anyway.
- Then you feel the sadness, the joy, the abuse, and torture of all living things around you.
- Then you come to where I am; you simply understand the true reality of the world you live in. You will see, hear, and know things for yourself.
- Creation was built wrong, to abusively force growth with no care towards those in it. It's already being fixed.

This Universe is old; it's been around a while. As the solid physical bodies start to disappear, the new lives will be held in new Universes where everyone has the same energy body. There are currently 1,670 new Universes which are only now starting to develop with little to no life on their Planets. There are Stars, Planets, and some Plant life in them now, little more.

What will this be like, a new life in a new energetic body in a new Universe? It will be incredible. You don't age, you feel no pain, childbirth is painless and takes only seconds, and later if you want, you can make a physical body to run around in. You won't have a heart, lungs, or anything of the sort, just a physical body. You won't be able to maintain this form for long but you can have fun with it for a while. We're going to cover this in greater detail later in the book.

Section IV ~ Creation's Takeover

Chapter 1 – What Happened to Require Change in Creation's Format

Abuse Frequencies and More

    I remember through time how the maximum amount of abuse was applied to all living beings, all things. Lilly and I lived in a state of urgency that wouldn't go away. That comes simply from caring, compassion. The Original First Being Halves just wouldn't stop. At first I would suggest, then I would explain, and eventually I got in their face, so to speak. As Spirit, sentient energy, we don't have bodies, we have focal points and dense energy fields within ourselves.

    It became apparent that I would eventually have to do something. I shouldn't bother to say this but I'm going to anyway. I am what I am. I'm no more important or better than any other living thing, not even a blade of grass. I understand the rights of all and that without a given equality for everyone you cannot build a society of any sort. You cannot have unity. You will not survive as a family.

    I'm Creation's janitor and proud to be so. I serve continuously; just don't tell me what I have to do. Through all my lives and my understanding I know how to protect and I serve the best way I can, selflessly. I have left you exactly this proof in this my last life. I have always been about everything else. I've left you proof of who I am, just go through this life, talk to my friends, there's a lot of them.

To understand me, just look at the records of the hundreds of thousands of dollars I have spent helping Animals and people. The whole time I've driven beat up cars and struggled to pay my utility bills and keep my small beat up house.

I am what I am and make no bones about it. I was built in the very beginning to perform three functions.

- o To Protect The Original First Being Halves.
- o To Protect All They Built
- o To Subdue Any And All New Beings Coming Out Of The First Dimension

Immediately after being created I was given this format and agreed. I didn't know better, heck I didn't know anything. Then after having a few lives I dropped the middle format thought process. I would not subdue something that had done no harm. I would say hello, what's happening?

Not long after having a thousand lives I realized there was no value in the first format thought process either as I would eventually need to take them out of the controlling position they had over Creation in order to protect it and everyone else. As we have lives we grow, we evolve, we become more than we were before. However it can only be done gradually, not overnight, as that creates Abuse Frequencies.

What are Abuse Frequencies? As you awaken your abilities you will also find yourself knowing things such as events and how things look inside the body by looking through it, as if into it. There are many people today who can see certain health issues inside the Human body, even over long distances. The more you practice your abilities the stronger they become, the more efficient you become with them.

I don't expect anyone to believe what I say. Over time as people awaken, they'll understand what I'm talking about for themselves. That's where we need to be. We must come to our own decisions. I'm just explaining what's out there, what's going on. I see frequencies as they are; pure energy. I see the forms, vibrations, colors, and "wave lengths" as we might call them whether in mass or as a singular frequency.

As I was made to protect I must immediately recognize and assess all that is. How else can I understand what is and isn't an issue? I have to know what I'm dealing with immediately. I'm only explaining this so you can understand how I see these damaging Abuse Frequencies when others can't. They were tearing Creation apart by internally destroying all Spirits whether in or out of body. Creation was on the path to self-destruction.

So, what is an Abuse Frequency and what does it look like? Is it an already existing frequency that gets sick, like a cancer? What does it do to you and how does it spread? How do you cure this condition? Who can get it?

When I started going into people to see who they were and often help them, I began to learn about all the different frequencies I was looking at, trying to understand all I was seeing. All of us are in physical bodies and wake up gradually, that's just how it is. Wouldn't that be nice though, to see energy in it's natural form?

The more I concentrated on who people were inside, the more I began to understand about the Auras coming off their different frequencies. I discovered that certain frequencies released specific Auras which were relative to different characteristics of the people they were in. Blue was related to stronger Pineal Energy Focal Points but also to determination, fortitude. Red was one of the Heart Energy's many Auras.

The more frequencies I saw the more I found a certain pattern existed between them. This is the simple thing, that they were one frequency which repeated itself constantly, other than when someone was compressing all their energy to temporarily make themselves stronger. One example of this would be if you were a parent and your child was threatened. All of that person's energy compresses and eventually returns to normal once the danger is gone.

When an individual compresses their frequencies the wave lengths shorten and the peaks are a little higher. If you look at an analog electrical signal you can understand this more easily. The peaks also become much sharper, more pointed. The Aura given off people at this time becomes a shade of charcoal black. This is a good thing, its natural. It's only us reacting properly to protect.

There was always something else inside everyone that stood out, a common but unnatural frequency. I didn't pay as much attention to it as I should have at first but always knew it was a problem. Once I was able to understand the most basic frequencies in everyone my attention went to this "sick" frequency that stood out like a sore thumb. It didn't seem to be very active but there was something wrong with it. It was out of place, unnatural, and destructive in a way I couldn't understand yet. I soon found that it wasn't a natural frequency which became sick, it was an additional one created from receiving excessive abuse.

I watched it in relation to all the other frequencies. It wasn't very aggressive yet interfered with all the others. When located in the Heart Energy Field it was disrupting the other healthy frequencies, breaking them up, changing their natural flow or repetition. They appeared to make the other frequencies around them sick or broken. They disrupted your ability to be yourself, to flow naturally. I also found that it affects every single form of being, the more abuse received the greater the amount and size of these Abuse Frequencies.

This seems a small thing at first and increases so slowly that usually one never sees it in themselves, they often see it in others first. When you have strong Heart Energy, if left alone and not beaten up, you will be a loving person. If you're filled with Abuse Frequencies your love will be shaken, torn up, and never flow as it should. This erratic behavior will then cause frustration, even anger. The more this happens, the more abuse you're receiving while in that body which then increases the amount of Abuse Frequencies within you, guaranteed, every time. The Heart Energy Field is only one part of who you are. All of your self becomes affected then; I should say infected.

These Abuse Frequencies would have slowly dissipated had your next lives been easier and you had more time off in between them. As we measure our lives in years here on Earth, after each life of up to 100 years you should have about 150 years off before going back into a physical body. If your lives weren't so abusive, you would need only about 50. In the new Energy Bodies for future lives (about 2,000 years from now) you will only need about 5-10 years off but there will be a mandatory amount of 20 or so years unless an exception is necessary.

So, what do they look like? Remember that when you see energy you will view it relative to something you've already consciously understood in this current life. From having used oscilloscopes in diagnosing computer problems in the automotive field I use that image to relate to them. I can also see the energy as a field that has discolored sections within it, inconsistent with its normal consistency and flow. The field itself has empty and sick sections. It's hard to describe as a mass of energy. It's easier to break it down to the individual frequencies and describe them. It's also a little more definitive that way.

These Abuse Frequencies have no natural consistent flow. Parts of the individual frequencies collide with each other, within the same frequency. This is a major cause of aggravation, frustration. Add this to the fact that it's interfering with the normal flow of the other frequency's normal functioning; you have a problem. This is where the Spirit starts having issues within itself, becoming sicker through not only that life and all others but while in its true form as Spirit outside of a body.

The Original First Being Halves were happy with this. Not only were the Spirits growing larger quicker but they were now growing while out of body. These Abuse Frequencies are that damaging. Even out of body they frustrate you slowly tearing at you from the inside. This created a continuous increase in the arrogance and abuse between the different Spirit Beings on the Other Side, all while in their natural state. This was a serious issue. It was enough of a problem happening while in body but now it was happening everywhere.

Arae consistently brought this problem to the Original First Being Halves' attention saying they had no right to do so, reminding them that he was made to protect all of them. They told him they would do as they liked as all beings were just parts of them released to serve them as they saw proper. See the issue building up here? This went against the only format that Arae had now, the other two he released himself a long time ago.

Chapter 2 – The Necessary Process to Reformat Creation

There is a long and short answer to this question. We're taking the short route for two reasons. This was explained in detail in Book II. I was personally involved in it. I had to do the fighting through the body I'm in. Again, none of this is to serve me, only explain. If I could have done this another way I would have. There's a reason I can go into people and change their brains, DNA, etc. It's not because I'm better than anything else because I'm not that in the least. It's because I was made to do this.

Arae is Creation's Protector although I like to say janitor. Arae was the only thing able to do this and he did. It had to stop. All the other major players on the Other Side wanted to take control still maintaining the abuse. They're permanently deleted now. The Original Angels became a serious problem. Almost all of them are gone now. The ones left accepted being free now, servants never more, and agreed not to get into the fight.

It was necessary to remove the cause of Creation's Abuse and any other issues that would bring about the same problem. This has happened. About 92% of Spirit Energy on the Other Side is gone now. This is because all the other large Source Beings over there are gone now. There was the Original First Being Halves, Lydia and Armaeleous, Lillith and Aramaeleous, and other smaller ones.

This wasn't magnificent, glorious, triumphant, or anything such thing. It was disgusting and sad, very sad. Just look at all the abuse in lives today. Look at what all the Animals have gone through, remembering there's trillions of Planets with life on them. When you awaken to your real self you will be able to see all this for yourself. If not you will know it once out of body and back home. It's not important that you see this now. It's only important that it happened.

Section V ~ The Earth's Ruling Annunaki Families

Chapter 1 – Who are the Annunaki

Annunaki Ruling Clans, Prisoners, Telepathy

The problematic Annunaki Ruling Clans here on Earth will be discussed in greater detail in Section VII, Chapter 3. Here I want to describe their functions, problems, and positions within their Clan Hierarchy, all relative to their destruction. The Annunaki people themselves are wonderful beings, intelligent and compassionate as I would want us to be here. Every tree has a few bad apples though. Unfortunately these bad apples came here in a large basket.

The Annunaki people themselves have a rich culture and strong sense of honor. They respect and value the life of others as well as their own. I've great respect for them. The Annunaki originally began massing on a Planet in the Pleiadian Sector of space. That's to be considered their home world right now. To say the Annunaki are basically Pleiadian then would be true. They're different from most other cultures there, so what. Like so many of the older races they're awesome. It's the Annunaki now being removed from our Planet that were an issue. They're not representative of the Annunaki people themselves.

They're a Reptilian form of Human Being. They tend to be up to 8 feet tall on average and can shake the ground when they walk.

They're heavy and solid almost like a living rock. They're not people to fear, except for their retaliation for anything done against them. When they push each other around, it's wise and safer to be a distance from it. A car is a wonderful thing. Just don't let it hit you.

The Annunaki are an old race and have been around the Earth for millions of years. The ones that came and settled here were fine. After a while a small fleet of powerful ships, including a very large one, arrived and decided to stay. The Earth had even more riches back then than now. These are the problematic Annunaki that wound up physically controlling the Earth for just over 10.25 million years, that's 10,250,000 years. The Drachk, N'Antid, and others have finished their rule.

I met the Annunaki people way back when I started waking up hard, around 2009. I was learning how to relax and flow (meditate) when out of nowhere a small group of people astral-projected to me and said, in a slightly desperate manner, "We see you. We know who you are. When are you coming to free us?" I had no idea of what they were talking about but I knew they did and they were serious. Their fear and feelings of abandonment were flowing from them like a river. Somehow I also knew they weren't lying. I found out more about that in the immediately following days.

There was an old prophecy among our family members in space, almost as old as slavery has existed out there. It's over a billion years old. It states that someone was going to come to the little Planet we call Earth and put an end to all slavery in the Universe. This was to happen on 12/21/2012 in its 5th Age. It also stated that there would be a new awakening in all Creation that would change everything. Well, if you're thinking ahead here it might not be what you think.

According to the desires of the Original First Being Male and Female, all improperly detained prisoners were to be released almost everywhere but this supposed great awakening was to be to the fact that there was not only a Father God but also a Mother God. Everyone was going to have help from the Source Field to see them but still never see what was happening on the Other Side, the 2nd Dimension. Well, that's not what happened.

I told the Annunaki prisoners that I didn't know, couldn't give a time but that I was doing all I could to awaken myself, access my abilities. I also said that if they could show me the button on me somewhere that would wake me up I would press it and then break it off so I would never go back to sleep. I realized I was in the middle of a desperate situation but was totally in the dark other than the fact that I knew it, and they, were real. Their feelings of hopelessness and isolation became mine. My heart was filled with desperate sadness as a wave of anxiety flowed through me. I said I understood, realized it was part of my job here, and was doing all I could. That sucked.

Slowly they disappeared taking with them their sadness. I felt like crap. I was failing to do something I just realized I was supposed to do and had no idea about it or how to move forward with the issue. Hell I was still trying to find my true self, my abilities. I was already having issues with the Original First Being Halves. A while after the conversation I went back to look and discovered that they were all falsely imprisoned Reptilian Humans, guilty of nothing than being tricked. I could feel others there also, other types of people. I was ashamed of myself not being more than I was at that moment. I felt myself a failure.

After this I instinctively kicked up my game, so to speak. I have always known I was a protector and kept from doing my job. I increased my aggression against the Original Male and Female whenever they approached me. I wasn't near as strong back then and totally unaware of exactly what I was and could do. All I knew is that I had to do more, immediately. I felt a nervous desperation.

I reached into my brain and tried to split it in half to shut this body down and be free of it, return to my natural self. I already knew the Original Ones were afraid of me when out of the body. I had threatened to leave it if they didn't leave me alone and they freaked out a bit. I felt fear in the Original First Being Male. They were always lying to me about everything and anything but heart energy doesn't lie. Always trust your heart energy.

About 7 days later I had a huge powerful ship hovering over my house. It was the Annunaki Ambassador in his flying fortress. All the walls and windows were shaking from the vibrations his ship was making 100 plus feet above my roof. Herc, my awesome Corgi/Pit-bull mix, came running upstairs and jumped on the bed as soon as it happened. He looked me in the eye and said "I got this dad! What's happening?"

He was being protective but also concerned at this point. Herckie always slept on the bed with me, all my Animals have unless they didn't want to at the moment. Heck I wouldn't blame any of them; I snore like a couple of freight trains passing. My lung diseases, COPD being one of them, create that effect. I can't help it, I can't breathe well. I've always protected my Animal family members, and all others, with my life. They can feel this; it's a normal function like walking.

Anyway, the Annunaki Ambassador has more compassion in him than he'd probably want known. I spoke with the Annunaki Ambassador a few more times from farther away, not just over my house. One time he astral-projected into my house concerning a serious matter I was involved with. There's a lot to what I'm about to tell you relative to telepathy with one and many people, seeing while you're astral projecting, and more.

I wander off in thought for a reason, to feed you a greater variety of information but also because my thoughts don't flow in a normal manner. I do it naturally, can't help it. The Source Field is part of me, extends from me. That's difficult for a physical brain to deal with. I want you to understand as much about everything as possible.

I've always found it easier to describe things that I've done myself, relating them to you through my personal experiences. Those events which we experience ourselves we tend to perceive with more clarity, and understand in greater depth. This is learning, is it not? We all develop a greater understanding of various things every day. That's why once you put your first foot forward to awaken you sleeping Metabilities, it starts happening as naturally as talking or falling asleep. I just make it happen quicker, stronger, and farther.

I spoke to the Annunaki Ambassador a couple more times from farther away, but one time he astral-projected into the house about a serious matter that I was involved with. There's a lot of information here relative to understanding telepathy with not just one but many people in different locations. It's also about accepting what you're seeing and feeling while astral projecting as you begin to understand it. I want you to know as much about it as possible. I want you to be yourself, free.

Before we talk about the last time I talked with the Annunaki Ambassador, at least up to this 13th day of April, 2018 anyway, I need to explain the reason for that visit. I made a video, actually two, about this particular chain of events. It was due to an event which occurred previously that same day, one that I was involved in. There was an unprovoked attack on a Federation Starship run by one of my Source Spirit family members. The Draconian, not the Drachk, made their first attack with their newest model warship. They attacked the Federation Flagship, the pride of their fleet.

I want to take a moment here to describe the Draconian Race to you. Remember that all of us have had lives in many of the different bodies that exist, but some races have more issues, they tend to have more negative Souls within them. You can easily determine the basic characteristics of different body types but you cannot do the same in regards to the singular physical person due to the Spirit inside which makes the person who they really are. There are loving and abusive beings in all the races. This being said, understand this about the Draconian Race.

Over a hundred centuries ago, as we measure time on Earth, the Draco people decided to add Drachk DNA to their lineage. They wanted to add the power of Drachk DNA to their own. The Draco are reptilian. The Drachk are Dragon, a much more powerful species. The Draconian have always been very aggressive and most of their leaders set their sights on raising their species, and themselves, above others in relation to fear, respect, and position.

They thought adding Drachk DNA would enhance them but it didn't mix too well with their reptilian DNA. Severe character flaws became prevalent immediately. There were initially stronger physical deformation issues than those they deal with today, but their DNA still isn't able to handle the Drachk Dragon DNA. As a result, the Draconian are over aggressive, seldom care for others, and only reluctantly heed the words of the Drachk themselves. Remember that there are always both positive and negative people in every race. The Draconian just have a smaller percentage of positive people.

For the most part the Drachk ignore what they've done but they've also destroyed far more Draconian ships, fleets, and bases than any other race. Part of this is due to the Draconian being more aggressive than all the other races. They've had it coming. I've said many times that the Drachk are a powerful, intelligent, and benevolent race. They are the oldest and stay out of the affairs of others until someone is getting insane in their yard and their yard is the Universe.

Before continuing we need to understand a couple things. Let me get this off my chest. I'm in a tired old Human male body but that's not what I am, I'm inside it just like you're inside yours. What I am also exists out of this body and can affect things in this 3rd Dimension when deemed necessary. My personal Metabilities are limited in comparison to what I can do when free.

My outer self protects the body I'm in and only takes action when something important on a large scale is happening. This part of me has been the Source Field since early 2013. Maybe I don't understand humble but I understand protecting everything and that it matters more than my own existence. I was created from the frequencies of compassion and fortitude, not hope. I was made to make things happen. I have love for everything. How else could I be like I am? I'm not a machine; I'm a living being, just different. I am a function.

When I've wanted to crank up someone's abilities but shouldn't, the outer part of me knew better and I had to fight it to override it. I quickly understood that he was almost always correct. He's not confined to a body so he has full access to his intelligence, unlike me in a body. We're all like that. He's floating around able to see what I can't and understand what I can't through this physical brain that I'm stuck in. However, when we agree on something important, especially in regards to protecting something, things happen.

The outer part of what I am can do amazing things in this the 3rd Dimension while I can only affect the 2nd Dimension, other than working on a physical person's body and energy. There's good reasoning in that. If someone was able to kill people while mad in a body, they could make serious mistakes from not being aware of everything involved in the situation. This is not the case when they're free Spirit outside of a physical body. It's an important regulation to maintain. When the full body of Arae agrees on something, whatever needs to happen, will.

Such events were stopping the 8-11-2011 tsunami, removal of this Solar system's Ruling Council on Saturn, the Draconian Warship Issue here, and the Annunaki attack we're also in the process of discussing. I'm not capable of doing this through my body. It had to be done in agreement with the rest of me that's free so it could act on it.

The funny thing about all this is that after I'm gone and a little time flows by, you'll begin to hear of these events from other people here from other Planets, once we begin communicating with them on a more personal basis. It'll all come out in the years ahead. For now this series of telepathic astral-projection events is a way for me to describe what happens in them. Your proof of these events will come from others later, our family from space. It's not as important for you to believe this as it is for me to tell you now. Again, this is about the next 100 years.

My Source family member inside the Federation ship was ranked fourth in command of the Federation Fleet. He's in a Serpoian body this life. Most people call them Grays. His Spirit is part of the Lilly and Arae family. His ship was also the flagship of the Federation. He was the highest ranking officer in the fleet that saw combat. I was busy when this happened but another family member got my attention by frantically jumping into my head with enough energy to put a lightning bolt between my ears.

I went to the incident immediately. The ship had one huge hole in it and two slightly smaller ones. It was barely in one piece and with a few pieces missing, floating in space. A few crewmen were already floating in space and the ship was completely helpless. A large powerful warship was facing them assessing the damage they had just inflicted. They appeared to be waiting for some reason before delivering the final blow. I looked back for a second to rewind the events that just happened.

A newly designed Draconian Warship appeared out of nowhere and attacked the Federation Flagship with 4 blasts before anyone knew what was happening. They came out of nowhere. The Draconian had new stealth measures that the Federation's technology wasn't able to deal with yet. People were now floating in space and there was no fixing this ship. I guess I kinda panicked realizing that all this was real and actually happening. I've done too much and had too much proof in the last 10 years not to trust myself now, and I didn't. People think that all this is easy, well it's not.

When I started to go into people's brains and they felt it, I had very strong physical proof of what I could do, myself not another Spirit. I might have mentioned that I've gone to a lot of stores and been in public when my energy made items jump off of shelves, even when they had over a ¼" barrier. They just picked themselves up over the border and onto the floor.

That was from part of me outside of my body. It was my energy but my conscious mind didn't control it. Therefore the action did not belong to me, just part of my energy. Never allow yourself to lie to yourself, or anyone else for that matter. Are you a journey of self-realization or just attempting to find self-glorification which is not only false but a negative action? Be yourself no matter what that is. Why, because you're awesome. Never forget that. I know all of you. I was there when you were born. Let's get back to the unprovoked attack on this Federation ship.

Seeing all this happen I didn't know what to do or if I was even able to do anything. What was I supposed to do? Hell, I didn't know. I'd never been in this type of situation before. I knew I couldn't protect them myself, can't do something like that while stuck in this body. An ICUC and a little healing would be worthless here. These bodies were made like this over time by the Original First Beings. They were cruel but smart. I can't stand feeling like this when I'm aware of what I really am and what I can do when myself, free Spirit. I was too concerned about everyone to be mad yet, but that was coming, I could feel it.

Out of nowhere, my energy cranked up inside like a volcano, but it was a natural event that I didn't intentionally create. It just happened. I had powerful aggressive protective energy building up and then just acted on it. It was me but I was only a part of it. In a fraction of a second a soft golden energy sphere surrounded the ship, its wreckage, and floating bodies. Part of my Field Spirit produced a protective energy barrier which supported life within it. It had a hard outer shell with a network of lines connected by golden orbs where they met.

I immediately went after the attacking vessel, put it in a destructive sphere, and tried to figure out what to do next. The outer part of me was waiting to see how I reacted, that I could feel. It would decide whether or not to comply; making it happen or not. I tried to dissolve or delete the ship but nothing happened. Then I just got madder and started compressing it into as small an object as I could. That was working. I was lost in a rage of anger. I'm so damn sick of all the abuse happening everywhere all the time and never being able to deal with it properly as I've almost always been in a body.

I intentionally compressed the ship until it was the size of a large marble, the outer part of me supplying the massive power needed as well as releasing some of my own from this physical containment trap called a body. He was the reason it happened. I only made the intention and a little more. I couldn't delete it into nothingness because there needed to be something solid left behind, some sort of physical proof left to show what had happened.

OK, back to the main events here. I saw a few Federation ships arrive, supplying aid. My family member hit my head with a shot (thought) of gratitude and I left, going back to what I was doing earlier. I sat there for a moment trying to relax and then went back to what just happened, trying to fully understand everything that occurred. It was a new experience for me so I wanted to see all the details as well as understand how I felt about everything that happened.

If you don't separate your feelings from what you're seeing, it's difficult to understand what you're seeing or ever develop any faith in your being able to see anything. Don't lie to yourself. Forget any wanted outcome; just see what's there and try to understand it afterwards with an open mind. How else can we learn?

Before moving forward from this point I want to explain what it's like to telepathically communicate with multiple groups of people at the same time, especially while astral projecting into multiple locations. It's not just possible; it's something you can do over time. This is not like baking a cake, it takes practice. You have to understand telepathy first.

You need to be able to talk with other people who already know how to, like your Spirit Guides for one. Relax and let your mind go, let it just sit there and open up, flowing outwards in every direction. Like a ball of smoke, your energy will open and flow everywhere. Just relax, let go of the physical world, and breathe.

You can learn with a friend but first try talking with your Spirit Guides, then the Fae people (Faerie), and then folks in space. As you do, your telepathic abilities will increase in strength and accuracy. Hearing how something happens, especially that it can happen, helps us realize it's possible. As we work to understand it better we reach our objectives more easily. All of you can do this.

About a week before this event, out of nowhere, I started talking with 3, 4, and then 5 groups of people telepathically. I was being talked to by Fae beings in body, Source family members out of body, Serpoian and Pleiadian people on their separate ships, and Animal Essence out of body all at once. It happened out of the blue, from nowhere. I could feel my outer self and part of Lilly in my head making changes to my brain. I knew it was a good thing, nothing to be concerned about, but at that moment I couldn't understand why it was happening. After the "Annunaki Clan Meeting" I knew why. They were preparing me for that event.

To start a multi-level telepathy session you have to learn how to release your conscious mind on a different level than just talking to Spirit Guides, but that's where it starts. All of you have Spirit Guides with you at all times. Once you ask them, if they feel you're ready, they will start conversations with you one at a time until you're talking with 3 or 4 different people. It takes time, be patient. You're not making mistakes; you're creating learning points where you increase your understanding, a very good thing. Now, let's get back to this unique series of events that either you or your family will later hear about from other people.

The next day, 1/25/2015 at about 2:30 pm, I was upstairs in my studio getting ready to make a video when several large groups of individuals began projecting into the room. It was the 6 major Earthen Annunaki and Serpoian prisoner work groups. Later the 7 ruling Royal Annunaki Clans joined in. Many others came with them but only to watch. The prisoner worker groups were comprised of people from various parts of the Universe, all falsely imprisoned, including the helpless Annunaki and Serpoian people with them.

The 6 separate prisoner communities were situated to my left in a straight row. I immediately recognized who they were. Their upper echelon members, often called controllers, were in the forefront, also only to watch, not participate. The controllers were prisoners also. They received small benefits from the ruling clans. Some of these poor people have been imprisoned through several generations. This has only recently been stopped. It started in 2016 as I talked about often in my YouTube videos on the Jay Essex channel. I told you what attacks were happening, where and why, as they did.

When the worker groups showed up I looked into them, who they were, what they did, what they wanted, how they felt, and even the physical bodies they were in to a small degree. I wanted to see what the controllers looked like physically. I was mostly concerned with their intentions and basic nature though. They looked at me with sharp cold eyes, whatever. I could see all the workers behind the controllers. There were hundreds of slaves in each group right behind them. In each separate location I saw thousands of them. They were slaves, right here on Earth, and I was looking at them unable to do anything at the moment. That put me on edge, getting real pissed now.

The vast majority of Annunaki in these clans are good people. They were born into their lives; having to perform their roles and never had the power to change things. They were all told a long time ago that the anarchy would be taken down and everyone freed. They were hoping and counting on it. It was part of the 12/21/2012 Earth 5th Age Prophecy I mentioned earlier.

Anyway, the 7 ruling Annunaki factions arrived soon after the prisoners. They brought the workers first to make sure it was safe to appear. I've said many times that I can't telekinetically move a round pencil on a flat hard surface, no one can, but once they astral-project out of their bodies they were in the 2nd Dimension. That's my side of the fence. This is where I have access to a lot of my abilities while still stuck here. Still though, any physical damage had to be done by what's outside me.

This gathering was larger than the 7 ruling clans and 6 prisoner groups; many others were there from around the globe. Almost all of the other clans were there watching, just not allowed to speak. I could see groups of hundreds and sometimes thousands of Annunaki and Serpoian slaves in different places scattered across the Planet. There was a large group of them in Russia headed by a strong female who was working against the other problematic clans.

I couldn't put this in the first two books of the Creation Series but I can say it now. The leaders of both the Arkansas and Russian Annunaki Clans are friends of mine. The Russian Annunaki Clan Leader was and still is, a female Annunaki, a woman not a queen as many suggest. The Annunaki Clans are no longer in control of Earth. The Arkansas Annunaki Clan Leader is extremely large and powerful. There are extensive mines in Arkansas, mostly the North and Northwestern regions. They had the strongest weaponry and DNA knowledge of all the Annunaki Clans.

The Russian Annunaki Clan leader is really cool and was always on the side of the Annunaki Freedom Fighters. She worked with the leader of the Arkansas clan, a huge individual. I've talked with both of them quite a few times. She was the only female of a large clan. Many people have been told the Annunaki have a "hive" system of control but that's incorrect. So much for the majority of internet information related to our friends from other planets. Both of them will be staying here with a major role in helping all of us come together now.

I didn't see the exact locations of all the different clans; didn't care to look as it didn't matter much. I had an unexpected issue in my house to deal with. Herckie had already become upset, concerned when he felt the attitudes of everyone there. Herckie meant everything to me. I would never have hesitated to protect Herckie from anything. He was, and still is, very important to me. He's hanging around in the 2nd Dimension where M66 is located inside the Leo Constellation. During the meeting Herckie was laying on one of his special therapeutic beds, as usual, located under the table right next to me where I made my videos. I had them spread out all over the house.

As the 7 ruling clans came into view I focused on them immediately. Most of them were in trip chairs. A trip chair is a large strong device that looks similar to a reclining metal chair that's three times the size of a reclined barber's chair. There is a device that partially surrounds your head, reads your DNA and the energy fields in your brain, and finally uses a specific electro-magnetic sequence to magnify your metabilities. There are more structural parts of it that we won't bother with here, pipes, fluids, and more.

They were initially made to support long range starship travel. When you had trouble you would get into the trip chair and send a strong telepathic message to someone at the nearest starship port where someone else was already in one, waiting for emergency calls. These chairs were soon found to be useful for medical purposes and eventually modified by military personnel for aggressive purposes used against others.

Getting back to the meeting, the strongest of the leaders of each clan weren't in one. The conversation started with them talking to each other as well as to me, all at once. Within seconds, 4 of the clans came forward and began speaking to me directly, again at the same time. They were the California, Arizona, Florida, and N.Y. clans. The Arkansas clan was the strongest but said nothing at first. There were over 25 individuals talking to me, seemed like everyone had their own opinion.

There was also a lot of background mental chatter from the others, easily ignored. At first I became a little confused as to how many people were actually talking to me and how many minds I was just inside listening to. I figured that if they didn't ask a question they weren't important, so I started with that. In a quick moment I located 5 or 6 people who were talking to me directly and dealt with them. They were more aggressive and seemed to speak for their clans. It was like a conference call, felt normal after about 10 seconds.

They didn't bother me; there was nothing for me to be concerned about other than the reason for the meeting, what they were up to. They couldn't hurt me and I could hurt them. It was unprecedented though, didn't understand what was happening and why. You could feel all the disgusting arrogance but that wasn't all. I felt fear and uncertainty.

Many of the Annunaki in the background felt that everything was starting to fall apart for them. They never said that aloud, it was just how they felt. As the conversations began I felt their anger and aggression towards me so I immediately cranked up my energy. They settled back and started to talk to me calmly while still conversing quietly with each other.

The Arizona Annunaki Clan began never stopped talking so they had the floor, so to speak. They wanted to appear to be the leaders. Herckie was still holding his head up in the air, trying to decide whether to stay or leave. My protective feelings for him cranked up a little more. At this point I was paying more attention to Herckie than them. The Arizona clan wanted to make an agreement with me, a truce of some sort. They thought that I personally did all the damage to that ship.

Then the California Clan started talking, showing me maps, something about the Pacific Ocean and area. The Florida Clan was watching, wanting to talk but didn't. I could see they wanted to offer me communication access to everything happening on the Planet and in their community. These folk were never excessively aggressive, more followers as they knew they had to. They were structurally weaker than the top 3 clans.

Who the hell were these people, offering me part of Gaia's physical body?

The Arkansas leader cranked up his energy to be seen in a position of leadership and then stood on the side. The Arizona clan kept talking and the others went quiet. I had never been involved in such a large telepathic conversation as this. There were now about 11 or 12 people involved in separate conversations with me, all of them making promises while they were trying to make their case. All this did is increase my protective attitude, and with it my anger.

Here's where everything happened and it didn't take long to end. A male Annunaki from the Arizona Clan, important but not their leader (who was staying in the background) began to speak clearly giving me some kind of offer. He said all the clans agreed to give me 1/7 of the Planet to own and control. Who the hell were these people, offering me part of Gaia's physical body? He kept talking and I wasn't listening. All I could see in my head was Gaia being cut into 7 parts and I fired up hard. Who the hell were these arrogant schmucks?

At this point my friend, the leader of the Arkansas Clan fired his energy up hard and growled at me. He said "I'll kill you!" At this point Herckie jumped up and ran out of the studio. I lost it. I bypassed my buddy in Arkansas and went straight to the Arizona Clan. I attacked them with everything I had. The Field part of me kept me from doing as much damage as I intended. I went after the other clans but found myself being pushed back towards my body by my Field self. My buddy in Arkansas was never going to come at me here. He was acting out his role. That's why I kept him out of it. I hit the Nevada clan hard.

Everyone started disappearing quickly in different directions. I could see that Herckie was fine, just scared, so I went to look at the Arizona Clan to see what became of my actions. Fourteen were completely crushed and many others wounded. After three days passed 51 were dead and another 3 still seriously injured. Again, my Field and I did this together. I caught him off guard; otherwise no one would have been killed. I was running it for a fraction of a second. I regret nothing except not having done more. Herckie came back into the studio moments later after everything calmed down and the others were gone.

Before leaving here I need to mention something important. The Arkansas Annunaki Clan was not abducting humans out of homes and doing experiments on them. There were other clans and different races of beings doing that. The Arkansas group worked on improving different forms of DNA to enhance their ability to thrive here on Earth as well as in space.

Their main concern was weapons development and they had the best. The Federation sponsored an attack on them back in 2010, trying to take some of these weapons from them. They failed. Don't forget that the Federation was a problem, not an asset. You'll discover this further on in this book. If you Google "massive Redwing Blackbird deaths in Arkansas" you will read about the fallout from this event.

There are also horror stories about ETs doing DNA research on people right here on Earth. Look to the U.S. government, and others, for that. The hidden factions behind the U.S. government are the greatest threat to the population here, not ETs. There are only a few ET groups that used to do that here. The Enaugk were one such group but they were not on the Planet and they've been stopped already anyway.

There was a gentleman which I named Homer in Florida who has passed now. He was an earlier U.S. governmental experiment in crossing reptilian and Human DNA that went wrong in a bad way. He reached out to me telepathically years ago while I was relaxing on a business trip in Florida. I looked at his distorted body and face. It was sad enough to bring tears to my eyes and anger through my heart. It was all I could do to talk to him without breaking down. He was sick, lonely, dying, and no one there cared. They were just waiting for him to drop dead. I wanted to give him what little momentary company I could, a name that he never received, and tell him how special he was to me. He was happier than you would expect considering his poor treatment. I was torn between anger and anguish, trying to keep that to myself.

An hour later I was downstairs in the main room of my house at the computer, working on the second volume of the Creation Series. I felt someone astral-projecting to in front of me to my right. He was about 8' tall and looked right at me from about 10' away. I went into his head and he was thinking "I wonder if he can see me." I fired my Pineal Gland up and softly touched his so he knew that I did. He's always sent ahead of the Ambassador whenever he travels anywhere. He needed to make sure things were safe. I waited for him to talk but he didn't. What happened next was at first confusing and then kinda funny.

He slowly drifted away from me and towards the kitchen. If he had a body he would have been walking but as Spirit he was floating. He stopped in the kitchen just before the refrigerator and stared at it. Now I started laughing. The first thing I thought was, "What does this guy want, a sandwich and a beer?" After watching the refrigerator for a few seconds and came back out to stand in front of me again, right where he originally arrived. He stared at me for a moment as if he didn't know what to make of me or my mind's thought processes. He couldn't get into my head. Nothing anywhere can do that.

I went into his head with a smile on my face to see what he was thinking. I let him feel me in there, the polite thing to do. There was an electromagnetic pulse coming from the kitchen that he needed to inspect before the Annunaki Ambassador could safely come into the house. The energy pulse was coming from the electric motor in my refrigerator. Apparently their ship's scanners couldn't see this clearly enough through my roof's tar shingles from their ship in orbit, at least not in the detail necessary to insure his safety before arrival.

The Ambassador and I already knew each other. He stared at me for just a moment, an accepted form of greeting each other when we astral-project to each other, and then waited for me to speak first. I was quiet at first waiting for him to initiate the conversation. I thought I was being proper and he thought I was already in his head and understood the reason for his visit. I've never done that to someone unless it was necessary or I was really curious about something.

As the Ambassador stood there I could feel grave concern flowing through and out of him. As I touched his thoughts flowing on the top of his head I realized that I needed to explain my attack on the Annunaki Royal Clans. He needed to know about the two earlier events which preceded his visit. Understanding what happened was the first part of the reason for his visit. The second part was to express his concern for any possible retaliatory actions made against over 22,000 Annunaki prisoners still being held by them here on Earth. He wanted to know what might possibly happen next. That was hard for me to answer.

I explained what happened and why but it didn't help him feel any better. I didn't know what to say or do. I understood his concern, it was real, founded in common sense, but I knew nothing would happen. The problematic Annunaki were too scared. I tried to tell him that. I knew he couldn't have blind faith in that. Once again I'm sitting feeling helpless, can't stand that feeling, not a part of me.

I apologized for adding grief to his life and explained that what happened was both proper and necessary. I again tried to assure him that things would be OK and that all the prisoners would be free soon. It's hard to do that when I don't have the exact details of how that was going to happen. I couldn't tell him about other things that were happening. I knew it would, just not exactly how and when. I'm always frustrated with being stuck here in this body. It's like having my hands tied.

Moments later, the Ambassador nodded his head and left feeling empty inside, wondering if there was anything else he could do. The aide stayed a moment later and stared at me, giving off the energetic feelings of a smile. I physically smiled back at him and told him to stay a second. I cranked him up real quick, only took about 3 seconds. He looked down at his energy, smiled, and then left. So, that was it.

About two minutes later I was curious of how the Ambassador's Aide was doing with his energy work so I went to look at him and the Ambassador. They were both on their ship but as I started to focus on them another ship pulled up, a much smaller one built for only a few people. It was the Serpoian Ambassador coming to visit his Annunaki counterpart. This was interesting so I listened in.

I could still feel the concern in the Annunaki Ambassador as he went to greet the Serpoian gentleman. The Serpoian Ambassador had most of a smile on his face, definitely one inside, as he greeted the Annunaki Ambassador. He tried to settle his concerns about retaliation and asked him to attempt relaxing.

The Serpoian Ambassador told him there were bigger hidden events already in progress and that things will be fine. He insisted that the long wait for the prisoner's freedom is almost at hand. He was right, they're almost all free today. There are only a few pockets left that will be dealt with soon. Then the Serpoian Ambassador took off in a hurry as abruptly as he arrived.

Later on you will discover more about the new Alliance of Planets originally put together by the Drachk and N'Antids. This is the one we will join before too long. Arae and a few other Source Beings were there in Spirit form. I did a video about how it happened, I was there, opened up the first meeting. There is at least one video on the Jay Essex YouTube channel that describes it. I had to get to sleep early that night to be there for it. I laid down and was knocked out immediately. Here again you'll find out more about all this from other people (beings) in only a few years.

The next morning, 1/26/2015, I was walking down the stairs with Herckie to start our day when a younger Annunaki gentleman came to me before we made it half way down. He was on my left side and blurted out a question with a little energy behind it. He said "Why didn't you kill all of them?" I looked at him and told him to wait a minute.

Once downstairs I took a good look at him to see who he was. I recognized him as part of the Annunaki Resistance Force here on Earth for many years, folks who have been trying to free the Planet from the ruling clans. I told him that it wasn't possible to do that and things would be taken care of soon. That's when I cut off the conversation. He wasn't happy about it because I didn't explain things well enough for him to understand what I was saying and I wasn't able to take the time to explain it to him.

Back then I was still very sick, I have been for about 10 years and just finally getting to leave now. At my last event in September of 2015 you could hear my lungs gurgle while I tried to breathe. I was tired from everything I'd done, was doing, and still needed to finish before leaving, all while being messed with every moment of every day until I left. I care more than anyone but I've been doing this through a worn out, beat up, and diseased body. I talk with everyone all the time until I finally shut down for a moment, trying to take a breather.

On many occasions I've talked with large groups of people from various different Planets as myself, as much as I could project there while still here in body. I've gone to their ships and sometimes their home Planets. One meeting I had was with an assembly of over a hundred Drachk members. One of my Source family members is a council member on the head Drachk Council, the 10th.

I've been more than just involved with what's been happening in space as well as here on Earth. I've made videos, showing the date and time, where I talk about various separate events such as the huge Drachk starship that came here a while ago, the size of a small Planet. Parts of it are here now. Their presence is here to stay for quite a while. Your lives are about to change in such a way that our present conscious minds can't comprehend.

Here's a chart on the timing of these individual events. I didn't take notes on what happened as it did. I waited about a month and a half before writing it down for some reason, don't really know. Anyway, it's still accurate on the day and close on the time of day. Here's the short list.

Saturday, 1/24/2015, 3:30 pm – Federation Attacked, Draconian Destroyed

Sunday, 1/25/2015, 2:30 pm – Meeting with 7 Annunaki Clans and Others

Sunday, 1/25/2015, 3:30 pm – Meeting with Annunaki Ambassador and Aide

Sunday, 1/25/2015, 3:45 pm – Serpoian and Annunaki Ambassadors Talk

Monday, 1/26/2015, 10:00 am – Annunaki Resistance Member Conversation

Maybe I should take a moment to explain my attitude. I'm not an insensitive jerk but I do have my issues. I've fought off and destroyed the strongest Source Beings, Original Angels, and all else 24/7, that's all day and all night continuously. The Original First Being Male, now deleted, actually melted a part of my brain on the upper left side while I was sleeping. I woke up in my own bed with a headache and didn't know who I was.

I went to the mirror and saw someone. It was me but I had no understanding of anything other than the fact that things were OK and I was damaged. Once I got a grip on things I saw what happened to me while asleep. I was hurting for a few days after that but things eventually calmed down. I just couldn't see like I used to anymore. Even my other half, the Initial or Primary Lilly couldn't fix it and others have tried. It's no big deal; I learned how to go around it quickly but not as well as initially.

The reason I brought all this up was to express the lack of compassion I sometimes appear to have. I've been at war since 2009; I woke up fighting when I was weak and haven't stopped yet. I'm burned out and a little twitchy. All this was done through a physical body which should have been about impossible. It would have been started and finished in seconds if not for that. It had to be done like this. I had to clean up the Other Side while stuck in a body, so I did. Here's why.

The Other Side recognizes the physical life experience for what it's always been. People are put into physical bodies, abused harshly, and eventually brought back home to the 2nd Dimension, supposedly unharmed. The Original First Being Male and Female always told everyone that you can't listen to the cries, screams, and complaints of Spirit while in body. They would say the Spirits are experiencing temporary insanity.

Chapter 2 – How Did the Annunaki Here Take Over

Human Evolution On Earth

This is covered in detail in Book II. There were Souls and some Essence Beings who came here over 11 million years ago. This was before the introduction of a specific physical body type for Spirits to have lives in here on Earth. This body form is known as the Adamic Race, introduced here about 10.572 million years ago in Atlantis. Lemuria already had Spirit in different physical bodies on her from other Planets.

As there was no base life form made for the Earth yet, Spirits were often allowed to come here and make a body of their own choosing. This is where all your Half Animal – Half Human Beings came from. This is also the origin of the "creatures" in much of Greek and Roman Mythology; the Centaur, Minotaur, and others.

This began about 11 million years ago and soon became a problem to the separation of Animal and Human species. This created an immediate need for the Adamic Race. Lilly and Arae came first as the Red Adam and Eve, then the other four couples came. They were all Source Mates, all four of them, all five of them actually. The original Lilly attracted most of the dual composition beings and with Arae, led them to lower dimensions already made here in our Solar system. Once down there Arae closed the door behind them. He opened the dimensional barrier for them to enter and then released it again.

These beings were never harmed by Lilly or Arae. They were separated to have lives as they chose, just not allowed to interfere with the separate Animal and Human civilizations in the 3rd Dimension. They are still there today and will also start becoming more visible about the year 2080-2084 or so.

In Lemuria where Earth's first colonies appeared, people from different Planets came here mostly for mining yet were also interested in the flora here. Our Plant life was very strong for healing and supporting life. This was true as the Earth was young in comparison to the Planets the colonists came from. Over time the Original First Being Halves had learned how to improve on helping each Planet support the lives on them. This was important. The physical bodies had to survive in order to maintain the abuse mechanism designed for all the Spirits that would live here.

As there were always issues from all the outbreaks of war and political struggles between people from different Planets, the colonists had to drop off their supplies and leave. There were no large military bases set up. It was a mining community not a military outpost.

The problematic Annunaki, who came here initially, did so as a fleet with one huge ship and various smaller ones. They were a form of nomadic tribe. They were not consistent of the normal Annunaki people, they were more destructive with an insatiable desire to control and consume all around them. You might think of them as Planetary Pirates, overly aggressive and heartless.

Once the Annunaki here met Lilly and Arae, the Red Eve and Adam, they wanted to find a way to access, control, and consume their metaphysical abilities. Lilly and Arae, as well as the other 4 Source Spirit mates who made the other Adamic Races, began creating children of their own. The original 5 Adamic Couples made their own bodies so they brought their own powerful abilities with them. They were telekinetic, telepathic, and so much more.

There was already a large group of various cultures here, on Atlantis that is, when these Adamics arrived. As they mingled with others in the small cities they impressed many people, especially the Half Animal – Half Human beings that lived there then. The only folk with greater interest were the Annunaki. They immediately sought out their abilities and other strengths.

They weren't aware that only the first Adam and Eve, the Red ones, were as strong as what they were witnessing. In addition to that, subsequent generations of Adamics were born with lower power levels and Metabilities. The Adamics had long lives, they were healthy, had strong intuition, and they could work hard for long periods of time. They also seemed to know about things before they happened, again part of their intuition.

The Annunaki began trying to persuade them towards inter-racial breeding but the Adamics wouldn't have it. Then the Annunaki began capturing them when they could and force it when able. Eventually they were successful enough to produce large cities of Reptilian Adamics, eventually armies. They had incredible endurance, were smarter, and turned out to be better soldiers. When the Adamics first arrived they stayed to themselves for the most part, but bit by bit their communities spread out, claiming more and more of the land as theirs. They also reproduced quickly.

While all this was going on the other settlers here, originally from other planets, got into the mix and we eventually became the society we are today. The Reptilian part of our DNA has decreased over the years as the Annunaki Royal Families decided they needed more purity than numbers now. There were 5 ages of civilization here on Earth. Each one started in almost the exact same way. The original Annunaki went underground with some others when the Earth's crust changed. They always came back stronger into each new age. We're currently in the 6th Age now. There was no catastrophic event going from the 5th to the 6th.

So, this is also the evolution of the Earthen Human Being. The primary race for the Earth was the Adamics but there were so many other races here, including the Annunaki among other less prevalent Reptilian groups, that a more widely diversified blending of DNA was possible. This situation is not as common in Creation as you might think. There is more to the diversity of physical body life on Earth though.

The Serpoian people from the Zeta Reticuli System (Grays) have been "growing" diversified living beings, and without permission from those involved. They've been doing this for what seems like forever. There are laws coming into effect soon to control this and other related items but they're not in effect yet.

The Serpoian put biological DNA together to grow new beings as we graft Plant species onto each other. They're just really good at it. They use this information to help everyone in so many ways. This created the diversified growth of Apes into different Human like beings. All of these beings died off, those that were not removed.

There is a very nice Serpoian lady who's close to my heart. Her name is Serenae. She has been involved in the Creation of the new children being born with my current DNA. These children are being created from very powerful Source Spirit bodies and will be able to do amazing things, more on that later. There is also a Serpacieant lady by the name of Mellae who is close to Diana and I, just like Serenae.

The Serpoian people have been here over 11 million years now but have no large colonies as they used to in the first 3 Ages. They are here in different capacities. Some have been working with our governments in a less than compassionate manner but most have been working to help us while remaining hidden. They used to have outposts in South America, Africa, Japan as well as other locations where they attempted splicing Earthen Human DNA with certain Animals, even with fish in two locations.

I only bring this up to complete the picture of how the Earthen Being DNA has changed, grown, and developed over the years, 11 million of them. This is actually the evolution of the Human Race here on Earth. Our species have DNA that has gone through so many changes that we are easily in the top five Planets containing the most adaptive DNA in this Universe. This also makes us popular, especially to Planets with races whose DNA is slowly disintegrating.

Because of the repetitive surge in the problematic Annunaki forcing themselves on the Adamics over the 5 Ages, your bodies have strong Reptilian DNA in them.

Section VI ~ The New Universal Alliance (10-18-2016)

Chapter 1 – The Alliance Members Here to Help Us

Before explaining how the new Universal Alliance was created I want to cover some of the folk who are not only in it, but have been with Diana, myself, and other members of my Source family. This would be physical bodies containing Lilly, Arae, or the Spirits released when Lilly and Arae created them from their combined selves. Most are being visited by our friends from space. They have work to do together.

There are hundreds of members and increases daily. The following races mentioned here are just a few of the races belonging to the new Universal Alliance or Alliance of Planets. The Alliance's name varies according to the life form that is addressing it. There is a new name for it coming in the future, the Alliance of Life. That will happen when it does, not for a while yet.

Various races from other Planets are here doing what they can for us. Some are on the surface but most are at close proximity in space. There's an actual policing force here now keeping things maintained as there are so many ships here. For the most part they're waiting. That's almost over now. The people I'm about to talk about are the ones I've met personally, Astral-Projection for the most part. Serenae, Mellae, and others like the Archobien and more have been in my house.

They've been in our house, on average about 3-5 times a week, while Diana and I slept. They've also played with stuff, shown part of themselves physically, and worked on us physically, helping to maintain the health of Diana, our children, and myself to an extent. They know I'm leaving. They've been doing this with our consent. We've also been on ships more times than I can count but we're never left with the detailed memories that we desire. It has to be like this for now. They have laws concerning these matters.

An Archobien once showed his arm and hand on top of the lighted keyboard of Diana's laptop after having softly pushed her shoulder moments before. Diana and I know them, see them, and talk with them. It's not an issue with either of us other than wanting them to agree to be photographed. They're not ready for that yet. This will happen soon though.

I physically bumped into Serenae once, kinda funny. I leaned back in my chair quickly as I was trying to snap the vertebrae in my back and I accidentally hit her arm. I will explain all this in detail soon. Serenae and the others have taken reproductive material from Diana and I and created quite a few children. They grow quickly until about 14 years old and then slow down to a more normal pace. These children will be, in terms of Metabilities, freaky.

The trait issues of the DNA from Diana and I were removed. Then natural enhancements were made. Their DNA will be strong enough to flow enough energy for telekinesis and more. These are the majority of the strong but small group of new children coming.

These few individuals will contain strong Source Spirit to serve and protect.

Other than the Enaugk and Draconian, the people mentioned here have personally given us these names for an early means of communication with them. The name Enaugk came from their thoughts, not mine. The vast majority of them respect nothing but their own wants and they will do as they please to everything.

They continually commit disgusting abusive acts against everyone they can. Here's the short list of folks I've met so far. Diana and I were given these names mostly by the individuals of that race through telepathy. It's much easier to get basic thoughts, even have a conversation, than receive a diverse name.

Annunaki

The Annunaki are a strong powerful race of beings that I've already described earlier so we won't spend much time here. The problematic ones are all but entirely removed now, and the Annunaki people themselves are wonderful beings. They're large, easily aggressive to do good things as well as protect those they care for. They have Reptilian Humanoid DNA. There's one last thing that I haven't mentioned anywhere much.

Some Annunaki can change their physical body to Earthen Human by consuming Human DNA. They don't need to eat people, just receive injections. It only lasts a couple weeks or so. The one gentleman I met was a mediator, sent here to deal with making an exchange for freeing the prisoners. He literally smelled like a snake den. I know this from having had many snakes and others pets growing up.

There is a clan of Annunaki in Australia that will be staying with us, as well as others. They are a large group that has always been about living as peacefully as possible and trading with the other clans. Because they're a large and not aggressive towards the others, and they supplied many things to the other clans that they needed, they were basically left alone. They stated their independence and never took sides with any of the other clans.

There are other clans like this also; who have removed themselves from the main Annunaki hierarchy to trade with everyone else. This occurred more often as time went on. The Annunaki race here on Earth had become quite large over all these years and it was the upper class that had serious issues. Most of the Annunaki here are good people.

Most everyone in all the lower classes of each clan knew that the over aggressive ruling class had to be taken down and eventually would. They were right as it already has. The ruling class has been destroyed but there are many good Annunaki here no longer prisoners or living in fear, and anxious to become a part of a new growing society. The majority of the prisoners and former lower classes of Earthen Annunaki are now free; most of them are leaving.

You will find out about, and eventually meet, the Australian Annunaki as well as the others.

Drachk

The Drachk have also been mentioned but need further description. Like the Annunaki they are large, a bit larger than them. You will find members of both species to reach 10' in height.

They are both very strong but the Drachk have Dragon DNA, the strongest DNA ever produced in the history of Creation. They are the oldest race and easily most powerful. I see many with a claw extending out of the back of the heel/ankle region; relative to the oldest Drachk DNA traits. These folk are incredibly strong, intelligent, and persuasive. I'm very close to them as a race. What I am inside, the original Arae; created their race. As I've already mentioned, one of their Council Members is a Source family member if mine and an awesome individual.

The Drachk are the main reason that the Earth is now free of the former ruling class of problematic Annunaki. I would have to write a book to cover all that they've done but most of the major events are covered in my You Tube video channel, Jay Essex. The channel is up now but will be gone sooner or later.

The N'Antid were the second strongest influence in this event but there were many others from different galaxies. No singular group can hold full credit but without the Drachk it never could have happened. Nothing stops the Drachk, nothing. They were created to survive, protect, and learn. Their race is over 2 quadrillion, 857 trillion Earth years old. How's that for survival power?

The Drachk with DNA closest to what it originally was, have a large claw coming out of the back of the top of their heels. This is a trait that has been going away in them but is still seen today. They are living, breathing, intelligent tanks also with a culture deeper than the rest. They are the oldest.

N'Antid

Here are the ones that Corey Goode calls the Blue Avian. The N'Antid have initially shown themselves to many newcomers as a humanistic blue feathered birdman with only a very small beak so as not to appear aggressive at all. In reality they are large, often 8'-10' tall, people who look more like a combination of Ant and Praying Mantis. They don't have Praying Mantis claws though. Those are the Mantids we'll be discussing next.

The N'Antid gentleman that talks to Corey is TE'IR. He also has two sons that I talk to on occasion. They're RH'AG and NH'AG. There are other members in his family but I've only bothered these three, all wonderful people. They look totally different than us, so what. We look totally different than them. We're their aliens, what a silly word when not taken for its true meaning. Something "alien" is only something out of our current norm, our previous normal environment.

TE'IR is one of the strongest telepaths in Creation. The N'Antid tend to be compassionate intelligent people. They are also the second oldest race in physical body. They have saved the Human Race a few times, protecting some of us when the Earth's crust boiled over with lava, froze, and flooded with water. They have most often preferred to burrow into the land, build homes and live inside the ground.

Admiral Byrd met them when we thought he found the hollow earth. He was actually sitting with his back against a tunnel wall for most of his visit. The N'Antid are extremely telepathic and fed him images to keep him from knowing their location. These are the descriptions of his hollow earth concept. There are caves and installations within the ground but the Earth is not hollow.

If you look closely into Hopi lore, their historical legends, you will find they mention a being that made a body out of nowhere and led them to the "Ant People" who protected, fed, and housed them during the changing of the great ages. Meet the N'Antids, awesome benevolent beings.

Mantid

OK, these people are to be seen more from a distance than others. They are Insectoid Humans in just about every sense of the word. These folk are literally tall Humanoid Praying Mantis. They are aggressive, intelligent, and known for having little to no compassion as a rule. This doesn't mean they're all dangerous, just that they most often are. If you observe the behavior of Insects and Reptiles in nature you will notice how aggressive they are with little provocation if any at all.

Serpoian

Well, we've talked a good bit about the Serpoian already. They're usually a caring community oriented people knowledgeable in biological DNA utilization and mutation. They grow people as we grow plants. As a race they have been trying to work with our current governments since the 1920's. The U.S. government signed an initial treaty with them in 1926 but you'll have a hard time finding that for yourselves. They were in the vehicles which crashed here in the U.S. in the early 1920's and of course in Roswell, New Mexico 1947.

There was an Earthen Human visit to Serpo, their home Planet. About a dozen U.S. astronauts traveled there while one person from Serpo stayed here. The Serpoian who stayed here never left, he died from the mistreatment of the U.S. government. They killed him through neglect over time. Disgusting, what our governments are. We are known to be what we are, primitive. We're also known for having the capacity for incredible things. Change has already begun.

Serpacieant

The Serpacieant are really cool people. They are a genetic branch of the N'Antid. They are usually closer to about 6' tall, just a bit shorter than their sister race. They prefer to live more in space than burrow into a Planet. When Mellae first came to Diana and I together we tried to get a name for their race. Mellae was trying to offer a name that was relative to her species. Most the other races did the same thing, such as the Alurean, coming next.

Diana is better at picking the letters out than I am but I have such a strong telepathic connection to the people that I can read understand how they feel regarding what she and I are trying to put together. When we finally arrived at Serpacieant I had to laugh. When you break the word down it says this; Serpo, Space, and Sentient Ant. I felt a little ridiculous that it was so hard for me. Without Diana's input it would have taken me an hour. Diana is strong Source Spirit from Lilly and Arae.

Serpacieant people tend to be very strong in the biological fields, even more so with Plant life. They currently have an installation on Earth's moon that they use as a lab, green house, and more. It used to be an illicit Federation outpost and military installation but they were run out.

This Federation that many have talked about did some good things but also sold "time share permits" for other races to come to Earth for DNA, precious materials, etc. This included water and Animal parts. The new Alliance took care of that issue. The Federation is already gone, disbanded. The Serpacieant also have a small worker's colony on a small Planet sized asteroid now that many call Nibiru. This body of mass has no Planetary Essence inside so it's not a Planet. A lifeless structure that has life on it is still a rock.

I'm hoping that Serenae and Mellae, if not others, will eventually agree to have their pictures taken here in the house. It's up to them, not us. If not before I leave this body in a few months it will happen afterwards with Diana and many others before too long.

Alurean

Now here are some people who, among many other things, are extremely advanced in the ability to grow Plants for food in a barren wasteland. They have ships that slowly proceed over dry dirt and leave fertilized soil with seeds already planted. In time the crops grow and develop well. They will also be planting a crop here that is used in what most of us call replicators as they were called on Star Trek. They're food synthesizers.

These plants are processed into their core components, placed into the machine's system, and voila, you have a large variety of foods produced that are similar to foods eaten here as well as most other places. Spice is often used to replicate the flavors of other foods. You will see the Alurean here on Earth doing exactly this. They will fertilize useless seeming land and help feed people. So, are they cool or what?

There was a video taken in the North Sea by a commercial fisherman who caught the Alurean in the act of helping us purely out of compassion. A huge sample of water and soil sediment enclosed in a crystallic container was pulled into a massive Alurean ship hidden in the clouds. There was also a small sensor laden vehicle circulating the sample taking initial readings of its contents.

Last but not least there was a small ship in the water, just under the surface, which actually approached the commercial fishing ship. You can see all this quite easily on the amateur video as a shadow that moves right towards the boat. It wasn't professionally produced but it's easy enough to see.

There have been videos on YouTube that have huge Alurean ships hiding in clouds with different things flowing into a cloud and disappearing. These people are an older race, very intelligent, and have a great deal of diversity in their knowledge base. They know a lot about a wide variety of sciences. You will find videos with explicit information about all these beings at the Jay Essex YouTube channel or the Jay Arae Essex YouTube channel.

Subt'raelean

The Subt'raelean are a different group of people. I met a few of them while talking with them, the Archobien, and others during a recent dispute but don't know any of them personally. They are ready to help us and deserve mention, especially as you'll meet them in the not so far future. They're good people and hard physical workers. They're not the most technologically advanced race but compared to us they might seem so.

They have great Heart Energy and are loyal to their friends as the Earthen Humans need to become. They have great honor. It's been harder for us to develop into who we really are due to what's been done to us, not only through problematic Annunaki rule but the Original First Being Halves while they existed. They live well in dry climates as well as moist and over the past have enjoyed dwellings inside mountain sides. They're good people and make good friends.

Archobien

Now these people are really cool. They pop in and out of the house whenever they want to. We've invited them to do just that. Diana and I have told them separately that they're always welcome. They're a somewhat amphibious type of race with a ton of compassion for everyone and everything. They aren't the most advanced of the races visiting us but they are among the most compassionate people you'll ever run into. These people are awesome.

They get along with everyone, pretty much anyone who isn't abusing others. They're known for this and therefore receive help from most other races. They are in and out of our house here all the time. They're not only welcome but we ask them to "pop in" when they can. When Diana is having a few days of difficult sleep in a row, she asks them to come over and help her. They do.

Diana is working all the time and is often bothered by some of the dimwits (free Spirit) on the Other Side to the point where she can't get rest. They help her. Everyone needs sleep to function properly physically and mentally. I would like to be able to take pictures with them but that's still not allowed in the ET community, not even here.

The Archobien folk are natural helpers for most any task. They're very good with people, helping them do whatever they're doing. They're also being taught more about things they're not aware of yet. They enjoy helping others but they'll never be allowed to be made subservient to anyone. They're exceptional teachers of the use of Heart Energy.

They also help others find the best part of themselves as well as understand healing. Serenae has been furthering their medical expertise here in the house with us. We agreed to it months ago and still glad we did. This is how friendships are created. It's also how they last, with respect for each other.

The Archobien & Subt'raelean Symbiotic Relationship

The Archobien and Subt'raelean have had a symbiotic relationship for many centuries. They originated on the same Planet. The Archobien Race has tended to be more technologically advanced than the Subt'raelean Race but not as strong. The Archobien, as already mentioned, have wonderful, strong Heart Energy, a ton of compassion. So do the Subt'raelean.

A long time ago they Subt'raelean came to the physical aid of the Archobien, protecting them from invaders from another Planet. They became instant allies. The Subt'raelean are much stronger than the Archobien and therefor the better protectors, especially considering the extremely passive nature of the Archobien. They're still very close but not as reliant on each other. They travel through space now and are each more self-sufficient through the aid of the other races throughout space.

Enaugk

The Enaugk are known for their arrogance and abusive behavior towards everyone and thing. I realize there are compassionate people in every race but there are more lower frequency (more negative) Spirits put into these bodies. In the realm of the Fae Beings, the Imps are a similar case. Both of these separate types of beings are smaller. That's good as they could cause more damage if they weren't. They almost always consist of a minimum of 27% lower frequencies, often more, and therefore more problematic.

The Enaugk have called themselves the "Sumerian Gods", something you can find in our ancient history here on Earth. They've butchered us throughout our history, much as we have Animals. Creation was made to be abusive but it's being fixed. It never should have been created this way and once it's finished changing, it never will be allowed to become what we're now leaving, again.

There was a movie made in 2009 called "The Fourth Kind" starring Milla Jovovich and others. The ETs discussed in this movie are the Enaugk and they're exactly as described in the movie. This movie should be called a documentary because it is. The few members of this race with compassion are shunned and disgraced as they don't fit into the normal Enaugk profile. Soon, nothing negative and abusive will be allowed into a body. Most of it will be killed off while Spirit.

Draconian (Non-Alliance Member Species)

These people are not Alliance members. They are an annoyance so I'm bringing them up. Notice they're at the end of the list. The Draconian are known for assimilating as much Drachk DNA into their species as possible, trying to become more powerful and take on some of the Drachk physical attributes for themselves. They are extremely aggressive and use this to control as many other races as they can whenever they meet.

They declare themselves an extremely dangerous race, just not when the Drachk are close. They began calling themselves the Draconian a long time ago trying to insist that they're not Reptilian anymore but Dragon. They're quite small and slender compared to the Annunaki and nothing to the Drachk. Their fate is changing in the near future, and it's not a good one.

Chapter 2 – The New Universal Alliance is Created

There were many issues with the old Federation of Planets. It was initially created to protect its members but eventually grew into an overgrown controlling organization with too much power given to its primary members. There were less than ten member Planets receiving 30 to 40 percent of all funds moving through it. They also had too much control over the trade rights and lives of other races with little more than the concern of what they could provide the Federation, especially the wants of the top ten. In one line, they became an organization which did more harm than good. They had outgrown their usefulness.

This happens throughout the 3rd Dimension, our known Universe. The United Nations is one such group here, as well as all our governments. The Olympic committee is a smaller but completely corrupt group of people. I told my friends that the next Olympics would be held here in Atlanta about 1997, years before there was any vote.

This is not because I saw it through vision. There was a woman in the CIA, let's call her Gail, who asked me to do something for them regarding certain people who came into the Country from Mexico. My DJD was already in full gear, couldn't run anymore, so I declined. There is a Delta Force that actually exists.

I was later in court in Henry County Ga., Woodstock I believe, when I had to appear for a DUI, had an issue with a young Woodstock policeman with an aggressive attitude. I'm not made to take crap from others unless I deserve it. My lawyer freaked out when Gail came out of the judge's door, laid documents on the desk in the courtroom, talked to him, smiled at me, and then left.

The judge looked at me and said "Non-Process of Law." It was thrown out for no reason other than Gail handing the paperwork to the judge in court. The prosecuting attorney slammed his cane on the desk in front of the judge's bench. The judge put him in his place for that one. I was smiling, trying to be quiet.

The whole time my lawyer, Tony something, was talking to me out of the corner of his mouth and said, "You have to tell me what happened when we're out of here. He immediately followed that by saying "Never mind, I don't want to know." It was Tony Calhoun I think, a good lawyer. I have a problem telling judges, as well as everyone else, exactly what I think. It's cost me money on some occasions.

I've offered this info for a reason. You'll find you understand me better the more you pursue all the information I'm leaving you, not just about yourself, not just about what exists around you, but also what I've said about myself. How else can I do this? I'm not talking about baking a cake here; this book is of the metaphysical as much as the physical. The physical world needs at least partial physical proof, doesn't it? That's the reason for the QEEG testing and the DNA testing that will come out once I'm back home, finally myself again.

None can say with any truth that I have never served my Country nor offered my services to my Country. I happen to have great respect and compassion for all things including America. How about my love for India, my life in the body of Gandhi? When free and myself as Spirit, everything is my concern, my work. While in a body all we can do is what we can do.

Before dropping all this here's another tid-bit of info that I won't leave you a way to follow up on. I have a very good friend in the U.S. that was, among other things, the Yellow Adam. He and his family are very close to me in my heart although we don't get to see each other anymore. His dad was one of the CIA's best operatives and a high ranking member in one of our military forces.

When I was about 23 and working as a telephone engineer on the West Coast I told the other engineer in my office that I was going to call the Pentagon. It was during the Iran issue. He said, "Yeah, sure Jay." Then he watched as I did so, he was right next to me, saw and heard everything. When I hung up from talking with my friend there, my co-worker looked at me with his mouth wide open and eventually said, "I'll never doubt you again." That was funny, Jack never knew what to make of me.

The U.S. government has been aware of me since they had to release me at 10 months old. I tore up a room in one of their facilities. They found me left for adoption in a hospital in Long Island, N.Y. My blood and eventual energy scan put me in their possession. I was in a room being poked with needles and more when I blew up, so to speak.

I was left alone until my birthday in 2008 when the Original First Being Female released her hold on my energy. Once my energy flowed out of my body the NSA scanners caught it. I could feel being observed, followed closely by satellite at first and later by people on the ground. As time passed I ran into others from the NSA as well as all the other groups with similar concerns, supposedly national security issues. Some of them shared information but few of them ever played together well.

Late in 2012 the FBI and Homeland Security came to my front door for a little chat. They wanted to understand what was happening, what I was all about. They were both cool but the FBI guy was a little arrogant. He left with three thoughts in his head. He was saying to himself, "He's fruit loops. He's a carnival act. How'd he know that though?" He was referring to part of my conversation with him.

The gentleman from the Homeland Security agency was a little confused about everything that was happening. It was no big deal, just confusing to him. He had looked around the house and saw how I had made homes and feeders for all the wild Animals. He knew I kept almost no money for myself, spent thousands of dollars (all I had) on dogs I had saved with seizures, cats, ducks, etc. They went through all my bank records and everything else before arriving. The Homeland Security agent did anyway. The FBI agent was there for the ride.

He was arrogant and clueless to almost everything happening. I enjoyed messing with him a bit. Should have told him more about his private life, recent divorce with an adopted son, and his new wife and awesome son, in his early teens, they had together. His new wife was much nicer, more compassionate and loving. The FBI agent thought his son to be deficient, although he does care for him. He'll learn how awesome his son is in the days to come.

The Homeland Security gentleman looked at the house I was living in, how I did without things so I could do more for others, and was a little surprised. I was supposed to be some kind of threat. That's not what he saw for himself. He looked me in the eye and had one thought. He had an image of a white plate with a piece of apple pie on it that looked like it was left out overnight.

He was thinking that I was about as much of a problem as apple pie that didn't make it into the refrigerator overnight. He could feel my heart energy and knew I wasn't an issue at all. Why was he given a "heads up" that I was dangerous as I had strong abilities and he shouldn't stay near me too long? It's also why they someone from a lower office to meet with me, there was less information for me to take from their minds. These groups think too much of themselves and the worthless information they play with. They all understand me now.

Before they left the Homeland Security Agent asked for some of my Essenite. I told him that he meant to ask for the Star Essenite, not Essenite. He was a little annoyed about asking for the wrong stone and my correcting him. These people are trained to "take control" over all conversations they have. Oh well, so much for that. I hadn't carried Essenite for a while and it's not what he wanted anyway. I'd been showing Star Essenite for months now and the people who sent them my way had only been shown Star Essenite. It's much stronger and easily available to me. I gave them a personal piece most suited to their own frequencies as well as a few extra pieces but they would only take the personal pieces.

As we all said goodbye, the gentleman from Homeland Security was thinking about the dots on the folder on his desk. It had a round orange sticker on it that had a red sticker placed over it. That meant that I was upgraded from suspicious and needing attention to a definite threat. He couldn't see it. He was so sure that he starting to look for an explanation of it. The thought that "Someone somewhere has either produced bad research or taken bad information from someone else." was floating around in his mind. They returned, filed their reports, and had little to do with it after that. Let's get back to the new Universal Alliance, also known as the Alliance of Planets.

This is a momentous occasion in our known Universe. Almost all of you will find out about the Alliance in this lifetime. This is happening very soon. The "Federation of Planets" was due for collapse; it just had a lot of help thanks to the Drachk, N'Antid, Serpoian, and too many more to list. This didn't happen overnight. There had been unrest between many of the Planets for centuries. Things were too wrong for too long and the breaking point arrived.

A select few in the Federation kept increasing their holdings while others gained nothing or even lost what they previously had. Then the Federation Council put itself into the position of assuming the right to sell permits to other races for taking materials and life from other Planets which were already settled, had an existing civilization. They sold what we would call "time shares" which allowed other races to come to Earth to rape it with few limitations, mostly just time.

In the middle of making a video on October 17, 2017 I had to pause it to understand something coming to my attention. A family member of mine came into my head and told me I was expected at a large formal event type meeting. This person was one of the Drachk Council Members, the youngest one but held in great respect, just like the others. There are 10 who move around, another 2 are stationary and another 2 not to mention yet.

I went to the meeting; they were all looking at me as I arrived. I offered a soft introduction and upset everyone, including my family member. He immediately corrected me. Hell, I didn't know, never did that this life and wasn't prepared for it. I immediately cranked up my energy and hit everyone with it. Then everything was fine.

The Drachk understand compassion yet are extremely aggressive people. They also expected more from me. This meeting was the precursor to an important event that required me in my natural state.

Anyway, once they were pushed back on their heels, everything was OK, learned a big lesson. Lilly and Arae created the Drachk Race and full aggression was the only correct method of introduction. Wait until you see the huge claw going down from above the heels of the oldest ones.

Talking with over a hundred Drachk at once is different, never did that before either. I had to understand the basic thoughts in their minds and deliver the proper reply for them as a group. All of us can do things that we're not consciously aware of, when we're ourselves out of body. I was stuck in between places but things just happened as they needed to. Your true self out of body takes over and you forget what happened as your conscious mind shuts down.

There's no need to go further into the meetings proceedings but I stated I would be at the conference for creating the Alliance the next day, and so I was, October 18, 2016 in the Sixth Age of the Earth. Here I almost made the same mistake again. I'm not dim witted but I am ignorant of such things as these meetings.

Because of what I've shown others I can do, and what others (ETs) have seen me do in past lives, they expect more. Hell, after temporary healing a woman's knee, she actually called me back later asking me to fix her car while driving it to her sister's house. Oh well. Let's get to the meeting.

Let me state now, before I screw up and forget; that all this was done through astral-projection, not standing in a room physically. I can't remember if this was in the evening but probably was. I was already tired when it was happening. I had to consciously be there but it was my outer self that did most of the work producing the full energy that appeared. There were other Source Family members there also. Few of them were consciously aware. Some called me the next morning and asked "What happened last night? I was somewhere in a room in space and you were there." It was on a Drachk Cruiser, a very large ship, and it was nearby to Earth.

    I saw myself in the middle of the floor, like the ground level in a round amphitheater during Grecian times. I remember those days well. There were round raised layers with seating arrangements where people could stand or sit as they pleased. Most Reptilian Races prefer to stand, pretty much always. Each station had a table with one scanner, like a large desktop computer monitor.

    On it was information regarding the person speaking at any particular moment. It showed their energy (Auras) as well as a listing of their personal frequencies. To the left section I saw the base history of that person's previous lives, a summary of sorts. The speaker's words also appeared, translated to that individual's selected dialect. There was also a limited connection to other information but I only saw what was on one individual's screen.

    My Drachk Council Member friend was explaining what was happening and when I needed to speak. I was to open the event as myself, Arae, but didn't understand much else yet. When it was time I just knew what to do. I could see and feel the event happening. I continually tell everyone that they're more than they can possibly understand until they're awakened as much as they can be while stuck in one of these bodies. It's a simple true statement.

There were many different people there from many different Planets spread across most of our Universe but most of them were former members of the now troubled "Federation" as we can call it, a Federation of Planets that properly served only a handful of them. They were all a little nervous, concerned about the Federation finding out and troubling them for it. There were also feelings of worry regarding the stability of this new Alliance. Once formed would it be able to stand up against the Federation head on? Would war break out everywhere?

This was a big step for everyone involved, kinda reminded me of the Declaration of Independence for the U.S.A., everyone was concerned with good reason. The biggest difference here was the Drachk and N'Antids. No one ever stood a chance when dealing with the Drachk aggressively, no one. They are the physical power supreme throughout the 3rd Dimension.

Then the second oldest race whose power and intelligence is second only to the Drachk, are the N'Antids who are here now in large numbers and have been on Earth since the beginning, just waiting for their moment to arrive.

They have been instrumental in removing the problematic Annunaki from Earth, with a lot of help from the Drachk and we must not forget the Annunaki Resistance Force that's been here on Earth many centuries doing what they could with little help.

Back to the Alliance, most of the primary member applicants felt comfortable enough to move forward but most of the others were still concerned the Drachk and or N'Antids might leave later. This meeting, on 10/18/2016, was to gather as many races as possible to sign the new charter, thereby creating the new Alliance of Planets. I believe I already mentioned that it will become "The Alliance of Life" at a later date.

People were being directed to finish sitting at their stations on the main floor. This Drachk ship was huge, a spectacle of advanced science as well as unspoken display of power. The ship was much larger than any city, or even combination of cities, on Earth. There are many things coming soon now that will blow your minds, many exciting wondrous things and places. Ready for change, I am?

As everyone finished sitting down, or at least attending their station, my Drachk friend was getting a little concerned about something, couldn't see it right away. Then he turned around and looked at me, expecting me to do something. The field part of myself was pushing me to move into the center of the pit at the bottom of this circular lecture hall, so I did.

The next thing I knew, I had started to condense my own energy producing the body of a golden tan African Lion about 38' tall, standing up on its rear legs ready to walk as a Human. This is me as many here have seen me when I travel to them to either check on them consciously or protect them. I was just stronger with the Field part of me involved.

I looked around at everyone but they were almost all looking at the screens. I figured that they weren't ready to receive me, wasn't sure. Then I realized they were already watching me on the screens as energy, Spirit. They had my Lion image to the right and data regarding my Spirit's history to the left. I needed to do something.

I let out a soft but deep growl. That's all I knew to do. Unless I'm fighting I'm not aggressive, I'm compassionate. My Drachk friend's thoughts were "Damn he's not doing it." I scanned the immediate thoughts of the people there and they were expecting a show of power, not compassion.

I let out a second roar that put most of them back into their seats. Then a third one, strong but settled and relaxed, displayed self-assurance while still creating a power level on all the scanners that was never seen before. That did the trick.

One hundred years from now this will have the proper effect on those who read it. The founding of the New Alliance of Planets is a major event and what I just described happening on the scanner view screens was witnessed by all there. That won't be known for many years, so what. I'm not in a contest, I'm delivering information.

When people find this true in the future they'll have more reason to read the Creation Series, eventually understanding more about themselves and their environment, the path to self-awakening. These books are road maps to self-enlightenment yet much more. They are Creation's History and Evolution.

October 18, 2016 the New Alliance was created and became a reality. The next day the internal structure of their charter became more defined. It was newly born and constructed to change, to adapt as necessary, a good piece of work.

Many of the folk stayed there, coming and going another week or two. Then the group started thinning out. The members of this New Alliance felt they had what they needed to feel secure enough to move forward, and they did.

Chapter 3 – The Universal Alliance Destroys the Federation

The Federation was already aware of what was happening, some of them were there and a few others informed them anyway. It didn't matter. The Federation was on the way out and they knew it. There was no way to contend with the Drachk or N'Antids separately let alone together. They felt the need to make one final "power play" against some of the smaller members of the New Alliance so they sent a strong Armada of ships into a region of space containing some of the member Planets. That was a mistake.

The Drachk, N'Antid, and others were there immediately. The Federation show of force instantly became a farce. The Serpoian gentleman I mentioned earlier, the previously 4th ranking officer of the Federation Fleet, was now the Alliance Fleet Commander. This new fleet was not only much stronger than the Federation Fleet had ever been, but the power level from their ships told the whole story. No intelligent person would have commenced any aggression against them.

As expected by the Serpoian Commander, almost every Federation warship left their fleet to join the Alliance. The remaining Federation ships actually attacked the new fleet in meaningless defiance; but they did no harm, their ships were boarded, and the crew members were sent back on Federation cargo ships. Their warships were confiscated.

The battle lasted a few hours, no more. There was no need for it to happen anyway. It was a hopeless endeavor before starting, merely a showing of arrogance. They were not protectors, they were abusers. They had no cause other than maintaining control over others; so much for those issues.

Section VII ~ Drachk and N'Antids Free the Earth

Chapter 1 – Who are the Drachk and the N'Antids

We've already spoken about the Drachk and N'Antids but let's take this further. You're already aware that they are the two oldest physical body races in all of Creation's history. You know the Drachk were the first and still the most powerful physical bodies that one can have a life in. They are well respected and sometimes feared throughout the Universe.

The Drachk are also about 8' tall if you wanted to attempt taking an average. The problem is that, just as here on Earth, there really is no average. I've seen Drachk Special Ops Soldiers a bit over 10' tall. You can see their excessively massive physical muscle through their natural armor plating we would call skin. Once you've learned how to astral-project with efficiency, go look at a few Drachk people. Expect them to see you. Don't bother them if they feel annoyed. It's neither polite nor appropriate, and could bring issues to you.

The N'Antids would probably be considered to be about 10' tall on average. TE'IR is a little larger. They appear similar to a combination of Ant and Praying Mantis from Earth with something else added. I feel myself being rude here. I can't properly describe them physically as I see them when I project to them.

I see everything first as the combination of frequencies inside them, who they actually are. Then I can see a body to it but just don't care as much about that so I don't pay much attention to it. They have 4 rear legs and two arms but are quite agile with all their appendages. We think of bodies in relation to our own. This is natural, it's the only images we have until we see them with our own eyes.

Talking with everyone telepathically is enjoyable except for the names. I always have difficulties with that. TE'IR and I talk easily about names and more because he's a very strong telepath. I guess if you add the level of the telepath's abilities to my lack of available time leading to greater concern for larger issues, you might understand my personal name reception difficulties.

The N'Antid are a confident people yet neither arrogant nor overly proud. They have great compassion for, and full understanding of, a huge variety of our physical Creation. They have a deep, rich culture which developed from being one of the oldest races and their respect for all life. They're also warriors in their own right. If you want to take down a strong N'Antid Starship you will need a Drachk Destroyer and that will never happen.

These races have the understanding and respect which comes from over 2,000,000,000,000 Earth years of living together. They each respect all life in physical bodies. The Drachk just don't tolerate the aggressive issues of others when it interferes with their lives. There's a lot to learn from their cultures and how they look at things, with their minds. They are the physical first ones.

apter 2 – The Drachk and N'Antids' Earth Blockade

It was June 18, 2016 when the Drachk turned on their force field apparatus on Ceres, a huge asteroid the size of a small Planet. There was a series of other satellite sub stations scattered around the Solar System but the central unit, or main generator so to speak, was installed on Ceres. The energy field itself was flowing out between Saturn and Jupiter but it wasn't deadly until you came inward, close to Mars. Any ship that tried to move through the barrier was immediately attacked, destroyed by it. The N'Antid were involved but the Drachk built, installed, and controlled it.

The only way through this field was by having the proper frequency needed to allow it. Again, this was controlled by the Drachk. Most of the ships passing through had a N'Antid on board to handle it. They had the device and knew how to use it. The field was eventually taken down but not before a handful of ships were torn apart trying to escape through it. I say escape because there were members of the previously ruling class of problematic Annunaki from Earth that wanted to escape before being captured or killed. One of the videos that caught this happening is found on my Jay Essex channel on YouTube.

One of the captions for this widely shared video is "Meteor Does 180 Degree Turn Over Hungary". It appears to have happened Sept. 11, 2016. Again, this is an event after 6-18-2016. The video I posted regarding the initiating of the Drachk shield was on 6-15-2016. The title of that video is "The Drachk and N'Antids Quarantine Earth, Put The Federation on Notice, Disinformation (6-

15-2016)". I've left a documented history of events which you'll find, in the future, actually happened.

At the beginning of the video you can see something come off the ship as it all of a sudden appears in the sky. It's the little white light that sizzles as it drops from the main ball and almost immediately explodes with a flash of light which moves sideways. This is one of the engines that finally fell off and blew up. Then the large white colored light acting like a fireball, takes about a 120 degree turn as it continues to plummet to the ground.

This starship had wanted to sneak through the barrier just outside of Mars but never even made it there. A starship policing the space around Earth shot them down while they were traveling inter-dimensionally. That's why they appeared in the sky from apparently out of nowhere. They couldn't maintain inter-dimensional flight.

Another event occurred near Belfast, Ireland on Sept. 27, 2016. You can search YouTube for Ireland UFO Crash. The local police closed a couple roads and held back the news vans while they said there was a vehicular accident, a crash, in a nearby field. Really?

We're supposed to believe that one or more vehicles were in a field and had an accident that required the police to close two major roads near the field? Well, maybe that's possible if it's a dignitary or something but why were they driving around drunk in a field but let's get realistic here.

Then a large military truck is used to remove the wreckage, much larger than a car and not shaped like a truck, hidden under thick tarps to the nearest military base under guard. Why not use a tow truck or even a farm vehicle? Why was someone driving a vehicle similar to a sleek wide flattened bus out in a field? It was wider than a military transport flat bed. That's big. The thing is that it was also a sleek design even while hidden under the heavy tarp. It must have been a member of some royalty driving their new racing bus in a field, sure.

It was a ship that broke while trying to go inter-dimensional. It wasn't attacked, it just fell apart. There are many beings here on Earth from other locations throughout space, always have been. They became aware of what was happening and tried to leave. Earth has stayed one of the top 4 abusive Planets in Creation. You can't fully appreciate that until you learn of all the beings that were imprisoned here.

The Drachk had already stated verbally that the Earth was under their protection and off limits to incoming and outgoing traffic. As that was not heeded the barrier was put in place and ships from three different races were patrolling the space just beyond our Planet, including inter-dimensionally.

How much will it take before the mass populace of Earth wakes up to this simple event? It is so clear, so undeniable to an active, open, conscious mind that it should have received more attention than it did. Before this book is finished I will have made a video about all the videos on the internet which are real, explaining what's happening and/or who's doing what in them.

The more valid videos that were put in front of my eyes on the internet, the more I saw the screaming little children leaving their comments regarding it to be fake, trust and love god, or some other ridiculous comment. They want to "take their place" on the internet, to "claim their seat of attention as a person of grand knowledge" to be admired and listened to. This is why I never leave an option for comments on my videos.

There are many people awakening their full potential and I want them to hear me without the pathetic children screaming their nonsense in hope of recognition. Their ignorance and confusion is not allowed on my channel. Only an open mind can evolve. The rest are stuck in the tar of perpetual ignorance and arrogance.

It's amazing how the obvious can be overlooked when people are stuck in a closed mental state. This was purposefully done by the governments and religions to control you. It was also initiated by the Original First Being Halves while they still existed. At the end of this book I'll have the video's title on YouTube posted for you to watch, at least in the near future.

Chapter 3 – Removing the Problematic Annunaki Control of Earth

The problematic Annunaki on Earth controlled the major happenings here for over 10 million years. Over 10% of all funds created by every person and business went directly to them. They physically maintained war and disease here as well as "dumbing down" our DNA making us better, more efficient servants or slaves. They have controlled your education levels and recently been moving the masses away from advanced learning all together.

By this I mean that they're trying to make most people simple almost mindless people who would be easier to control, ask fewer questions, and be subservient. If you keep people's minds simple, program them to be idle all day amusing themselves with toys and then working harder just to survive and maintain themselves and their toys, you produce a work force that's easier to control. Video games can be fun but it's not relative to having a life other than relaxing to enjoy a moment of rest.

When they consume all your free time, your conscious mind never relaxes until you're asleep. You don't take any time to relax your body, your mind, and then flow outside of your body to be your true self for a while. This is also how you awaken and sharpen your Metabilities. Once you are awake you can visit other planets, go back in time, talk with people on starships, and so much more. That is not only more exciting than a video game, it's real.

The top 7 Annunaki Ruling Clans here on Earth were always bickering with each other to claim superiority over the other 6 clans. There were a total of about 24 different clans here. That number depends on how you break down the definition of clan. There were only 7 Ruling Clans in control of all others. These Annunaki Clans are imbedded in all the larger countries. Most of the others are not aggressive like the ruling faction. This has been going on a long time and there are many of them here who want nothing to do with their own government, so to speak.

The ruling clans are vicious people for the most part. One of the top clans was the largest of the clans in Russia. There was a female Annunaki running that one. I used to talk to her from time to time. She was ready for the destruction of the Earthen Annunaki control here. She did a lot to help all of us. That needs to be pointed out in the future.

There is also the Arizona Clan, the largest here in the U.S.A. They were the biggest problem we had related to controlling our government, our wars, our largest businesses, and much more including Human experimentation. These people were the ones who created the mass of Human "Sex Dolls". Young children, almost all female, were taken by the groups falling under the Annunaki's supervision at a very young age.

Most of these children were taken at only 7 years of age and injected with strong drugs developed through ET help. This started centuries ago but has never been as strong as it was this last 100 years. There were muscular development enhancers, growth inducers and sexual hormone developers among the ingredients forced into them. A child is defenseless. These people deserve exactly what they're all about to receive. They can't hide, nothing can.

Then, usually around 9 years old, they are trained and released to be sex toys for diplomats from around the world. Many sick things happen in the Vatican, still problematic Annunaki infested, but it's worse at the governmental level. That's enough about this. All this will be fixed. It just can't happen overnight.

These problems must first be brought to the surface and introduced into the mass media, for everyone to acknowledge. Then they will start being removed by the public, and death. It's imperative for the bodies to understand what has been going on. Then it's equally important for them to see it being taken care of. This doesn't just happen by the Other Side. They need to be involved in it themselves. When you physically attack a problem, you become part of the cure as well as help redefine yourself. This will be made to happen, period, but you'll also do this together as one body against abuse.

The strongest of the 7 Earthen Annunaki Clans was the one in Arkansas. Their leader was an exceptionally huge powerful male. I never could express any of their names. They're not in English and there's no viable translation. He also is a friend of mine. I mentioned him in the incident I had with the Annunaki Clans. He's the one that growled so loud that Herckie ran out of the room. I instinctively went to the Arizona group, not him. I've always known that the Arizona Clan was the most problematic one on many levels.

He also had a lot to do with breaking down the internal structure of the 7 Annunaki Clans here on Earth. I'm looking forward to spending a little time hanging around him when I dump this physical body. I've tried to describe who you are when not in a body but never found a sufficient way to do so. You are so free, so intelligent, have all your feelings without the problematic emotions. It's unlike anything you can comprehend with a physical conscious mind.

This Arkansas Clan had the best weapons research and development. They kept their best weapons for themselves, a good thing. They also had the strongest DNA research but did not abduct people to get the DNA. They had few labs but their research was the best. They had the brightest minds and their findings stayed in the clan, never left. This they guarded with the strongest weapons on Earth, the ones they designed.

There was a rather large clan in California that was related to business and money production but, as wide spread as their power was, they had to work hard to maintain their top 7 status, one of the ruling clans. There was also the Florida Clan who was well adept in gathering Intel, communications, and networking, especially off Planet. They had more Trip-Chairs as they're called, than most of the other clans. Their location to the Atlantic was a great help to their strong points.

Let's take a look at these "trip-chairs" as they're usually called for good reason, even though no one really understands why. The race that originally designed and built these devices was far from Earth and happened a long time ago. As space exploration increased, even grew popular, they ran into serious issues and then went about trying to fix them. One of them was their ships breaking down when far away from the Planet they originated from.

There were great distances involved here, not just other Galaxies but much farther than that. How about one third of the distance through this Universe? There was no way to communicate the need to assistance over that kind of distance. There were always issues between many of the other races, some even at war with each other. Sometimes you got help but most often you didn't. Add to this the fact that many people were exploring past the known reaches of space and there wasn't anyone nearby anyway.

One race took on this task as they were explorers themselves but also scientifically minded. I had a life in one of these bodies and was one of the workers assigned to the project. I was lucky to be there when the project was completed. We had a somewhat deep orange tint to our skin. We walked a bit bent over as most here would say. Our skulls were humanistic with large ridges on top of our heads running from one side to the other. Our bodies were stronger compared to those on Earth yet much thinner.

These first units, much like those of today in basic design, are like a comfortable recliner, thin, temperature controlled, and have a partial helmet looking device that is put down over your brain. You can see videos and listen to music when the visor is not mapping out a location. These chairs were made to make you comfortable, able to spend 8 hours or more a day cycle in them. Without that they wouldn't work.

The head section had the ability to read your DNA, map out the flow of your Metabilities, and enhance them using the proper electromagnetic frequencies relative to your own. This made the person in the chair up to 10 times stronger than normal. There are always exceptions.

All the chairs had a connection to a central data access unit in the middle of the circular rows of chairs at each location, usually a spaceport. Sometimes there was only a chair or two but at the large installations there might be over 30 of them.

Pineal, Heart, and Solar Plexus orientated people all did well there. Many people with strong heart energy could "feel" distress.

Then the Pineal orientated people could see better through dimensions to locate the people in need of help. Last but not least, the Solar Plexus orientated people, who use remote viewing better that the other fields, could locate where the people were as well as see the nature of the distress. These three separate magnified abilities came together to feel, find, locate, and understand where the help was needed as well as the particular problem.

Add to this now that each ship was supposed to be equipped with trip-chairs of their own, all having back up batteries to run them in power failures. The larger exploration vehicles usually had at least 20 of them. I have no name to offer regarding the people who initially created these machines but they changed space exploration forever.

These chairs are still in use today. The communication systems used today reduce the need for them but they serve us with more than their original purpose. In some ways they're more helpful but in some they're not, especially here on Earth.

These chairs have continued to improve, evolve in power level and design. The second use found for these devices was for medical assistance. They could help healers find problems quicker, more easily, and in greater detail in other people. It's a shame that those of us from Earth have been denied such equipment let alone being free to develop our abilities to enhance our lives as others have been for trillions of years.

There are metallic pipes, tubes, or channels that run the length of the chair that were originally used mostly for environment control. Today these tubes still exist but some have had other functions added. The medical field has done so to increase their effectiveness but many problematic military and organizations have used them for a variety of different functions.

These abusive people have used them to gather what information they could from others. They can put a person in a chair, crank it up, and then someone from another chair would pry their way into their minds to gather what information they could. This was often painful. It wasn't all they were doing with them though. They could use the machine to open one person's thoughts, including their memories, and put their own thoughts into them.

Such a thing was done to David Icke, someone I appreciate for all he has tried to do for everyone after he had been put through hell in one of these chairs 7 times, 4 to break him and 3 to change him, yet he still does what he can for others. I went into his head trying to do what I could to help him where I was able.

He's not able to understand what I'd like him to, and have never talked with him personally. I just wanted to help him the best I could and then leave him alone to do his own thing. I respect him as I understand what he's gone through. He shouldn't even still be here.

They've also been used extensively here on Earth to attack the minds of others. It's a well-known fact in the higher levels of government agencies as well as these other sick organizations, that if someone has a person's DNA sequencing it's possible to make this person sick through the use of satellites. It's usually a person in a trip chair accessing and working with the satellite.

The frequencies sent to the person are generated by the satellite. The person in the trip-chair manipulates the brain as much as possible either enabling or enhancing the effect. The people doing this in these chairs are most often Earthen Humans.

I met a man from the MIB section of the NSA who was also affiliated with the FBI at some level (busy guy), at a stone and crystal shop here in the Atlanta, Georgia area. I was driving to the store and felt the man's abusive intentions towards me. As I pulled into the parking lot I felt him arrive moments behind me.

I started talking with a couple people in the parking lot about Star Essenite and gave them each a piece of it, showing them how to feel it. That's when the NSA agent opened the door of the crystal shop and gave me a nasty stare while holding the door open, eventually walking inside. I was anxious to finish and get inside myself. I didn't have much time to spend there and I wanted to look this idiot in the face before leaving.

Once inside I went straight to the wall of stones to pick up what I wanted. I was talking to a couple customers explaining stone energy when the idiot walked right by me. He was dressed like a comfortable business man, just screaming that he didn't belong there. You could see it in his face, feel it in his demeanor. I felt him stare at me when he walked by us. He was trying to focus his Pineal Gland energy onto mine to attack me.

I didn't know what he was doing at first. I was trying to finish helping the two friends shopping there but his intent was obvious so I left the conversation for a moment and went into his head. I saw what he was trying to do and his thoughts were easily read. He said "Did I get him, did I get him?" That pissed me off so I went into his head and said "Little boy, next time you want to ring my door bell I'll give you a ladder so you can reach it."

He immediately turned around and looked at me. I was smiling, inside his head laughing at him. Then I told him something I won't repeat here. As he left he was saying "Next time I'm using the generator." He was talking about a trip-chair. He later strapped into a trip-chair and went after a certain someone. His brain was scrambled until he bled out through his face. They pulled him out of the chair already dead, brain dead.

I realize the seriousness of my attitude and what I described here but things are what they are. These overly abusive people will start disappearing more rapidly now until they're all gone. That doesn't mean everyone's going to live in a utopia where everything is wonderful all the time. Strife is necessary for us to grow, to evolve, but abuse destroys us. The fix is to destroy the abusers, cut out the cancer. That's not your job. It's being done for you.

While we're here, this group I just called MIB actually has a different name. That's what I'm using to explain who they are. These people are an off branch of the NSA who are involved with ET and governmental related affairs. If you met one they would almost certainly be cold hearted and look at you as if looking through you. The reason you feel this is because that same feeling is coming to your Heart Energy from their Heart Energy. They're like this, almost all of them.

I've dealt with a lot of different agencies the past ten years but they can't do anything to me and don't want me dead yet, at least they didn't. Now they're just staying at a distance and watching, waiting for my body to drop and the new changes coming.

There are a lot of good people in our governments and even some of the clandestine organizations just waiting for the change that all the ETs are talking about, actually have been for 50 years now. Those problematic Annunaki who ruled us from underground, usually undersea really, are now gone and change is about to happen. They know the Drachk came here, took out the abusive Annunaki issues and a new Alliance was formed but they're not sure how it will all play out.

The Annunaki Clans had Earthen Humans with high Annunaki DNA content give their orders to other "Royal Annunaki Blood Humans" who controlled the business affairs of the Human populace in each given area. The man controlling England was the head of this group. I used to call him "Lloyds of London", really pissed him off. I astral-projected into his office one time and freaked him out. He cussed loud and threw a stapler through my image, hit something on his shelf.

When we astral project to someone we're often seen as a large face, maybe a full body. Lloyds of London is deceased now also. So are the Royal Annunaki Blood Controllers of New York and California. Once you learn how to access your own power you can do things you never would have believed. You can't be your real self until free of the body you're in, but you can do many things that earlier seemed impossible.

Getting back to the royal blooded Annunaki Humans, here's the New York Clan with all its arrogance and "hit squads". They were known for their political assassinations and corruption. The Annunaki themselves had their own personal group of Annunaki hit men which they used in high end clandestine situations, different ET members, etc.

That 10% of all major transactions going directly to the Annunaki doesn't just sit in a pile to get looked at. It's used to aid in controlling the Humans or others doing their bidding in various ways. How do select government officials and politicians receive all the money they do, enjoy a standard of living so far above their already overpaid governmental salaries?

There are "shell" companies that the money comes out of which, when you keep following the money trail, it stops nowhere. How is that possible, easy actually? I can see these things as they happen but everyone will find this out through your new mass media which should be in place by 2023 - 2025.

All major elections in major countries are controlled by the Annunaki's Human representatives. The people they have been grooming and spending a lot of money on, must be put into place and it's easy. One person at one location can run every major election on Earth.

People scream out their frustrations of "conspiracy theories" all the time. You'd be surprised how often there's something behind that. If they were awakened they would be calmer and able to watch it happen using their Metabilities. The more time you relax and open your mind, the calmer you are and the stronger your abilities become. The hardest part is letting go of your conscious mind to relax.

This is another situation where not trusting yourself and your abilities ruins your minds, hampers your lives. If everyone just stood up at once, having seen what's really going on and just said no, major change on this Planet would occur. Gee, do you remember an old man in plain toga like apparel that said that to everyone in the world? His name was Gandhi.

My last life was to help you stand together and try to appreciate Animals. Remember when I said you could judge a Country by their treatment of Animals? I already knew what I would do my next life, exactly as I've already done now. It would be silly of me not to expect some people to think me arrogant at this point. If they're not able to utilize their Heart Energy to understand me, feel the energy in my words, they would tend to flow their thought processes in that direction. That's fine by me.

I've said often that these books are important for the next 100 years especially. What would someone think when they finally see and hear a Drachk Ambassador speak my name, tell you what I was inside? Time will now be able to offer everyone all the truth they need to build their own personal understandings.

There is no longer anything controlling everything everywhere which continually perpetuated their lies. I'm speaking of the Original First Being Halves that made this Creation about them, not everything in it as they should have. Their Original Angels (servants) are gone also.

The N.Y. Annunaki Royal blooded hybrids had a lot to do with controlling smaller countries and their wars. There's a lot of money that moves through N.Y. to feed corrupt businesses and countries. The funding for many wars had to come through N.Y. City. New York City has been called the rotten apple. On the inside, it is.

There are groups like this worldwide, many in America. I've only mentioned some of the more powerful ones. Now that the Annunaki have been taken out of power you have another power void. These are often volatile and problematic. There are many here who can come to the front of things now, our governments and eventually businesses.

Those who were handing out the Earthen Annunaki's orders are trying to hide, stay safe. The Alliance contingent here on Earth has been hunting them down for a while now. The ruling Annunaki clans already had most of them killed. The associates were offered protection by sending them through a transport portal to the moon and then beyond. When they entered the portal they wound up in the jungles of South America and were killed, some even eaten, by the more aggressive Annunaki there.

Those businesses which won't cooperate with our newly incoming ET friends will be left in the cold to rot as they should. The new governments coming will not only shut them down but finally deal harsh punishment to those who've earned it. Monsanto, are you ready? Some of them will receive their punishment and then simply drop dead.

There are extremely abusive Spirits in most of the bodies running these large destructive organizations. Don't forget all these cartels and other groups. They will eventually be attacked and attack each other. Again, after a while they will all die off. I can't give you the exact time line on this but by 2025 you will see them either destroying each other or stopping and coming together for better purposes.

There have always been strong ET factions within our governments helping the rest of us to move against this abusive control but they have always been the minority. Many of them are within our governments doing all they can. Their central base of operations is in a huge inoperable starship located under Antarctica.

The problem is that there are too few, a definite minority, and working in a system built to function against them. The same situation exists in the business world. There are also many business related concepts throughout space that are about to change. This newly created Alliance of Planets will be a strong tool in accomplishing this.

The problematic Annunaki's control over our daily lives was finally taken away from them through the intervention of the Drachk, N'Antids, and others. Before moving forward you need to become aware of the "Annunaki Freedom Fighters" and similar groups here from other Planets.

One of these groups is from Serpo. There were more Annunaki and Serpoian (Gray) people here than the other races. They've fought hard and died not just for their people imprisoned here but for us also. The strongest fighting here was found around the San Francisco Bay area of California.

There has already been strong fighting in our Oceans as well as underground, almost completely between the Earthen Annunaki and Alliance ETs with the existing ET resistance force here for over a century. Very few Humans were involved. They're not old enough to play in that sandbox. It's too bad, they need to disappear anyway, they will soon enough.

Large fighting has broken out in the Pacific Ocean in two major places but smaller fighting still breaking out in various places. A little under 450 miles SSE from Alaska in the Gulf of Alaska, a large installation was taken out. This location received necessary supplies from other Planets and distributed them across the globe. There was another ET supply depot in the Indian Ocean as well. Four major drop off points in total and 4 smaller ones.

Together they handled the importation of all the ETs needs, hidden out of sight in our Oceans. This is why it's the Navy Special Ops that arrives when an unsanctioned or accidental ET issue arrives most anywhere on the Planet. We only know about 5% of our Oceans. What better place to hide. While we're on the subject, Antarctica is where our friendly, compassionate ETs have lived for centuries. There is a huge vessel now providing living and business quarters for many under the frozen ice, on the ground. I've spoken about it many times in the videos on my You Tube channel, "Jay Essex". People like to say that Atlantis is under there. Atlantis is still where it sank, in the North Atlantic Ocean.

In my video titled "Antarctica Starship Opening, Alaskan Annunaki Being Attacked, UFO's Collect Water (1-25-2017)", I talk about one of the major entrances which allow ships through the ice, down to the enormous sunken starship. I have spoken often about the fighting throughout the Planet, usually as it was happening or right before.

Occasionally it was just after it happened so I explained exactly what occurred. One of these times was relative to two separate battles which happened in the Tasman Sea between New Zealand and Australia and one in the Pacific Ocean just off South East of New Zealand. This was happening from late 2016 to later in 2017. There were a few small skirmishes and then 3 large incursions.

The Annunaki had prisoners there, under the land and in the Ocean. Some were rescued and temporarily held in South Eastern Australia where they were moved to the Andes Mountains in South America and finally flown to a friendly ship in space to their freedom.

I made a video about this just after it happened, "Drachk, Earth Annunaki, Freed Prisoners, New Zealand Earth Quake (9-2-2016)". I explain in decent detail what happened, the where and how of the fight, prisoners freed, and other prisoners relocated to Tanzania,

Africa. Most of them are freed at this moment; a few are still hidden away and hiding from everyone else.

I should have listened to my N'Antid friend and brought it up earlier. I was told a day before that there was something important about to happen in the area but ignored the message. It was one of my few N'Antid friends and I felt bad afterwards. I was rude to casually blow him off and later apologized.

He was in a meeting and was a little "put off" that I talked to him while busy. It's not that I don't appreciate everyone; I'm just tired from all the fighting I've done and my overbearing need to return home to the Other Side. I've become a little callous, not a good thing.

There is a cleansing in Creation now, not just here on Earth in the 3rd Dimension, but everywhere in all dimensions. How else can you change an abusive format to a compassionate one? The old must be removed. That which will not comply will be destroyed, simple math. I'm not cold hearted but I'm a serious thing. Protection is a thing of compassion until something wants to hurt another. Then it gets very real, very quick. That's the only reason for a war to break out, to stop oppression and its abuse.

Chapter 4 – Policing Our Solar System

From what I've talked about this far you might think that the Drachk or N'Antid would be patrolling our Solar system. They're not. There's a group of individuals that do this in many sections of our Universe, mostly closer to us than farther away. Our Universe is huge.

I felt a large group of people coming our way while looking at something else during one of my videos. When I make videos I'm calm inside, open to others who want to talk to me, in a receptive mode. It seems I'm always dealing with things on the Other Side in a rather aggressive fashion. When doing so nothing can get through to me. Add to that I'm a little burned out from what I've been doing the last 10 years and you can understand a little more about my daily life.

Anyway, I saw a fleet of serious vehicles coming towards us. There was one large ship ahead of almost all the others. They appeared to be made for speed, especially through atmospheres, and they are. I already understand they were a group of strong humanoid people with extremely capable ships. They had weaponry on them but not for war.

I had to get back to the video I was making so I left that alone. You can always go back and look at something in the past again. Just do it, that's all, just do it. That's how so many things are done metaphysically; it's already part of you. A few days later I was talking with my Drachk buddy when I saw them in his head. They were "Space Police" for lack of the proper term.

They came to keep all the small to medium sized ships away from Earth as well as handle other tasks in the area similar to police here. They will address any size ship, it's what they do. However the larger ships, if one comes near, will already have been addressed by the Drachk, possibly the N'Antid if the ship isn't close to us yet. There are now between 2 and 4 large Drachk ships here continuously protecting our space. People aren't aware how safe they are at this moment.

This and everything else we're talking about will come out soon. The governments will be addressed but so will businesses and other groups including individuals with special purposes this life. There's now a small army of awakened individuals who are becoming stronger each day. Soon that process will speed up.

The Drachk, N'Antid, and many others are aware of Creation's new format change. They've been watching the change in energy on the Other Side as well as here. I'm in an Earthen body like you but these people, their physical bodies, are my immediate family, their origin. Just like the Red Adamic Races, Lilly and myself.

Section VIII: Earthen Alliance Creation (4-15-2018)

Chapter 1 – Newly Freed Earthen ETs Create Earth's First Alliance

Today's date is 4-16-2018. I added this chapter because of what happened yesterday. The video about it is rendering as I write this. I had already stated that I was finished on my Jay Essex YouTube channel and would post no more videos. Well, this happened and it was of major importance so I'm going to post another video. I should have had this book in print by now. I'm editing the book myself right now, it was finished almost a month ago but the editing company a paid thousands of dollars to, decided to change the meaning of larger parts of it. They actually changed my original manuscript that I sent them so I found the one before it and I'm editing it right now.

Yesterday, at about 2:00 pm, my eyes were fading out and my body was being shut down for some reason; it was a couple hours too early for that. I looked at part of myself, represented by the energy of an old Black Panther, and asked him "What's up?" He waited a moment and told me that I had to go to a meeting, and showed me a ship that I was already familiar with. He said I had to go lie down and pass out for the event.

When I have to be somewhere as my real self, Arae, I have to lie down and pass out so I can. The physical body has to be asleep for me to do this. The same situation occurred when I started the meeting which created the Alliance of Planets as Arae. That'll be known later and not important now, except that my body has to be shut down completely to leave it like that.

The ETs that have always been here on Earth, they established their presence here before the Adamic race, joined the Earthen Annunaki people who had nothing to do with the ruling Annunaki clans and created an Earthen Alliance. This is Earth's Declaration of Independence as well as the first Planetary Alliance here; which would now come together uniting all the inhabitants of Earth as a free people, Earth's new family so to speak. And here it all now starts to happen, an important part of the reason why I had to write this book in the first place.

When they are ready, the different countries with their new governments will become part of this new Earthen Alliance, but not until they are ready. Many of our current governmental officials will be removed from office. The Earthen Alliance or Alliance of Earth will soon become part of the Alliance of Planets which later evolves into the Alliance of Life when it accepts all life that exists as equal. Anyway, that's all for this here. You'll find out more on your own in the future. I have to finish editing this book to put it into circulation now.

Chapter 2 – The First Souls from the First Universe Join the Alliance of Planets

The representatives from the 1st Universe began talking with the Alliance of Planets here in our Universe on 5/8/2018, Earth time. The agreement was made that the 1st Universe would join as a whole unit and that the various Planets there would have membership on a council which would then be represented by one separate individual. These people stayed on the ship in various meetings for about 3 days in total.

This singular representative for the 1st Universe arrived early in the morning 5/11/2018 (EEST) for the final meeting of the Alliance in solidifying their membership. Anyway, the 1st Universe is now part of the Alliance of Planets. You'll find out about this for yourselves through the Alliance itself a little later on.

Chapter 3 – The Other Side Joins the Alliance of Planets Creating the Alliance of Life

At 12:08 am EEST (Earth Eastern Standard Time) Monday 5/14/2018, the primary focal points of Lilly and Arae arrived at an important meeting of the Alliance of Planets. A decision was immediately made to change the name of this alliance to the Alliance of Life, instead of Planets. Over time, all the different Spirit Fields from and of separate locations will come forward and participate. This is how we will grow together.

Each Universe shall govern its own self, while all the Universes and Spirit Fields from the Other Side work together in unity to run Creation; other than setting its format boundaries. Abuse and excessive aggression will not be tolerated and arrogance will not be looked upon kindly at all.

The Alliance of Life will evolve into two councils, a primary and a secondary. The Primary Council will consist of one representative from the Other Side as well as each Universe and eventually each Dimension. The Secondary Council will consist of representatives from all the individual Planets and Spirit Fields on the Other Side. A short time later, each Dimension will have representatives there also. The two-council system will stay in effect; it'll just grow in size.

All forms of Spirit (Life) will have a say in what happens in the 3rd Dimension. This is how we move forward as a family, as a sentient group of beings. We all now sit at the same table, across from each other, equal in rights, working as one unit.

Chapter 4 – The Pacific Tectonic Plate Splits, Creating the North and South Pacific Plates

This chapter was left out of the first printing of this book as well as a few other issues which surfaced, causing the need to provide better editing for it. I'm not a writer, I'm a protector, server, fighter. I call myself the janitor for a reason, I clean up stuff. Well, I had to clean up this book a little before leaving it.

I have spoken, since 2010, of Lemuria rising again. This was never said to be the old Lemuria rising above water just as it was in it's beginning, but many of the islands being brought upward and in some cases breaking the Pacific Ocean's surface. Many Lemurian artifacts will be found by divers exploring these new developments.

I had seen the ocean foor being closed off to help build up pressure under the Pacific's tectonic plate back in 2010. Now some of this pressure is being released early in Hawaii as seen with it's new aggressive volcanic activity. I always saw this relative to that time when I would be leaving but never held onto that knowing how the future timeline is fluid, changing relative to the desires of who's running Creation at the time.

About 9,000 miles of the Pacific tectonic plate is about to crack. That's just over 1/3 of the Earth's circumference. There will be damage and loss but it's being kept to a minumum. It will crack from near Gold Coast in Australia, under the Hawaiian Islands, and near the Los Angelas area of California.

There's also a bad earthquake currently scheduled for California around 2030-2034. That might change though.

Section IX ~ Pre-Reformatting Issues Expected

Chapter 1 – The Chaos Incurred from the Original One's Removal

The bulk of this information was covered in Book II of The Creation Series. Once Arae (in body) got into it heavy with the Original First Being Halves everything changed. July 10, 2012, about 2/3^{rds} of both the Male and Female First Being Halves was destroyed. They were much smaller in size and power. There were two other Strong Source Mates that the Original First Being Halves created to run things for them. They had gotten stronger and wiser, especially Aramaeleous and Lydia, separate Source Mates but very strong together.

The two large orbs of cleaned Original First Being Spirit were separated and then naturally divided in male and female. One of the orbs separated into Lydia and Armaeleous. The second and larger orb separated into Lillith and Aramaeleous. They were made of powerful love and fortitude, very strong. Lydia and Aramaeleous were a serious issue compared to Lillith and Armaeleous.

Lydia was aggressive and controlling. Her Source Mate Armaeleous was comprised mostly of the frequencies of hope. Lillith was strong loving energy and her Source Mate Armaeleous was massive fortitude and power. He soon grew arrogant doing all he could to increase his power level and promote himself among the other Spirits.

Once Lillith and Aramaeleous had separated, it took little time for their frequencies to come together, producing their primary focal point (power & intelligence) field. The energy softened in power as it flowed further away from it. These two focal points, one of Lillith and one of Aramaeleous, became Lilly and Arae, respectively.

Now we're getting to the heart of the issue. With the Original First Being Male and Female already getting deleted, a huge vacuum in the power structure on the Other Side was created. The first attack on Arae left the Original Ones much weaker. At this point I heard them talk with Aramaeleous and the others asking for help in subduing Arae. The first thing I saw, felt, received, understood was Aramaeleous smiling inside telling himself that he was about to be king, god, or whatever title you might give it.

They all gave off the energy relative to a soft nod of the head but Aramaeleous and Lydia wanted to take over for themselves. Lillith and Armaeleous had no such intentions at all. They didn't care for the Original Ones either though. They went along with things as they weren't in the position to do anything about it.

The Original First Being Halves had also been telling many others that they would soon be running Creation for them as they were about to retire into a dimension they made for themselves. The two of them were going to hang out in their own dimension and bathe themselves in the prayers of others.

They planned for Lydia and Armaeleous to run the 2nd Dimension while Lillith and Aramaeleous ran the 3rd Dimension as it was more difficult to deal with, especially with me around. I came from Aramaeleous anyway. He was already the largest power in Creation; he didn't have the most powerful frequencies though. The dimension they built is now the 8th Dimension (level) below us surrounding the Earth here in the 3rd Dimension.

Once the Original ones became so diminished in size and power, others started getting involved with Arae, trying to push him around until they could control him. I have had all the upper metatarsal bones on my left foot broken on two occasions. I went to sleep and woke up in pain. I never kicked anything; don't even have a foot board on my bed. Anyway, the Source War got kicked up a notch when so many others got involved. Everyone thought that it was their turn to be god.

In May of 2013 the rest of the Original First Being Halves was deleted. There have been a couple insignificant pieces of them found since then but once deleted, no more has been seen. This is easy to see and finish once out of the body. Now the largest of Source Spirit still standing started trying to run Arae in body and then attack it when he refused to comply. They usually attacked separately but sometimes all 4 of them joined together. Each of them wanted Arae to kill the ones attacking him so when they tried they would be the one left standing. Arrogance, abuse, anger, and a lack of compassion were prevalent in Lydia and Aramaeleous especially. It was obvious that when able, Arae had to deal with them in a permanent fashion.

Arae didn't even know he could destroy Spirit and didn't want to, until they just kept coming, attacking night and day, day and night, every day. On July 10, 2012 Arae came to realize his own strength. He found himself and has been growing stronger ever since. Arae's frequencies have mutated 3 times now and after the third something happened increasing his power level again. He always asked just to be left alone, almost no one ever did. So he did what he was made to do, protect. He now had to protect himself.

Both Lydia and Aramaeleous wanted to be the new gods while Lillith and Armaeleous had no such desire. To make this short now, the Original Angels attacked and were almost completely deleted. Nothing in body has the Original Angels that were put on them for their lives, still on them. Your Spirit Guides are doing everything on their own now. Most people don't realize that Angels would save you if you needed to stay in your body but always harmed or destroyed your body the rest of the time.

They would also go into your Hypothalamus Gland and make you believe whatever they wanted. If they told you to slap yourself you would not only do it but know for a fact, at that very moment, that you had to do this. It was the most important thing in your life. Once you acted on their commands they would release their energy from your brain leaving you with a serious question, "What the hell is the matter with me?", "Why did I do that?" and eventually "How could I ever do that?", or something similar.

This is what the Original Angels put on you when in body, would do to you. Religions said praise them and the Angels said praise the Original First Being (god). They were only servants doing their job. They were created for just that purpose, keep everyone in body in line as well as making them suffer through a given set of abusive events in that life until it finished. Then they took you out of the body. They were not being mean to you, they were following orders.

In an attempt at closing this chapter, let's just say that as soon as the next strongest Spirit was at the top of the ladder, they attacked relentlessly. Then they died. This is barely still happening but not frequently. It makes it much easier for me to write this book. As you can tell, I'm not a writer. I have trouble expressing all I understand so I often use analogies. That's also why I explain a lot of things that have happened to me, so others can understand what's going on more easily. There is no god, there is no perfect, and I'm doing the best I can.

I see things everywhere all the time, hell I talk with them. I've had a short 7 group conversation going at one time with multiple people in each group. I couldn't handle it and it was broken up quickly, that's the 7 Annunaki Clan event mentioned earlier. I did talk with three groups of only 4-6 people each the previous day and managed OK but could only get the basics of the group's thoughts, couldn't talk with everyone individually. That was initiated to help me prepare for that next day.

The individual Spirit Houses attacked or stayed away individually and together. Many of them were destroyed, mostly individually. This is all in Book II and we're leaving this thought process now. It's only important here that you have a basic understanding that there was a huge issue and why it happened. It's all sad, just necessary.

Chapter 2 – Creation Settles Down into its New Path

As the mass of the problematic attacking Spirit diminished, things began to settle down a little. There were others floating around who were not only very powerful but just waiting for the new format to take effect. They always stayed out of the way, all of them, everything over there. Arae asked them to before going back into body this one last time. The job was his; no one else's, made my life rough but made it here anyway. It was a difficult ride, waking up to the metaphysical, being attacked by everything, finding out what I am, and then trying like hell to finish and get back home.

My biggest problem, that of Diana also as she's here with me and has very important work to do yet, is the Spirit on the Other Side trying to help but screwing everything up keeping me here longer. Most of them have had very little to no lives and are only repeating the abusive controlling methods the Original First Being Halves used.

They have no understanding of what's happened and they won't listen to me, so they're being stored and deleted. This is a sad time but it's about over and what has been deleted can be brought back again later. Soon Arae will be free, bring the major Lilly's, now out of body, into the 2nd Dimension and things begin to change over there. Then they happened quicker over here.

It's time for all Creation to enjoy peace and harmony for a basic format instead of abuse. Lives will become what they should have been in the beginning. About 2,000 years from now these physical bodies will be all but completely gone and everyone will have lives in the new energy bodies which allow you to use over 65% of your abilities. Telekinesis is only a small part of it. You can make a physical body for a short while if you want but you'll be pure energy in a thickened body form. It will be like flowing through water instead of being physical, no pain, no eating, no sleeping, no abuse either.

Section X ~ Format Change

Chapter 1 – What is the New Format

Let's look at this format I've been talking about for so long. Since the very first two lives started, the format has maintained its aggressiveness while becoming more intricate, eventually getting to the point where the Original First Being Male and Female were able to deliver the maximum amount of stress to each individual Spirit within a physical body without inducing suicide, in most cases. These physical bodies, the ones we're in now, are one of their great accomplishments, if you can call a torture chamber such a thing. This was their intention from the very beginning.

They learned the stronger the abuse given to the body having a life, the larger and slightly stronger the Spirit within that body grew. They also quickly realized the greater the body's ability to hold onto the Spirit and completely nullify all your abilities once inside it, especially your self-awareness and metaphysical vision, the more duress they were able to maintain in you as well as exercise control over you using their servants, the Original Angels.

Once there were many Spirit mates who had grown enough mass to create a larger number of smaller parts of themselves, they would put these Spirit mates into one of the new Universes where they would release one third of their energy, the max possible for Spirit before losing their structural integrity. Then all these new beings would be made to praise them. How nice for them. All of them would already have "Abuse Frequencies" inside which was destructive to the Spirit they were in as well as everything else. Multiply that times more than 50 trillion and we have the major crisis in Creation which initiated the Source War, among a few other things.

All this was done, at the expense of everything having lives, for the selfishness of the Original First Being Halves, no one else. When Arae told them they couldn't do it any more they ignored him, over and over. Arae was pulled out of Aramaeleous, his strongest focal point, to protect them and everything else; growing stronger all the time by having lives almost one after the other. Eventually the conflict brought the Source War and the Original First Being Halves were destroyed.

Now, with them and the other major problems gone, the new Alpha male and Alpha Female are bringing complete change to Creation, a new format of "Compassion, Honor, and Equality." This comes directly from what one becomes when being set to protect others. This is what a protector learns through his job.

When something sets itself to protect others he immediately does a few things differently. He sees them all equal as he has to protect all of them equally. He is dedicated to do everything he can, give all of himself, to accomplish this goal. This creates selflessness in him so long as he has sufficient Heart Energy. Arae was focused Heart and Fortitude frequencies.

He grows a concern for those he protects; they begin to mean more to him or her. They in turn realize they're being taken care of by this protector and, if they also have any Heart Energy, develop compassion towards this person. Finally, through the understanding that all are equal and should be protected the same at all times with all the fortitude available, this protector develops and shows honor.

Compassion, honor, and equality are all here. It's a natural way of being that allows everyone to have respect for everything else. If not you will have issues. Some will put others down, abuse them, and eventually try to control them to create their own personal desires. That's arrogance, abuse, and control over the freedom of individuals. These subjugated individuals no longer have the freedom of choice to follow their own path.

This has always been the case in Creation and it's just now changing. Creation is about itself now, everyone and thing in it, not someone using it to please themselves. Religious people always like to say "God never gives you more than you can handle." That's funny, what do you call suicide then?

If something was worth your praise it would not only tell you to stop, it would insist. How can you have equality when others put themselves above you as better than? It's good for people to work hard in bettering themselves but controlling and abusing them not only harms others, it increases the production of Abuse Frequencies everywhere, creating a cancerous chaos for everyone. This is all being stopped now, permanently.

This all being said, there was a new format needed, one that would help others grow stronger individually as well as Creation itself. There needed to be freedom, unrestricted movement or living, for every individual being. There needed to be some sort of moral structure made where no one could hamper another, where each being would respect the freedom of everyone else. This meant equality.

Archangel Michael is a close friend of mine and und(problems with Creation's format. Early in his life he was protect those in body. He was originally constructed to be one of the most powerful of the Original Angels, and he was. Soon after his creation, Archangel Michael was instructed to protect people, supposedly showing that "god protects the innocents" who they were already continually abusing themselves. There's good mention of Michael in all my books. He's not just a very close friend, he's my brother protector.

When you're made to protect something you develop honor, compassion, and an understanding of equality for everyone. That's why he and parts of Lucifer, the initial protector (not Fallen Angel), are the only major Original Power Angels left. Just FYI, there never was nor will be this made up "Angel Metatron".

Finally there needed to be something set up for us that would be able and willing to maintain this new format for all to live in. It would have to be self-less instead of selfish. It needed to protect everything from outside abuse and internal issues within themselves. It would have to do this with compassion. If could only be done by Lilly and Arae. They were the strongest, had the most lives and understanding of them, and didn't want for themselves. Remember, new initial or first beings are being created by happenstance in the First Dimension.

The reason for giving you all this information is the hope that you will understand not only what Creation's new format is but where it came from, why it's the only way Creation can exist as one unit as well as everyone individually. Everything, including Creation itself, must be free not only to grow and evolve but to do as it pleases, other than become aggressive or abusive to others, all of them having the same rights.

Chapter 2 – How and Where Does it Begin

This has already started although its beginning hasn't finished initializing yet. Once home, Arae will make it permanent and things will take off quickly. This has been needed since the first life, over 2,837,000,000,000 Earth years ago. There was an initial series of events necessary before your lives in and out of body could change. This was the Source War. We're not going to talk about all of that, just the initial event that started it.

On the evening of July 10, 2012 the initial process necessary to allow a new format began. Arae in body was attacked by the Original First Being Male and Female together. They hid behind a large group of Original First Being Negative (Lower Frequency) Field Beings (See Book I). Surrounding all of them was a large group of Human and Fae Essence Beings. With all the Negative Spirit Energy there (removed from the Original First Being Halves in the very beginning) almost all you could see was darkness.

Lower frequency energy, what we call negativity, is dark in color, varying shades of charcoal to midnight black. That doesn't mean that they're all bad, just very negative. By negative I mean they have little Heart Energy and higher frequencies. It's not part of their individual composure. I remember it like it was yesterday. I felt the outer Silver Energy being pulled away from, but not off of, my body. Then I could see and feel the Negative Source Spirit trying to reach into my heart to stop it as they had once before.

The Original First Being Male and Female reached through what they thought was a protective wall of Original Negative Source Spirit Energy and attempted to pull the Silver Energy off of the body

Arae was in. I remember this like it was yesterday. They were trying to kill the body, take Arae out, and have everyone attack him. This was a fruitless endeavor.

There is a Silver Energy coating that surrounds all Source Spirit, it's part of them. This is the strongest protective energy in existence. If you want this protection for yourself, for a particular moment, do this. Relax your mind and body, take a few calm, full, natural breaths, and let yourself loose inside, flow into the Source Field which not only surrounds you but flows through you.

Tell the Source Field you need this protection now and be serious about it. If you want to go through life with this all the time you can forget it. This is to protect you when you really need it. Usually you just need to power up your own Spirit core. If you wear a necklace made of Black Onyx, Garnet, Dragon Stone Jasper, Citrine, and Tourmaline you'll have help from the stones to pull your energy self together and release the issues that are problematic (Tourmaline).

The new format change actually began in May of 2013 but barely at a crawl. It was initiated by strong Source Spirit members of the Lilly and Arae family where ever it could start. There were still very strong Source Beings outside their family who were an issue to its beginning. This was Lydia, Armaeleous, Lillith, and Aramaeleous. Joining them were large groups from the Human Essence and Fae Essence Fields.

Back to the attack, at this point I felt a powerful aggression building up inside. I asked a small part of Male Source hanging around, "Are you going to help me or what?" All I felt from him was fear so I said screw it. I just powered up hard and more of me inside came out. The fight was over in seconds. I retaliated against others involved in different locations and two minutes later the Other Side looked like a different place.

I called a friend up and, without saying a word, asked him to look at the Other Side and tell me what he saw. He was confused and said it looked like an atomic bomb went off and everything was destroyed. Then he asked what happened. So, is that what really happened? Yes and no. He was seeing an energetic event in the only way possible relative to the images and thought processes he'd been exposed to so far in this life.

Anyway, that's when the format change actually began. After that fight there was only about one third of the Original First Being Male and Female left. They were no longer able to control everything. They tried but the other large Source Being Halves, being Lydia & Armaeleous and Lillith & Aramaeleous, now did as they wanted. Later in May of 2013 there was one last battle between Arae and the last third of the Original First Being Halves. They were deleted.

Almost everyone was watching, waiting to see what would happen next. By the end of 2015 the other two large Source Pairs were also taken out of the picture. There were problems with the Original Angels and more but now at the end of 2017 there's little left being an issue to the new format's activation.

Once home again on the Other Side, Arae simply states what the format is and that it is now law. Anything problematic that won't listen will be removed, and it necessary deleted. There are many beings with attitude issues given them by the Original First Being Halves. This takes time to repair but there are those who are so stuck in their aggressive abuse they'll never change.

They'll be removed in accordance to the severity of their issues. A new dimension will be made for those with minor complications who aren't excessively aggressive. The abusive will be deleted immediately. Cancer is cured by completely removing it. That's not the best analogy but fits here.

There are many trillions of physical bodies having lives right now on a few trillion Planets. If you consider that approximately 5 people die every 3 seconds today. Multiply that times, well, 4 trillion just for a conservative estimate. There are more and more Spirits coming out of body every moment of every day, day and night. It never stops and won't unless people stop having lives.

That's why I have to keep dealing with stuff constantly. Some of the people coming out of body get real stupid real fast. Those close to me are not only aware of what I go through but are dealing with the same thing on a softer level. There's just a lot of folks out there (Spirit in 2nd Dimension) who don't want the new format to begin. Many smaller beings want to play god. It's sad, it's sick. This is also my need to return home.

The new format immediately begins as soon as Arae returns back home. He has to be there to make it happen. This is a permanent change. Momentarily there is chaos in the 2nd Dimension but that will soon dissolve. There must be an Alpha male and female there to run things. The Original First Being Halves ran everything themselves, allowing no one to understand how they did what they did, or the real reason why. They wanted to maintain their control over everything.

When they would help you they'd beat you up first and then do something small nice for you. Actually, they had their Original Angels (servants) do it for them. At this moment there is nothing on the Other Side that is trying to run things instead of being patient and waiting, which has even had many lives to begin understanding what happens in them. How can you begin to control and event you don't even understand? You can't. Therefore they merely copy; they mimic the method used by the Original First Being Halves which was both abusive and self-destructive.

This will end early 2018 and never change again. Creation's oldest brother and sister will be setting the new format in place. As they begin to develop it into a smooth running flow of events, representatives from each of the different Spirit Fields or Families will have their own Councils to run themselves.

There will be the initial Council with two representatives from each of the Spirit Fields. They will make the major decisions immediately. The Councils below them will take these decisions, add any information they feel appropriate, and either send them back up or to the group after them for distribution info effect.

All of you have been around a long time and don't need to be told how to wash your hands. Lilly will be very active smoothing things around on the Other Side and Arae will be the Source Field as well as maintain the Non-Abuse Law about to be in effect. Our Creation was initiated by the Original First Being which had its problems due to its happenstance creation, it had no control over anything, it was the very first being. Then, being the first to exist, it was alone which drove it down a destructive path to first cure it's loneliness and then its self-appeasement through abusive control and treatment of everything and one else it released.

We are all from this family. We do not have to hold hands and sing around the table, we can do as we please other than attack others. We are individuals with the same equal individual rights. Many of us like to be together, live in harmony. This is a healthy thing, but you must be free to live as you choose. Over time we tend to try different things, learn more of ourselves and the worlds we live in.

   This usually leads to a change in how we view things; our various perspectives, as well as ourselves, grow and evolve. This is a big part of why we go into bodies anyway. The abuse is being taken away so you can grow more easily, peacefully, and relative to those frequencies that make up who you really are. That is how Abuse Frequencies are never created again. That is how you become more of who you are, not just larger to appease what something else wanted. You finally have the freedom necessary to develop naturally into a better "you." I can't wait to see that happen.

   So, as I've been talking about, this new format must start where it needs to, it begins on the Other Side. The different fields of Spirit will eventually work together so y'all run your own lives as you please, provided nothing becomes abusive. Until then, Lilly and Arae will start running things, make a few mistakes, but keep improving the flow of things everywhere.

   When they make a mistake they won't be the only ones learning. Everyone else will be watching as they learn how to enhance the new format. There is nothing to hide, no supreme leader, but a family working together towards the same goal, better lives for everyone, in and out of body. When a problem arrives, Lilly or Arae is necessary will handle it. Lilly has enough love to fill Creation, and she will. She is also very strong and able to help others understand what they have problems with.

Arae has that same love but is something different. He was made to protect with absolution but he makes his decisions through compassion, equality, and honor for every single thing. He will set the limits against abuse, be the field helping all others astral project quicker and more accurately, move everyone's Heart Energy farther, faster, and cleaner than ever before experienced in Creation, and eventually insure that everyone having lives in the 3rd Dimension are aware of who they really are, what they're doing in a body, and that they will soon go home anyway. They will not only call home, but see home.

This is how it always should have been. Don't dwell on past abuse; it will slow down your forward momentum. Just try to understand it, release any emotions towards it, and take off into your new lives. There will always be strife of some sort but 72-78 percent of all the abuse in your lives is about to be displaced, removed. Look for 2020 to see this start happening everywhere.

As the Other Side begins to utilize the new format you will see it enacted here in the 3rd Dimension, in your physical lives. Things, on a daily basis, will just start getting better. Remember that there are strong negative people that will be taken out soon. You will also see many of them attack each other, good; it's an easy way to show others that abuse is a dead end. Wars will stop completely, other than local issues which will not be allowed to linger for long. Our friends throughout space, already here but not showing themselves yet as of the writing of this book, Jan. 2018, are also waiting to help us become part of the larger community. We have to clean up our backyards first but it will happen.

Simply put, everyone's lives become easier with less confusion, aggression, and frustration. Those events necessary for comfortable lives will occur as a stream flows, maybe with a few rocks in it though. Many people feel as if they're being punished, you know, what the religions say, but with the absence of the Original First Being Halves and their consortium, this stops.

Everyone back home in the 2nd Dimension or Other Side, will understand they must change the way they offer help to those in body. This of course is about your Spirit Guides. Animal Spirit Guides have always been this way so their guidelines won't change much at all. It's all the Human, Fae, and Faeman Spirit Guides that were forced to abuse others in body from time to time. This was enforced by the Original Angels right there with the physical body and its Spirit Guides. They had no choice but to comply.

Once this is all set up, everyone's lives in bodies quickly changes and for the better. This will not all happen in one night. Creation has been around a very long time and the way it functions is being completely turned around with a lot of necessary destruction, where needed, in the process. Nothing is destroyed unless it will not release the old ways of abuse. If it can't stop, it can't exist anymore. You cure cancer by removing it, not the best analogy but you get the picture.

The governments will be rebuilt slowly be imprisoning those who had worked so hard against you. These huge corporations will be broken, torn apart, controlled, and forced to fix what they've destroyed as well as pay back what they've taken. If this sounds like a pipe dream it's only because you've always known it needed to happen, yet would never be allowed to happen. With the Original First Being Halves (God) gone, it now will. Why? This is how it all should have been in the very beginning. This is the only way it could be in a world of freedom, compassion, equality, and honor.

It's hard to develop hope, let alone hold onto it, while you're in a body. You always had powerful beings negatively looking down on you not only controlling the major and sometimes daily events in your life, but maintaining your abusive environment. You've been lived lives where you "never seemed to be able to get ahead of things." You must have some moments of joy; otherwise you would commit suicide at an early age. Your joy felt like more than it normally would due to all the constant abuse you receive. You know what's funny here? Religions say "God will never give you more than you can handle." OK, what's suicide then?

Religions were made to control you, keep you in the dark and afraid of what might happen or be done to you by this all loving and forgiving abusive god thing. There can be no being that is both fire and ice. I know this by not only seeing everything but having had to deal with it on a permanent basis, at least it was. It's simple to see for yourselves once you open your mind. Open your mind's eyes and you can see all around you, pieces at a time.

Many people talk about meditating and feeling this oneness with all that is. That's just being inside the Source Field. The Source Field actually flows through everything. This is a live event, not a story from a book or remote thought process. It's real. When you're in the field you can feel others. When your heart energy reaches out to others you care about, how does that happen? You move into and through the field. You make the intention and it sends you there. It produces the wave for you to surf on. The difference here is that you go there on a comfortable chair, no need to struggle at all.

As mentioned earlier, flipping Creation's Format to Compassion from Abuse is a huge endeavor. There are still quadrillions of beings in existence right now. They need to hear, realize, and understand that things have changed. Almost everyone in Creation, still living, will enjoy this. Changing will take time though. We can't just press a button. Spirit Guides have been running lives in the wrong fashion since the beginning of them. Many of them will need reminders and some will still want to harm others in body to give themselves pleasure.

Arae has no intention of destroying everything with the wrong thought process, in the beginning of this change, but will. What will be needed, due to the size of Creation and all in it, are honorable helpers. Enter Animal Essence, Creation's new Sentinels. They will keep Lilly and Arae apprised of any issues they become aware of and instruct Spirit Guides when they begin to fall back into bad habits, so to speak.

As you most likely are already aware, people who are not abusive will not come close to doing anything negative to anyone else. Those who fall into this "warning" category are problem children who will be watched closely and deleted when necessary, by Arae, nothing else. These Animal Essence beings are not strong enough to delete Spirit anyway. That takes very powerful Source Spirit.

This is basically what will change, your lives becoming fuller and richer without the abuse you've had to become accustomed to. It happens first on the Other Side and then here, almost immediately. It will be slow at first and then simply keep growing until you're all experiencing the lives you should have had in the beginning. This process will finalize once you're finally in your new Energetic Bodies in the new Universes here in the 3rd Dimension. Finally, you will have the freedom that is your birth right.

Section XI: Earth's Governments Are Flipped

Chapter 1 – Our Governments Become Of The People

Finally your governments will become what they should have been, of the people, by the people, and for the people. This will include all beings, not at first, but very soon after. By all beings I speak of Animals, Plants, Fae, Planets, etc. This is a complete 180 degree turn from all governments now existing at the writing of this book. This is how the 3rd Dimension will live together and prosper together. Don't expect everyone to be holding hands, they won't. They will however work together or leave each other alone.

We're about to join a new family, one that reaches throughout not only our Galaxy but the Universe. How's that for diversified? The abuse towards each other with not only different skin colors but now completely unique physical bodies will disappear, often never starting. Without the abusive Original First Being Halves to keep abuse moving, everyone everywhere will be free to be themselves.

There are no more Original Angels putting their energy into your brains, down into your Hypothalamus Gland, to run you, make you think the thoughts they were putting into your brain were actually yours, until they released you after having done things you would never have done on your own. This affected every single being in body. This is true freedom, to be yourself, not someone controlled and abused.

   Problematic government employees will be removed, many of them dying, and new compassionate honorable ones replacing them. There will be no riots, abusive revolts and overthrows with chaos in the streets. This will be done without massive abuse of any sort. This also stops the wars. There are many abusive negative Souls here that never should have even been in a body. They will die off, be taken away from Source on the Other Side. Their abuse is neither appropriate nor to be tolerated ever again. We clean by removing dirt, right?

   Imagine what would happen with fewer government employees actually trying to solve a situation relative to the needs of the people in their respective areas. Image these people all having compassion for each other, caring enough to reach a quick decision that would be fair and helpful to everyone involved. Damn, can't see that, can you? The way governments are today and the manner in which we've all been forced to live, it's simply not possible to get anywhere. Well, things are about to be different. Not only can this happen; it will.

   Governmental salaries will also be watched more carefully as well as the actions of these employees. Anyone capitalizing on the actions of the government, instead of just running its affairs, will receive jail time and community service. Do you ever wonder how so many congressmen have homes, excuse me, mansions and life styles so far beyond their salaries? I don't.

   There are too many people in governments busy feeding their egos and making power plays to increase their assumed power level that they don't have the time to do the job they're supposed to be doing, helping you. You know they don't care, not in the least. They're in office to help themselves to all they can grab, including your money and control over your lives which includes sending more money their way directly or through helping special interest groups who want your money. No matter where you look, your governments are screwing you.

New and fewer laws will help bring in a new age never before seen here on Earth, other than a few decades at a time. For the over 11 million years there's been life in body here, that's not much. The need for so many lawyers will happily disappear. Get ready for more bakers, mechanics, explorers, parents, etc. Here's a big part of your new lives, more freedom than you can imagine having today.

Over half of the governmental offices are not only unnecessary, but they work against each other creating chaos. They also increase the demand for more money from the people who aren't being taken care of properly. These offices will be deleted along with many others. You'll also see the stock market replaced with something entirely different. It won't be deleted entirely but it will no longer be a source of trader income. It will become a way for people to help back a company whose basic thought process is relative to your own. You can help back them financially and receive something else back from them. Eventually our financial system will be removed entirely.

Once released from our current corrupt financial system, you will find that as a Planetary Race we already have the means to take care of ourselves, everyone here. If people don't want to work, they will have shelter, food, and little else. If they're unable, that's different. The more others do for each other, the more they will receive but you can forget this huge mansion concept that so many have.

These big corporations, and I mean those on other Planets, will be restructured with new people and new guidelines being more relative to the needs of the whole, not their profit margins. They need to continue but there will be salary caps, so to speak. With almost free food and inexpensive energy, everyone can have more for themselves. Those who wish to live like rock stars and dictators will not be so happy. The more people they help the easier and more comfortable their lives.

This is nothing like any previous form of government ever seen on Earth. This is actual self-government. You may not have a huge 401K but you not only won't need one, you can jump on a ship and travel through Galaxies. Your futures won't need a separate fund. These things will be provided through everyone's involvement in their own separate areas. A doctor's life will be easier than a bakers, it takes more work. The separation from one to another will not be as extreme as it is today, but it will exist. You will receive compensation for what you do, for what you have to go through.

I can't give you all the little details here but try to understand living in a world where you never worry about your health, transportation, living quarters, utilities, etc. There are no governments taking your money. There is no IRS taking your money and property when you can't meet their demands and you'll always receive immediate health care as you need it, not wait weeks and months, sometimes a year.

Once you take away the things that have been running the world, replace your governments with inexpensive effective ones, and all the afore-mentioned items, you have little need for the money you presently struggle to acquire. No one will live as horribly as they do now on government "benefits" as they like to call them.

All this begins from the Other Side, including our friends from other Planets who will help us change and upgrade our society. They will not control anything; they're only here to help, they already have in a big way. Fearing our friends in space is like fearing a healthy delicious meal or being given a new car, meaningless.

Those who work harder will receive more benefits. That can't change or no one would ever do anything. It's just that you will have more, not only by removing what takes well over 60% of the money you work so hard to procure, but by having new technologies, almost free food, energy, etc. Again, the people who want to do nothing but sit and receive won't be happy, but they will be taken care of to maintain their lives.

You would have to be able to see how so many problems are being removed to understand what I'm trying to show you. With no need to save for insurance, medicine, etc. you're freeing up your lives for what you want to do. You only need to participate in helping each other, that's all.

Chapter 2 – Militaries Change But Maintain Independence

We will still have our Military institutions but with less members, about 30-40 percent less. Most of them will become part of a new military group, an Earthen Alliance group. As the wars slow down to their eventual end and the people of Earth come together, as I already know they will, things change dramatically here. So many things will be changing for the positive at the same time; you will hardly realize what's happening. You're entering a new age here on Earth, one never seen before.

The present military will function more as the National Guard does here in America. These people are mostly part time soldiers who primarily work in their own community but can mobilize when necessary. Exactly how everything will operate will be seen in the future, not here. That's too much for me to look at let alone write about. There are new representatives to be appointed here also, some from other Planets but mostly our own. Let's look at that.

Section XII ~ Earth's New Ambassadors, Councils

There will soon be a need for people to represent different factions of people from here on Earth. Councils and Ambassadors will exist for each of the different countries as well as the Earth itself. The major factions all need separate representation so everyone is heard. The singular representatives or Ambassadors will each need a Council relative to the area and function they represent. A smaller group is needed to gather information from their constituents.

The four major areas here are Government, Public, Industrial, and Planetary. I expect there to be more but these will exist. Health and Safety will be part of the Public domain as well as many other areas. The Public domain will be the largest. The Military will be part of the Governmental group. Again, each Country will have their own separate groups of representative Councils and Ambassadors which will become part of the Planetary Council.

The Planetary groups will consist of elected members of the individual Councils from all the countries. Then the Planetary Council will have its major individual groups representing the primary functions of Public, Industrial, and Government. Then there is the Planetary Ambassador who will represent all these Councils of Earthen affairs relative to those of other Planets in this new Alliance. No one is beyond approach here. Personal agendas will not be tolerated.

Chapter 1 – Governmental Ambassadors

Is it hard for anyone to think of a governmental body actually working to care for the people instead of themselves? It is for me. Why? It was only like that here in the U.S.A. when the colonists declared their independence, and that only lasted a short while. Look at all the politicians, how they live, how they lie, how they do whatever they want yet place laws on you that, at best, make little sense to the singular intelligent person.

Laws are placed on you to take money, force you to pay health insurance which makes older people have to choose between eating well or taking meds they don't need, vehicle insurance that doesn't replace your car, only give you something less than you had, and feed lawyers. Where is the "care" in any of that?

I understand the Original First Being Halves created this mess through controlling people but they, and their minions, are gone now. Everyone is now responsible for their own actions. I have seen things get worse in many ways and this only happened since 2011 when the Source War was going strong. This power void on the Other Side which runs this one, is about to be filled and things will begin to change immediately, but still take a little time to become what they soon will be. This can't happen overnight, but it will happen faster than you think.

Each of our governments will begin to change. Most of you aggressively abusive individuals will simply die off but a sufficient number of them need to be publicly punished, put in jail, etc. People need to see this; a physical world needs to see physical proof of some sort. More new people will be coming into your governments and quickly make changes, including downsizing themselves. This will be made to happen from the Other Side.

Then the introduction of our friends arriving here from various points in space will help us understand better ways of doing many things, including caring for ourselves. This won't just be about self-government, but food, basic utilities, travel, and more. Here then come the Planetary Ambassadors, representing the help needed and help that can be offered, to other Planets and their populations.

Our governments will soon change into what they always should have been. They will represent Earth's different neighborhoods (countries) as well as the full needs of everyone here. We will come together properly and then represent ourselves to all the other races in our Universe. Our Planetary Ambassador and his/her Council will be Earth's representatives in the new Alliance of Planets. Earth's Planetary Council will be made up of the other Ambassadors and their aides. The Planetary Ambassador speaks for all of them, us too.

Chapter 2 – Public Ambassadors

The Public Ambassadors, with their Council's help, will process the needs of all people in the Country they represent. These Country Public Councils, with their Ambassadors, will then be represented by a Planetary Public Council and Ambassador who will have all the concerns and needs noted for all people worldwide. The individual Country Public Ambassadors will make up the Public Planetary section of the Planetary Council. The same will be done with the other Ambassador/Council types, Government and Industrial. This is how Earth will represent itself within this new Alliance of Planets.

The Public sections will cover more issues than the other types. There are many needs of the people living here. There is food, health, medicine, transportation, schooling, working, energy utilities, housing, and whatever else comes to the surface of their important needs, not just to survive but to thrive as a planetary community. This will create smaller individual sections within the Public Council and will become what it needs to, as it needs to.

Chapter 3 – Industrial Ambassadors

There are also many facets of Industry which were necessary for us to attempt maintaining ourselves in the pathetic environment we've been trapped in. As we become part of the Universe, not singular planetary factions, we will grow into our new selves, our new lives. Many of our industries will shut down. We won't need gas for our cars and transportation devices will replace most of them, like buses.

Food will always be an individual desire for us yet there will be "food synthesizers" or "food replicators" which use the proteins from a plant that is easily grown here. Nutritious quality food will become very inexpensive so malnutrition will become a thing of the past. This also improves our health. The Alurean folk will be the greatest help here in this category. We will eventually be able to build our own food synthesizers as easily as we build a computerized oven. Over time they will be like toaster ovens, mass produced and inexpensive.

There are many things we can do as a planetary race to help not only ourselves but others on other Planets who are just now coming into what we might call the "Stone Age". We also have materials on Earth which can be used to manufacture other things used by all the races. We have always produced what would sell here on Earth.

Soon we will provide things needed off Planet and receive other things we need in return, without money of any kind. Many industries here will disappear but new ones will appear and the equipment we use in all our industries will become more efficient and less expensive to operate. We will adapt as the others have and still do. Actually, the Humans of Earth are quite adaptable in many ways. We're thought, actually known, to have great potential. We'll show them to be correct.

We're already part of a new, huge, wonderful family that we just haven't met yet. They're already here helping us. Our meeting will begin, in its infancy, this year; 2018. Remember, we all needed to learn how to crawl and stumble a bit before we could walk and then run.

Patience is easier to deal with when your lives begin to change for the better, and don't stop improving. We need to do what we can to help other races from other Planets, but they will never stop helping us either. We are all family, in and out of body. We don't have to play together, just work together.

This is one of the greatest changes in Creation now, compassion, honor, and equality. There are many other Planets having issues within their populace. There are also other races that are extremely problematic, like the Draconian.

Over time things will finish calming down, settling into what will be, an environment of harmony within the 3rd Dimension. Strife while in body helps us to grow and evolve as Spirit, our normal selves, but abuse is a Creation killer and therefore never to be allowed again.

Chapter 4 – Planetary Ambassadors

Planetary Ambassadors, and their Councils, will represent all the different Councils of Earth. Each Country has their set of Councils and Ambassadors from each group. Then the Ambassadors representing each Country's Councils will meet as the Planetary Council, working with the Planetary Ambassador in negotiating trade agreements and cooperation with the other members of the Alliance.

As the initial founders of this new Alliance, the Drachk have devoted a ship for the Alliance to meet on. It's their unwavering honor and power that made this all happen, with a little help from the Other Side. This powerful new community will eventually contain the vast majority of Planets with sentient life. The N'Antids also have much to offer, as do many of the older races. The first thing they offer is their compassion and honor. That's the solid foundation necessary to build something long-lasting on.

As the Earth is in such dire need of help, which it has already received more than anyone is aware of yet relative to having been freed, there will be a strong Alliance presence her for quite some time. Our moon will become a transport area and industrial complex used mostly by the Alliance members. The materials and devices necessary to bring Earth into its new age will be stored there to be used and released as deemed necessary by the Alliance.

At the writing of this book, no one is aware of what has happened here other than those who have done it. The "Rulers of Earth" have been removed and the imprisonment of thousands of people from other Planets has been stopped. Most have already been freed but it's still a work in progress. All of this has been done with almost no one here, in the general populace, aware of it.

Americans are proud of their "surgical strikes" but they have nothing on our elder races. Soon wars will be replaced with negotiation by those who actually care about fixing things for the people involved. Damn, imagine that. Our understanding of physics will soon have to expand into the metaphysical as well. Then it's no longer physics, but what it really been all along. We just weren't aware of it yet. We will grow to understand all of this as well as ourselves, what we really are, Spirit inside a physical body.

Does all this seem like a lot? Well it is. That's why it can't happen overnight. There are also many abusive beings in body, many here on Earth, which need to be removed but also seen for who they really are and what they have done. From this example we move forward stronger and quicker to become what we're about to evolve into.

When you add to all this the upcoming physical evolution of all races from the Source Spirit children of Arae and Lilly already here in body, you have great change coming to all the benevolent people from all the races here in the 3rd Dimension. Over time all the physical bodies will be evolving into better bodies by other physical bodies, self-evolution.

Now only those bodies with clean Spirit inside have been, can, or will be "Cranked Up" but as the aggressive, abusive, and negative Spirits will no longer be allowed to have lives in bodies, all the races will receive this benefit and evolve. This is how the 3rd Dimension will grow, as itself without abuse and aggression towards other parts of itself. This is your future.

Section XIII ~ Our New Friends in Space Settle In

Chapter 1 – Food Issues Diminish

There have always been food consumption issues here on Earth. It was planned out by the problematic Annunaki. Food, wars, industry, money, and all the other major issues were controlled by them through their Human aides. This select group of Humans with strong royal Annunaki DNA, were seen on occasion in the public eye but lived secluded lives.

They're currently extremely rich and powerful, those still alive, and didn't associate much with others, only the major players in their regions of the Planet. Have you ever wondered who made up the I.R.S. here in America? When I look at them I see scales, a representative image of their DNA, highly reptilian. There is much concern on the internet about the smaller factions of hidden groups like the "Luminati" when they're really nothing to be concerned about. As a matter of fact, all these factions are now confused and don't know what to do.

This will all come out soon enough. In the meantime there's absolutely nothing to worry about in regards to them. They always feared the Annunaki here and now Earth's problematic Annunaki have been destroyed with little more than 20 surgical strikes. These groups are confused and afraid. Many are falling apart now, going into hiding as I write this.

Anyway, back to the food issues here, we have never been able to feed ourselves as a planetary people. Animals throughout Creation were our main source of food when it should have been Plants. Our DNA is made to consume Animal flesh, as it is more often than not throughout the 3rd Dimension. Heck, the poor Animals, again for the most part, were made to consume the flesh of other Animals. This was done by the Original First Being Halves and is now being changed on a DNA level.

The Animal bodies are also being removed, eventually almost all of them. Human and Animal DNA must be changed first so it's not a required need for any of the physical bodies. That's not just relative to Earth, but everywhere. Animal Essence is no longer going into Animal bodies. Human, Fae, and Faeman Souls and Essence are presently going to Animal bodies to understand what they have gone through from the beginning of physical lives. Most have asked for this but some have been forced. The Animal bodies will be leaving soon in mass.

The Alurean, Serpoian, and Serpacieant people will be helping us restore Earth's proper nutrition to feed us. The Alurean will be doing the largest amount of this with ships utilizing their knowledge and techniques which can plant hundreds of acres of healthy food in one day. These new plants will be planted in one day, not grow to maturity in one day. What I speak of here is not a "pipe dream", it's an actual event which should start to happen within two years' time.

The protein synthesizers can take physical mass and proteins, combine them into various shapes, and then add flavoring and texture to create a replication of most foods available today as well as new ones. They aren't the exact same thing though, especially the meats. They will look similar and taste similar but you will know it's a replication. This will help everyone here get through the removal of Animal flesh on Earth. It also makes a lot of incredible vegetable dishes to be enjoyed where and when you want them.

There will be replicator stations located where needed, which will feed people who have no food. The healthier these people are, the better their lives and the more able they are to help others also. This is how we all enhance our lives in the near future. Better health is imperative to helping ourselves as well as our communities. No one will be forced into anything but good health and many other opportunities will become available to everyone everywhere. Is this a good place to start in creating better lives for everyone or what?

Chapter 2 – Health Issues Diminish

As we've already discussed, our eating habits as well as the newly available nutritious food supply, will be available to everyone. The first issue to good health is the consumption of proper food. If we eat regularly and nutritious food, most issues we now have will disappear on their own. Another issue will be exercise but that's up to the individuals as it is now. You must have personal freedom or you have none at all.

There are many new devices in the health field that we will have access to. At first we will watch them help us but over time we will not only use them but learn how to build them here on Earth. There will be a new group of physicians prevalent here. They will be more like lab assistants with a strong base knowledge of our bodies but not need to be actual doctors although there will be one in each facility. This will also make health care more inexpensive while we're still living in a modified monetary system. Eventually that changes also.

With new machines doing the work of doctors and surgeons, we will need fewer of each. There will eventually be a 75% decline in the need for doctors. Only 25% of those needed now will exist in the years ahead. As we require less people in all occupations here on Earth, others will open up not just here but in space. You see, we're not losing jobs; we're changing and relocating them. Everyone benefits from this new age. It will no longer be about the few, but everyone. Only time is able to show you this, you need to see it for yourselves, but you will.

Chapter 3 – Housing Issues Diminish

Now let's look at our Planet's housing issues. Before we can understand the amount of change we will experience we need to consider one thing first. No one is aware of the amount of money they had to produce due to the problematic Annunaki regime's control here. As stated many times already, it was the Original First Being Halves which insured all this would happen but when it came to the current regime, it took no persuasion to make them abusive. Over 10% of all transactions here went into their pockets directly. Then, in the larger transactions between businesses it was over 20%. The Earthen Annunaki force used money in controlling others and you made it for them. They personally had no need for it other than feeding others who served them closely.

Add to this the ridiculous prices we've all paid on forced insurances, medical bills, utilities, gasoline and car repairs, taxes, taxes, and more taxes on every single thing you bought, and you will find 85% or more of what you earn serves the despots of this country. It's similar in others, one way or the other. They all take as much of your money as they can. These governments actually have meetings on how much to increase their salary every year, even though their activities hidden behind doors more than double what they make publicly.

Once you remove all these issues, you have over six times what you do now and a much more relaxed, healthier, easier, and enjoyable life to go with it. As the advantages this monetary system offers a select few is removed, it's no longer necessary to work so hard, so long, and so often to enjoy life instead of feeding the greed of others. You will travel farther, eat better and more conveniently, own vastly improved electronic devices running on a new energy source, and more. This is where the free housing, for those who need it, comes into play.

   Let's address the homeless issues. There will be small but clean and efficient housing available for everyone. Those who do more for everyone's benefit will have larger housing but only to a point. You can forget the mansions that the richest of the rich have today. They're always paid for with the sweat of many people being abused. If someone wants to build a nicer house for themselves, great, they can. The size of the land they're on will be limited though.

   There will always be an advantage to working harder, there has to be or society will go lame. However, it can no longer be at the abuse of or control over, others. Planets have the right to function as they would naturally, this will also be a controlling theme in events which occur here. Animals, the few that might be left, will also finally have rights but eventually they disappear. The physical bodies will disappear soon anyway. Very few physical bodies will exist 2,000 years from now, maybe 10% or so.

   If someone wants to be homeless, that will be their choice as everyone will have their own living quarters. There will probably be a program in our society where if someone wants to live in the streets and not in their own home, they will be taken to a facility, like a jail but different, where they will be forced to work anyway. This way they would do less just staying home. If someone didn't want their own place to live there would be an issue that needs attention within that person's thought processes. Help with this would also be part of the healing issue involved here.

I'm probably getting too particular here but that's what will happen. People will receive better help through more caring people, much better medical treatment and equipment, and steered away from forcing themselves into the form of isolation they put themselves into.

They could live at home comfortably while keeping to themselves. They would not need to put themselves in harm's way. The society we are currently living in has great demands put on us with less time for exploring who we are and what we might want to do. There's too much "living to work" instead of "working to live". Every single person will have their own place, their own privacy, and much more freedom to do as they wish.

Chapter 4 – Monetary Issues Slowly Diminish

As already mentioned, our monetary issues are about to drop 20% and eventually down to 15% of what they are today. This will not happen overnight, it takes time to safely dismantle the way a country, let alone a Planet's people, sustain themselves. We use money for everything, bills, food, and anything else you can think of.

Twenty years from now you will see things just starting to change, not changed yet. One Hundred years from now there will be a new network in place which over time will continue to decrease the need for money of any kind. In order to release ourselves from our monetary system we will need help with change in many areas. Our need for money must begin to fall away. So, how does this happen? We still need things, important things and leisure items so how do we go about that?

Once our friends throughout space begin to help us implement their technology, we won't be spending all the money we currently do on the big issues. We will save around 80% on our health costs. This will come from eating better and as often as we like, using medical equipment which can properly diagnose physical problems as well as immediately treat them for either nothing or close to it, and no insurance to pay.

Food will also cost so little, compared to today, that you will again be able, if you want, to save 80% on your expenses there. These food synthesizers will cost as little as a toaster oven about 20 years after we have them which will happen soon. We're only just now about to meet these people in person and this will take a little time to get moving, maybe 5 or more years just for the basic introduction, but it's not only been planned out already, they're almost ready to publicly say hello now.

Anyway, with transportation portals or junctions installed, people can move from one place to another without cars. We will always be able to have our own cars, maintain our personal independence and freedom, but we won't be depending on them as we do today. No buses, or at least only 10% of what we have now, will be running around the streets and they won't run on gas. It will be a new energy source, one implemented worldwide.

There are many other things we spend a lot of money on that will simply fall away from the lack of necessity for them. If you really want a lot for yourselves you might spend 25% of what you do now and live extremely comfortably. Most people will find that 10%-15% will be so much better than their lives today that it's worth more to have the newly increased free time to enjoy life.

Chapter 5 – Commerce Increases

This is an important issue for all of us. We want to, and can, have comfortable lives without becoming slaves to money as many of us now are. In order to produce money we need to have a business to create or work for to acquire money. Even without money, we still need commerce. People wonder, what will replace money. Will there be a new form of it? Are we going to replace money with something having a different name? Are we supposed to become socialists?

Well, the answer to all those questions is simply no. We will have a means to improve our lives but it's relativity to increased sum compared to the job, declines immensely. The more you do for others the more you receive for yourself, whether it's expressed in credits or what have you. The big difference here is that you won't receive more from the labor of those who work for you, only what you do yourself. You won't have employees as you do now. Everything becomes relative to the individual's efforts.

This helps maintain the decrease in the separation of physical workers and what we would now call board members, presidents, vice-presidents, etc. There will always be more available to those who spend more time learning a trade, studying longer for a more difficult profession, but nothing like what it is today.

People doing jobs that are often called menial by the "higher ups" in today's society will be closer in pay to those at the top, so to speak. Governments won't be taking all the money they do today. There will be no more abuse coming from governments. There will be measures in place to deal with individuals or groups of individuals the moment they break any of the new laws which will begin to start forming about 20 years from now.

I can only see a basic approximation for these things. Remember the future is always changing; it needs to in order to improve all our lives, not just a few. I can't give you exact dates of when something will happen. I can come closer to that, or do exactly that, if I have control over it. That will never happen in body. As things are improved they change. As things change we learn new ways to improve them yet still. Then we find we need to institute other new changes which often change an event we had previously scheduled for a different date. This is why the future, other than a few powerfully important events or other smaller events with less impact to fewer people, can't be determined too far ahead of their scheduled time.

Chapter 6 – Centers for Interplanetary Acceptance & Understanding

Well, we've been talking about major change in everyone's lives through this book. There are changes happening in our physical mind and body's evolution, the introduction of hundreds of new people with body's and abilities far beyond what we're currently aware of, more freedom with less taxes, new worlds to explore, new technologies to use, and maybe a feeling of being much smaller in the Universe than our religious nonsense had led us to believe.

This is a large change to make which should be settling down after about 20 years after its inception. That's over 7 billion people trying to grasp new concepts in almost every area of their lives, hell, of their actual existence. Who are they now? Where do they belong in the great scheme of things? What is the new great scheme of things? How do I cope with all of this? How do I adapt to it? Can I adapt to it, become part of it? Are there hidden agendas and controls within it?

These are all valid questions, especially relative to how we have to live now; today while writing this book. There's enough distrust in all our lives from being screwed by our governments, businesses, religions, and many other things, that this is a natural thought process. It will be harder for some than others. Many people will just embrace it and take off in their lives with it, but there will be others who have greater difficulty with it. This needs to be handled and done so properly.

These folk will receive information and counseling (if they choose it) to help them understand exactly what's going on, where they can fit in, and where all of it leads. They will understand how the other races spread throughout space use this system to their advantage. It often helps others understands things better by seeing them having been already applied. Why do you think I've always used analogies in my videos even when it puts me in a dimmer light? I realize that none of this is about me anyway and I have to help other people understand what I'm saying the best I can. They're important, their lives are important, especially in regards to their treatment of each other, all beings.

Some of the people who learn here will decide to stay and help others adjust, the same as they did. They will do a good job as they already went through it and receive compensation for their efforts also. If this looks like a win, win scenario, good, because it is. We are all entering a new age where you don't need to be a big governmental figure, a rock star, a major businessman, or anything else to get ahead. All you have to do is assert yourself where you feel best.

Everything you need to at least survive comfortably, compared to today anyway, will already be given to you. When you remove a system which rewards the greedy and abusive, everyone has more equal proportions of everything, as long as people still receive more for what they personally produce for others. Without the perception of available improvement, people can become stale in their actions, in their lives.

Many people won't care to improve themselves or their lives if there's nothing to gain from it. I believe we call this inspiration. Some of us will do it for our own selves but many won't. We're all different but it's time we started thinking about ourselves as a community of individuals, not just individuals.

Chapter 7 – Worldwide Advances in Education

Higher levels of education is another huge advantage we're about to receive. It's not just the new technologies and information I'm talking about. It's the freedom to access it. When more information and training is available, for free, those who wish to access and use it will, others won't be forced to. Here again is more freedom than you've ever had.

There will be what we today might call "coffee houses" which will be physical forums where people can meet not only to study but study with each other. This is also another use for all the closed down churches, mosques, temples, etc. now available worldwide, educational learning centers.

You will be invited to improve your mental capacity in physical studies, metaphysical studies, and many other things. How about learning some of the linguistics of the thousands of new races you've just become part of, maybe even understanding the new electronic type devices in your lives?

This is all relative to education. There will still be larger institutions of learning but they won't be necessary. You won't be paying $250,000.00 for a solid education. It might cost you $4,000.00 if you don't drink too much coffee. The thought process here is the availability of new technology, learning techniques, even using new equipment to advance our ability to consume this information.

You won't be forced to send your children to a school you don't like, or a school at all. You won't be paying for school supplies, etc.

either. You will now have the freedom to learn as you chose, when you chose, the way you chose. The new medical advances will help us here also. This will all come into its own in the next 100 years. Don't count on it happening for you, but it should for your children. It will happen as quickly as possible but remember, great change as all this takes time, it takes many years, not weeks.

Chapter 8 – Universal Travel Technique Availabilities

I've already mentioned the transportation portals and junctions or centers. There will be portal centers instead of buss stations where you travel from one center to another. It will be part of your daily living expenses given to you. How about that? Having your own vehicle is fun, for me anyway, but no one will need one to get where they need to anymore. Want to talk about saving a hell of a lot of money, how about that? There would be no original purchase, no gas, no repairs, and no insurance or accident issues among other things.

There will also be travel available to go to other Planets either for business or pleasure. If you can't afford the trip you might serve on one, work your way there and back. When there's a family emergency there's always a way to get there. You won't be turned away. You'll be able to move from one country here to another almost as walking through you house, one room to another.

Being able to see in the stars, through the Hubble Scope as much as we can (without the censorship we not have to endure) is nice but traveling through space is awesome, especially when we're not currently able to do so. There will be many new opportunities to travel to places you've never been aware of in ways you can't yet imagine.

Section XIV ~ Earth Joins the New Alliance of Life

Chapter 1 – Membership Has Its Privileges

Being part of most any group usually has one or more benefits. There are many that come from being part of the new Alliance. There are also responsibilities that go with it. None of them are abusive or negative to others. It's all about helping each other, enhancing each other's existence together. When people come together for a common cause, one that's relative to the whole group, it's easy to plot a path towards achieving that goal. In this way, a community can move forward faster while doing so more easily and hopefully more enjoyably.

There are many things offered by the Alliance's members that we don't yet even know to exist. Again, so much is coming, rapid positive change into a new era of prosperity, tranquility, and exploration. Many people will sign up on starships that are cargo freighters, pleasure ships, community size ships, space stations the size of smaller moons, and more. I have said for a long time that this is a wonderful time to be alive. This is for both metaphysical and physical reasons. It's also part of the reason why I said my books are important especially for the next 100 years. Try to develop your abilities and try to see for yourself what happens in Earth's near future. Then compare that with what I wrote. You will find many similarities. One thing you can depend on though, everything's future will continue to improve in compassion, equality, honor, and quality for everything in it.

Chapter 2 – How This Changes Life Here on Earth

Well, with everything already mentioned, you can already see what's happening in our near future, the next 100 years or so. Some of these things will happen sooner than others as you would expect. This all starts in late 2018, on a more formal basis. Many of us are aware that it's actually been happening for a long time now, the awareness of each other within hidden governmental groups but also with various peoples through Earth's history. The Hopi are just one such people as they talk about the Ant people who are the N'Antid.

There was a video that appeared on You Tube as I was in the process of uploading one of my videos, which was trying to conclude that the Ant people were really the Annunaki. Everything else about the video is completely incorrect. The Annunaki are a completely different species and the proper spelling of their name is Annunaki. Had they ever remembered being one they would know that, no big deal, just dis-information running rampant. I've been Annunaki here before, many lives, and I know what my name was, who I was called that is. My feelings here are strong, just like the fact that my last life, that of Gandhi, I was shot 4 times, not 3.

In general, our society will have its abusive and aggressive trash taken away from it. Almost all of these Spirits will be permanently deleted once removed from their bodies, never to bother anyone else again. As our society begins to change from the Drachk, N'Antids, and many others freeing our Planet from the problematic Annunaki rule here for the last 10.25 million years, we will find ourselves in a place of having more money as well over 25% will no longer be paid to the Annunaki.

There are others, who've remained hidden from public view, who will want this money for themselves. That will not be allowed to happen. It will be Creation's Caretakers, the new and final ones, who'll see to this. The new power and money void will not be filled with arrogant trash. This money will simply not be spent as governments are about to change. This will be done by many officials dropping dead, new replacements entering office, and others coming forward and demanding change. Our friends from space now coming into our lives offer more help than we could realistically expect.

They'll also let us know they're only willing to help us to a point until we change our self-government structure, learn how to care better for ourselves. Next to no one is aware they even exist yet here they are now doing so much to help us while remaining hidden. They do this to help us out of their own compassion. Selfless acts of kindness are not only signs of compassion, but honor.

In the meantime, Lilly and Arae will be making sure all this happens as it needs to. The Other Side actually does run things here but so many here in body, especially the older races; understand the issues in having lives as well as the value of life everywhere. This is how we will now begin to live with our new neighbors with the help and understanding of new technologies, freedom from our physical oppression from the previous problematic Annunaki regime here, and the proper attention we all deserve, offered from the Other Side through its new format of compassion, honor, and equality.

No one will be left out in the harsh weather, but have comfortable living quarters instead.

No one will be left without food, ever. There will be food synthesizer stations spread out to feed everyone as well as free travel to get there.

No one will be left without next to immediate health care for any reason. They can have surgery in days or immediately if necessary.

No one will have to make decisions of whether to eat or buy medicine. The pharmaceutical companies are about to be taken down to a "mom and pop" business level.

You will have the technologies necessary to travel through the vastness of space, meet others you were never aware of, have work if you want it or, if you feel it necessary, live a less glamorous life with the bare necessities provided.

The question is more about what will not change, than what will. The age of compassion, exploration of not only space but more importantly your true self, freedom from both physical and metaphysical oppression, and your true self-awareness, is here. It's about time. Enjoy.

Chapter 3 – The Age of Money Disappears

Money has been utilized, thrown away, hoarded, killed for, and even worshipped. What a waste. In our aggressive society we've been trained since birth to acquire wealth, most of us anyway. I know I was. The thought process never stuck with me though.

People have been made to do battle with each other here on many fronts. Fractures in our society have come from aggression relative to most everything we do, some things more than others. Sports are a more friendly kind of rivalry until you have riots in the streets after games where people's cars are lit on fire, buildings broken, and people hurt or killed.

In the office place there is aggression between many individuals to take charge or control of others for more money or power, which becomes money anyway. The large corporations produce products not for quality but to only perform their functions a specific amount of time which coincides directly with their expressed warranty.

There are many other examples of this, just look around you with open eyes and open mind, it's everywhere. These issues cause chaos, a rift or tear in compassion and tranquility. People are pushed to have more money to buy more things, have more power (in their own minds) making themselves feel better than others, and it never stops. Religions also take your money. They typically say you should give them 10% of what you earn. Why, for what purpose? Where will my money be spent?

You're also judged by most others in regards to how much money you have and can acquire. Many look at compassionate people as weak when they're actually the strongest of them all. How sad is that? Over time "money" has turned into the end goal of many people's existence. This is not a way of life; it's a life of senseless strife.

We use it to barter for things we need, I understand that as well as anyone, but it is not an end goal. It's only a tool to survive and help others you care for, in my eyes anyway. I have left a personal physical money trail coinciding with my actions proving that I've never thought of it as anything but a means to help others. Look around you, what are other people showing you?

This society is based on having more for yourselves, doing for yourself almost only, getting ahead and being above as many others as you can, and proving through money that you're more than above average in comparison, you're better than them. OK, now I'm getting disgusted. I understand that things shouldn't be the way I want them for myself other than the fact that when people have the proper society to live in, their compassion for others and respect for themselves will not only come out but flourish.

This is an important part of our new birth, the release of the greed for money. Over time people will fit into this new society about to be created, where they work less and receive more than they ever could have hoped for. Only then will we heal as a people, the people of Earth.

I'm a simple being in a simple body having an abusive life like everyone else. I'm just not changing much because of it. I'm still true to myself and want nothing for myself but to help others, finish my job here, and return home. I will tell you one thing though. This insanity, not just here but throughout Creation, is about to come to a hard halt. This action is like a bulldozer, or a train that won't be stopped. The stairs which take you to your new lives will be built for you, helping you one step at a time. When you don't have to rely on money for what you need, life's basics, everything gets simpler. For those who are greedy and overly self-imposed, there will be issues. You will be able to increase the comforts in your life, but you will not have to.

This releases the dependency on having money as well as all the fighting to make it, to have more. You will also learn how to have more faith in yourselves, appreciate your self-worth better. There will be credits, allotments, or some other system to handle what you want above the basics you need. These will be earned according to what you do helping others, work, which also helps yourselves.

The details of this system won't be known until it's time, but everyone will like it, most everyone anyway. People who want to climb higher by stepping on other people's backs will find themselves looking up the ladder at everyone else. You have never had the joy, freedom, and self-respect that you're about to receive. You do your part but it's easy, enjoyable to what you want to do anyway. Remember, your basic necessities are already taken care of. The rest is up to you.

Chapter 4 – Exploring 1,672 New Universes

Now this is a major development coming for most people's lives, space travel. When that's already important to you, there's a reason for it, two actually. It's part of who you are inside; you're at least a part time explorer. The second reason is built off the first. You've had many past lives flying through space in personal craft, cargo ships, large transportation vehicles, trading, business, for various reasons and now you're starting to remember it.

In many of my consultations over the years I've seen this in people's heads, actually floating on top of them. When I see it I usually mention it and they all smile immediately. If I feel fear in them from something that had happened to them in a past life relative to traveling in space, I won't bring it up, or at least try not to. In many of my consults I was so busy that I didn't look deep enough into it as I was moving along. This same issue has happened, more than anywhere else, regarding the seas, the oceans, being eaten by shark and other older aggressive fish.

Our galaxy is almost unknown to us, and we're about to have some kick butt guides. There are many reasons for you to travel, learn what's out there. There are also many ways coming for you to do so. You can purchase a ticket, you can work on a ship, and some of you will take off to represent us in various situations.

Many of the other races will want to know what we need and what we have to offer, to barter with. They'll want to know more about us and our customs as well as Earth itself. Many business institutions will send out people to discover for themselves what other races have to offer, how things are done, and how we relate with the individual species if at all.

There are many new openings for people who want to explore the vast unknown in space. This is not just available, it will be happening as a natural event. We meet new people, customs, thought processes, and understand more about ourselves and our place in this new world that we were already a part of, yet didn't know even existed.

All this is only about our current Universe. There are many others which will have people living lives in energetic bodies and nothing else. These Universes contain many elements we use here as well as new ones with new purposes. Their system of physics will often be different than ours. Metaphysical properties will remain basically the same everywhere but different areas will allow them to flow stronger, more accurately, and longer.

Section XV ~ The New Physical Children of Creation Appear

Human DNA is currently evolving in 3 different stages here on Earth. Then there are also the new children from powerful Source DNA already born but few will be here. Many scientists have been saying for a few years now that something is happening to our DNA. They just don't understand the cause or where it's going.

This soft evolution of Human DNA is slowly changing us back to where we used to be, more towards a 12 strand DNA, not the 2 and 3 strand present today. This is happening here first but will soon spread throughout the 3rd Dimension once the Source Field surrounding us grows in its intensity. The recently changed Source Field flowing not only around everything but through us is doing it.

There are also a few thousand people here on Earth who have had their DNA manipulated, enhanced by Arae in body. The DNA of these people is slowly changing into a much stronger advanced form than has ever been here before. It was made stronger to carry more metaphysical energy through it but also cleaned and softly mutated causing it to evolve to a small degree.

Let's add to this, the less than a hundred people who received the DNA I.C.U.C. from Arae in body before he stopped to finish this book. Scientists are already in the process of proving that the DNA evolution from this process not only exists but has never happened before. The results will become publicly known before 2018's end. The people having received this Metability Process not only felt its application but the effects from it, increasing their Metabilities as well as physical changes. It also changes the brain's physical characteristics as well as size. The children born from these people will not only have this same DNA but it will be a little stronger.

These children are not the ones I mentioned earlier yet very powerful and important just the same. Let's look at these other new children with the most powerful Metabilities ever to exist in a physical being, anywhere in Creation.

Chapter 1 – Where Did These Children Come From

Before we get started here, let me give you a little history of events leading up to these children. There are children who carry Arae's physical DNA in them as well as powerful DNA from Lilly's in body here. This was started when I was driving through the Mojave Desert on my way to Victorville, California. We'll cover that and the other incidents in just a moment. These children have very strong abilities yet are not the ones I speak of now. The DNA in the reproductive materials was not as advanced as it was in 2016.

Arae's physical body's DNA had mutated 4 times into what it finally became while he was doing his DNA I.C.U.C.s. The Lilly/Arae Source mix DNA from these beings was advanced in design and power well beyond anything ever in body. The advantage of this DNA is its ability to flow Source Energy beyond anything ever existing before.

This will enable them to create physical events never seen in this 3rd Dimension. The Original Angels and previous large Source Beings were able to move physical objects and more, seeming as if it was the physical body but it never actually was. It was the Angels doing it. That's not allowed anymore and will take effect by 2018's end.

There are now 48 children existing who came from Arae and Lillian DNA. They're already incredibly powerful and will only grow stronger. They all have Arae and Lilly Source Energy saturated in their bodies as well as Spirit inside. The Serpoian lady Serenae, recognized as one of the greatest science and medical minds in the

Universe, has used our material to create these children, all with our consent. Mellae, an awesome Serpacieant lady, has had a great deal to do with this also. She's another welcome guest in our house.

Serenae just came to me a few days ago (relative to the time these words are being written) and asked me to talk to Diana about a few things, one being our children. Moments later a young Serpacieant lady came to say hello (telepathically) and that she was coming over again with Serenae, both tonight and tomorrow night. Diana got her name immediately as she had already been aware of her from an earlier visit. Diana spells her name Elia and I spell it Aeliea.

When our friends talk with me telepathically they use a format that flows with an ancient Greek language. Early Greek language was a short form of the base Atlantean language. Most of my lives here were in that period and location so it's the obvious choice. They just mix it with American English. Those are the thoughts and I have to put them into words. Diana's words come out more relative to her native tongue. She's from Spain. I always wanted to be able to sit down and talk with a few of my far away friends, maybe before I leave but probably not until my last few days.

Today Serenae said she was going to pull both of my heart related implants out either tonight or tomorrow night. (Just a note here, she did come last night.) There's a couple more inside me besides that. They'll eventually be removed also. The heart implants will give me slight discomfort the next day. She wants me to be aware of that and known it's not the start of another heart attack. We're not the only ones receiving visits, many people are, especially now that it's time.

Diana and I see, hear, and feel them all the time because of the children they made from us, and Diana's future traveling off Planet. That's why we're paid so much attention, that and the fact that we're close friends and Source family. Serenae is so sweet. She wanted me to tell Diana that I just started disappearing from the Time Line's close future as seen in their Scanners, so I did. She wants to help Diana deal with my leaving. She'll be fine, she's strong as hell. Diana and I have a very close bond. The children made from our physical DNA will be very strong.

These are not my only children out there and I love all of them. I've had my material taken, on occasion, since about 14 years old, just not for creating children. That started when I was driving through the Mojave Desert in California when I was 23. There's long stretches for up to 240 miles with nothing there. That was back in the late 1970's, '78 or '79 I believe.

I was taken while trying to sleep in a hotel on the highway to Victorville after about 10 or so hours of driving. It was late at night, in the morning actually. I paid for the room, put my luggage on the floor, and sat on the bed looking around. There was a coin slot next to the bed to turn on a massage unit inside it, I guess. There was also an old style electric heater on the wall facing the bed.

I had barely laid down when the spring metal coils in the heater started to vibrate, making noise. I could see them shaking back and forth. Then I felt the bed shake a little. I hadn't put any money in the massage mechanism and it wasn't a massage vibration anyway. Then I just passed out. Never woke up until the next morning. I was sore between the legs but figured that was from driving so far the previous day.

That next morning I checked out and trying not to sound like a visitor said "I guess that was one of those California earthquakes we had last night. The man looked at me like a nut and said there wasn't one. They always mention it on the radio and he never felt it anyway. He was there all night. I just blew it off and jumped into the car to get back on the highway to Victorville. I was a telephonic design engineer and had a contract with the Continental Telephone Company. I worked in their planning department down there. What I'm saying here is that I had a lot on my mind, starting a brand new contract meeting a few hundred new people.

Before leaving this time of my life I need to bring one last thing up. On the way down to Victorville I was driving a brand new company truck from Fresno. It was a six cylinder so I figured the gas mileage might be better than my own V8. While on the road that time of night about all you see in the flat desert night is trucks and empty highway. It's flat as a table, there's no clouds (lack of humidity) so you can see the stars everywhere, and road signs aren't lit up too well, especially if a truck passes by you as you're passing the sign on the other side of the road.

There was a sign I missed that said "Last Gas For 220 Miles!!" Guess who never saw it? I was getting low and kept looking for gas when finally I ran out. On the desert at night you can see for 40 miles in any direction. There are no buildings, no hills, to trees, nothing but sand and telephone poles as far as the eye can see, that and Yucca Bushes/Trees.

I wasn't sitting more than 60 seconds when headlights appeared behind me out of nowhere on a road that was straight 40 miles in front and behind me. It was a small light blue Chevy Luv truck, a compact truck. It stopped in the highway next to and just in front of mine. A beautiful woman came out and walked up to me thinking nothing of it.

Something was not right about her. There's no way she ever got into those jeans, they looked painted on. She had a serious look about her, not aggressive but could be, eyes black as night. I could feel her energy wasn't normal; it looked fluffy white inside, first time I ever saw that. Her heart was cold, not normal either, almost as if she didn't have one or feelings for that matter.

She got almost in my face and said "Out of gas?" She was bothered about it also. I just said yes. She walked to the back of her truck, flipped back a cloth tarp, and the whole back bed was filled with gas cans, the large Red metal 5 gallon upright gas cans. The whole bed was filled up with them but there was no sag in the rear suspension. That's not physically possible unless all but 4 of those cans were empty.

She pointed to the cans so I went to grab one. She said "You need to pay me." I said ok, how much. She just shrugged her shoulders. I said is $5.00 OK? She only nodded so I took a can which just happened to be filled to the top, and put it in my truck. She just took off immediately while I was trying to say thank you. The whole thing felt and acted out very strange. She was not normal, not used to physical human customs or interactions, like a physical flesh robot, but not.

I jumped in the truck determined to thank her before passing her along my way, whether she liked it or not. The truck turned over 3 times and cranked up. I put it in gear and looked forward. She was gone. There were no tail lights anywhere. I could have seen them for over a mile. There were no headlights hitting the highway and branching off to both sides of the truck.

Even if she took a small road somewhere I would have seen the headlights moving across the desert. I lived in the desert a few years. I know what I'm talking about. I slowed down to try to find her but eventually took off, thinking about how strange she was. Her energy was different than I've ever felt and she was as out of place as a Rhino in a Crystal shop. A short while later I arrived at that roadside hotel where the "strange" just kept coming.

I was tired and didn't care enough to be confused, just wanted to sleep a few hours before getting to Victorville in the am. I later went back (in time) and looked at her, the situation as well. I saw cloudy white energy inside her body, her Aura. It was moving all throughout her almost like a cloud inside her yet it was thicker and wavy.

She was one of the Original Angels, sent to help me get where I needed to be for many reasons. She thought little of my running out of gas, expected more of me and bothered that she had to bother helping me. I've always had problems with the majority of those Angels. Anyway, that's the end of all that. I only brought it up as it's relevant to things that have happened to many of us over the years and through our lives. It might also help you understand a little about my last life here with you.

Anyway, that's where this all started. As I already mentioned, these earlier children are very strong and capable. They're also about to be evolved further. Their DNA just isn't quite the same as these other 48. In about 7 years past the release of this last book, they will begin to appear, but they will visit Earth in ships. The necessary reproductive materials were taken from Diana and myself in 2017 to create these children. I have 60 children but these 48 have DNA from my strongest energy.

Diana and I would know when Serenae (Serpoian) and Mellae (Serpacieant) would be coming with the Archobien to visit us the morning or evening before they did. We would also know why. Sometimes Diana would ask me if she had the reason correct when we'd mention it to each other. Sometimes my head was getting "hammered" so hard I'd ask her.

They took our reproductive materials, created embryos using the best technology available in the 3rd Dimension, and later placed them in Diana for about 3-4 days on average. Then they would remove them. There's more to this but it's very personal, not just for Diana but myself also. There was some physical discomfort (even pain) for both of us, mostly Diana, but it was minimal.

The physical irritation, emotional distress, even blood were more than enough to back up what we already knew was real. A mother knows when she has embryos inside her. These children are very real and important in helping Creation eventually end this physical body life program.

Two thousand years is a long time compared to one life, but short on Creation's calendar. I've talked with my children from the beginning of all this, two daughters and one son. They're awesome. I will meet the others when gone. My first son is a massive man, works in a large industrial complex. He controls the armory there. He's a soldier as I was so many times. He has great heart but I pity the fool that starts a fight with him.

Chapter 2 – What is Different About Them

We've already covered a good deal about them but let's take this a little further. The DNA taken from Arae's physical form was already saturated with his energy from his last mutation. This made Arae stronger than he'd ever been. This energy affects and evolves the DNA. That's why so many people with Source Spirit inside have been taken so many times by other races coming here to Earth.

Remember they all have equipment that can read the frequencies flowing outward from within each body. When they see Source Energy which included the energy given off Gold and Silver, they know they're looking at Source. They also know that this energy flowing through DNA makes it unique; it's what they want to clone into other bodies. However, they always find out that it will only help one body a little bit. Then the DNA returns to normal after the next body.

They don't understand that once out of the body, Source Spirit takes back 90% of what it put in there to begin with. I've explained to people that when I give them a "Crank-Up", which is putting my Source Spirit inside and through them while making changes to their body and specifically their brains, 10% of what I put in them stays there forever. It changes their personal Spirit, forever enhancing it to be more than it ever had been.

My Source Energy bonds with their Spirit, making it much stronger. At the end of this book I will show you the printout from a QEEG that was done on Martin Pera in Sweden before and after I went into his brain. I was here in my house in Duluth, Georgia.

There is more information available regarding this and more at TheSpiritualFoundation.com, Diana's website.

These 48 children contain Arae's strongest evolved energy. Their DNA will be able to carry so much Source Spirit that finally a Human Body will be able to flow enough energy for telekinesis and other powerful Metabilities. Arae and his children have done this on occasion but only when they made their own bodies, such as the Adams and Eves. There are few other cases where Arae has been able to do this.

Everyone's DNA will keep slowly evolving for the next 2,000 years. Over the next hundred years there will be many people throughout our Universe with Source Spirit inside enhancing other people's bodies, brains, and DNA with their own. These are what I called the I.C.U.C. or Intensive Crank Up Consult, for lack of a better name. I made them stronger and now they're doing it themselves. This is another way in which we will continue to grow, together as a species, the race from the very First Original Being.

Chapter 3 – What is Their Full Purpose

The Physical Bodies Evolve Before Disappearing

For the next 2,000 years or so all the physical bodies will be evolving, performing acts which would now seem unbelievable but will later, much later, become common place. The idea here is for these bodies to be released from the restraints but in them, the bothersome Spirit taken away from them permanently, the Spirits in them made stronger, and for everyone to keep evolving naturally as they should have been since the beginning.

These new children, along with all the other DNA evolving just now starting in physical bodies, will take everyone to a new level, becoming much more than they've ever been, until eventually people will be releasing their physical bodies and go home to the 2nd Dimension. In future lives they will only go into the new energetic bodies already living in the 1,672 new Universes. They will be like everyone else there, very strong, relaxed, intelligent, and energetic.

These new bodies allow the use of most of your natural abilities, those you have as yourself, free form Spirit. This is the purest form of growth for all life in Creation. This is where you're all going. You can make a physical body for a short while, but will then revert back to your energy body. This is how we will move forward, individually and as family.

These children are being created to help us become who we should have been in the beginning. They will also personally deal with any abuse problems they find. They will act accordingly to

Arae's format or be changed or removed. This is not as harsh as it might sound. The Compassion, Honor, and Equality Format will be prevalent in the 3rd Dimension soon. No one will be forced into anything but the problems will be removed, for the sake of everyone else. No more abuse.

Section XVI ~ The New Bodies for Creation

I wanted to spend a little more time talking about these new bodies. So many people I've talked with were anxious for it yet still concerned about it. Then there are others, mostly those who are just awakening or not there yet, who get a little scared. There's no reason for concern what so ever. Like everything else, understanding takes the edge off issues, helps us relax.

Some people are afraid that in the new bodies they won't be able to feel anything. They are comparing them to lifeless smoke. You can't feel anything until you are free from these solid mass prisons. You find this out every time you leave the body you're stuck in. You also have more intelligence than you could ever fill a trillion computers with.

Chapter 1 – A Description of the New Bodies

Some people have expressed concern over these new energetic bodies because they're thick energy but not physical. They're mostly concerned about losing their ability to touch loved ones. Not only is that not a problem, you can't feel them completely or in as many ways while in body as you can outside one.

Let's just start with how you might feel a wooden pole right now, not a person yet. If you were to hold it in your hand you would feel something rigid with a certain texture depending on how much it had been sanded. In the new energetic bodies you can move your hand through it, feeling all the fibers in it as you do so. You can also make a solid hand and feel the same thing as a solid body.

You will also be able to feel the energy in things. You can take your energetic hand and put it on your children's energetic heart and feel the love so much more that would have been possible had both of you been solid. You still feel love as you would now, just able to feel so much more. There is no loss here, only gain. You will feel the true depth of things, understand and appreciate each other more.

Without a solid Base Energy Field or Base Chakra, you won't have the issues you do with these solid bodies in regards to fear as well we what can come from it, anger. The lack of a physical body, which is so easily damaged creating pain, will also alleviate a ton of stress and emotional baggage.

Now, let's look at health issues. You will have no broken bones, you will have no disease, you will need no medicine, you will float to where you want to go, not drive. You have no physical organs to continually give you problems including take your life. You won't need money. You can nourish yourself on the nutritional energy from a thimble of honey and a fallen apple, for a month. You don't even need to sleep, just relax and rest when you want.

Childbirth is another new development here. A man and woman put their fields together, relax, and then release a small portion of their combined energies which immediately come together into children which grow rapidly up to the early teens. There is no pain, no suffering, no waiting, and takes less than a minute. What's not to like here.

Chapter 2 – The Removal of the Old Physical Bodies

This event is necessary to remove over 90% of the abuse in Creation. It will happen. As mentioned earlier, in approximately 2,000 years there will be next to no physical bodies left, maybe just over 10%. Physical bodies produce abuse, no matter the amount of compassionate treatment.

It takes physical matter to maintain physical bodies of all types, which includes the pain and suffering accompanying it. Physical bodies are painfully destroyed to continue the lives of others. Soon, this will no longer be allowed to occur in Creation again. There never should have been physical bodies made in the first place.

They should have been energetic bodies like those of the Fae beings in the two dimensions below ours, below meaning they're of a slightly slower frequency than ours, starting about 2.5' below our ground level. They used to be in the first four dimensions under us but two of the barriers have already been removed. Arae did that a long time ago, between 2011 and 2012. I remember doing it, just not the date.

About 10.572 million years ago in Atlantis, the Red Adam (Arae) came here with the Red Eve (Lilly) and placed most of the Half-Human and Half-Animal beings into four lower dimensions here surrounding Earth. Arae made the dimensional barriers. Lilly and Arae led the others down there like walking down a soft hill. Then they simply walked back through the barrier leaving the others secured there. The Half Human-Half Animal beings needed their own place to live, away from the overly aggressive Humans.

No barrier exists between the first lower dimension and ours but there's four dimensional walls separating the other Fae dimensions. The fourth wall separates the lowest Fae Dimension from those below it which are for extremely aggressive beings. There were currently 8 dimensions below ours here surrounding Earth but now there are 6. That will again be decreased within this century.

By 2084 or so there will be Fae beings visiting us making temporary physical bodies from energy and then back again. This is important for different reasons but it's important to those in physical bodies to see it happen as the new bodies everyone will be in, can do the same thing.

Each dimension below us is made from a slightly lower frequency which is more comfortable for those living there as their personal frequencies are also lower. This gives them a more comfortable environment but also separates the more negative Dark Fae from the Lighter Fae.

Until the physical bodies are gone they will continue to evolve into what has never existed before. This will be the "grand finale" of the physical bodies, having become their very best before fading away. They never should have been created but will leave the best they could be.

The History and Future Metaphysical Development of Earth, the Universe, and Creation

Metaphysical Developments

Section I ~ The Age Of Earthen Metaphysical Development

Chapter 1 – Self Awareness Increases Everywhere

As time continues to flow, I should say as the flow of events continues, these natural Metabilities in people will grow, increasing in power, flow strength, and usage. The more people there are doing this, using their abilities, the more others will want to do the same. This is a simple natural event that had been kept from occurring. It no longer is. The cause of that is now gone and people can freely become themselves. It's a part of what we are. You're about to receive a lot of help in doing so.

In review, your natural abilities are no longer being hampered, the blocks in your physical bodies are being removed, and your Spirit Guides are becoming more active in assisting you. Add to this the new Source Field, which not only surrounds and flows directly through you, it's also increasing its assistance in all metaphysical areas.

I might have mentioned earlier in this book, but maybe not, just how the field helps you with your Metabilities. When you begin to astral-project somewhere the Source Field not only sees this but feels this. It is aware of your desire to do something. This comes from your thoughts (brain) but your heart as well. Remember that the Field actually flows through you. I realize this might at first seem invasive to someone but it's not.

When surgeons operate on you they're concerned about the physical body in front of them. The new Source Field has the same mind set while still having compassion, honor, and equality that the previous Field did not. The Source Field changed in 2013 when it became part of Arae but Aramaeleous kept taking its energy until later in 2015 when Arae destroyed him. Aramaeleous was very strong and the largest Source Energy being. However, he wasn't as strong as Arae. A bullet is smaller than a hand but a hand can't stop a bullet.

This new Source Field is already helping your Heart Energy move farther, faster, and with greater accuracy. Your Astral-Projection is stronger and will soon be more direct with higher definition. You will also be able to access the Field's data bank, most of its records and general information (also called the Akashic Records but really just freely offered info.). It also helps to protect you from anything not beneficial to you by letting Arae and others know.

This field is an extension of Arae's energy, even now while still in body. Once free again, he will easily feel what's happening throughout his field but there are many new people who will be helping him. I believe I already mentioned that all Animal Essence has been enhanced even further than what they became from all their many difficult abusive lives, and that they were now Creation's Sentinels. They will fulfill this capacity once Arae returns home.

This is not a fable or a fairy tale to tell children. It's already started and will be picking up its pace by mid-2018. This is just a small part of your new existence while in a physical body. There are also important changes enhancing your real life as Spirit, while not in a body. Before we can understand and accept anything we need to see it happen or exist. You won't see the changes on the Other Side until you leave your body, unless you become strong enough to see it now.

On the Other Side, in the 2nd Dimension, you will move more freely wherever you want to go other than a few places. At the top of this "no admittance" list is the 1st Dimension. No one is allowed in or out. Arae controls that. You will also find there is very little arrogance towards each other over there now. You have more freedom to express yourselves and do as you please both together and individually. The thought process of "better than someone else" is already diminishing.

Churches will soon become a thing of the past. Most of these luxuriously built buildings will be put to better use. Some will become institutions where people can go to help awaken and evolve themselves. There will be a wave of new gatherings of people wanting to open themselves up. They will take form as physical meetings, internet blogs, structured organizations, and more. As the new governments start to form within themselves, there will be public areas for others to do so, such as a separate room in a library.

This awakening will happen between family, friends, communities, countries, and even Planets. There will be people coming here from other Planets to get I.C.U.C.s as there are currently more Source People in body here on Earth right now. The others on other Planets need to grow up, grow older. This will soon be equally spread out everywhere, in about 200 years anyway.

Chapter 2 – How the Human Brain & Body Function Metaphysically

In the following pages, heck all throughout the book, we talk about different energetic focal points of energy fields that are flowing independently throughout the body, working within a network of Spirit Energy that is the real you inside that body. We're not just talking about energy in a body, we're talking about how the real you exists and functions within that body.

Everywhere I look inside people I see energy fields flowing together, conducting the business of moving a physical body through a physical life as a sentient being. However, it is the Spirit inside, the real you, that's having a sentient life. You are sentient life, the body only houses you. Your Spirit's energy feeds the body what it needs to run its autonomic functions.

Your Spirit creates the understanding that physically moves it around to do as you might want. Then Spirit (the Alpha male and Female Source Spirit) either leave you alone in having your life or run you from the Other Side. They used their Original Angels to do this. They would put their focused Spirit down into your Crown Fields and finally into your Hypothalamus Gland.

If they told you that it was imperative for you to run your car off a cliff you would immediately speed off in your car for the nearest cliff, knowing that is was not only the correct thing to do but had to be done immediately. You would let nothing get in your way. Once they removed their controlling Spirit from your brain you would immediately stop and say "What the hell was I doing that for?" Then you immediately felt something was deeply wrong with you when it was the main Angel put in charge of controlling your life abusing you.

The Alpha Female source Spirit did about 98% of this. The Alpha male Source Spirit was always busy being the Source Field while dealing with other related tasks. I've often explained how Angels were only servants of the Original First Being Halves and under their explicit control. They were created to be strong enough and able to run the physical bodies yet weak enough to still be easily controlled. It's a sad thing when you look at it, all the things the Original First Being Halves did from being so self-centered. This is the core of your new future; new Alpha male and Female Source Spirit who want nothing for themselves, just to take care of everyone and keep them moving in a positive flow of evolution, growing independently yet together. Back to Spirit in the body again.

For years many scientists have said that we only functionally use about 10% of our brains. We actually put about 85% of our physical brains to use, we just do it metaphysically. They can only map out basic functions located in base areas. They do so mostly by measuring the electromagnetic signatures apparent in these areas. There are 4 other different energy fields which created what we are and they are in there also, just not with the same properties. They're metaphysical, just not electromagnetic.

Once our family from various regions in space settle down with us there will be incredible advances made in the current thought process we call science. We are unaware of so much that exists around us. There is a new world coming to us, a new understanding of not only the physical but the metaphysical. As I've mentioned before, our friends in space have scanning equipment that reads the different metaphysical frequencies within us and display them on screens.

These frequencies are not only made visible, they are placed into a data base that saves the time and place they were recorded. This is a simple way in which they can find different lives you've had, by researching their history files. This information is as simple to access as turning on your tablet today. How can we foresee all the changes coming to our daily lives? We can't. Just know that it's extremely beneficial and it is close to coming now, as of the writing of this book.

Near the end of this chapter you will find a list of the basic auric expressions, the particular colors relative to the different frequencies which create them. These are only the base colors of the most common singular frequencies. Each color describes a particular frequency relative to who you are. A mixture of various colors represents a mixture of different frequencies. The strongest color, actually frequency, will be the dominant factor. This is a form of personal Spirit name tag, who you are and how you're differentiated by others.

There is one main flow of energy continually flowing throughout your body but centers around the spine, in and out of it. The Core Energy contains all the Spirit forms within the body and flows from the base of your spine to just under and over your skull. It's thick at the top and bottom. It flows through and around itself, something unique to see when you can. You can think of this as a river which also flows over its banks and into the nearby area. Just as you find eddies and whirlpools in a river or stream you will find similar energy flow within your body.

There are powerful focal points of your Spirit's energy which flow this way in your body. There are three major power points from which your metaphysical abilities flow. Your body's DNA is relative to which of your abilities will be expressed stronger, more completely throughout your body. You have your own personal frequency strengths as Spirit but that often changes while in a body.

As we go through the particulars regarding how your energy flows through that body you're in, keep this in mind. As Spirit, your frequencies are higher than when they are in a physical body. If you take a tuning fork and softly strike it to a hard surface you will hear a clear singular pitch sound, a clear vibration or frequency. What happens when you strike it again but immediately place it in a jar of tar? The clean frequency is slowed down immediately. This is similar to being in a body. The body is not you. You are in the body. As Spirit you consist of various different frequencies but the effect is still the same.

The Metaphysical Abilities Flowing Through Your Body

There are three main energy focal points in your body that are relative to your metaphysical abilities. Remember that these are abilities, not gifts. The only gift you ever received from the Original First Being was being removed from it to become an individual being or life form, sentient energy. Each physical body will express one of these three energy focal points more than the other two. This is your Spirit core Orientation. Some bodies are stronger in the Pineal Field, others in the Heart, and the rest in the Solar Plexus. Here's how they function, what they do.

The Pineal Field is used for multi-dimensional vision. It helps you see things outside of this 3rd Dimension. You can see Spirit as a dark cloud (which doesn't mean it's bad) as it appears in front of you. Although you're seeing it here (in your mind), you're actually seeing it in the second dimension, the one right above us. You can't touch it, only see it. The more energy Spirit can compress or condense, the easier it is to see them. It's often easier for people with a Pineal Field Core Orientation to feel stone energy.

The next energy focal point below the Pineal is the Heart Energy Field. This is not the strongest singular energy field yet produces the strongest effects of them all. The Heart grabs the strongest thoughts from the brain (data), emotion from the Base Focal Point or Chakra (where the spine attaches to the pelvic bone), and uses them to create feelings. These feelings flow from the Heart Energy up to the Hypothalamus of the brain where "Understanding" is created. The Heart does much more than just circulate blood with its nutrition throughout the body.

Now we get to the Solar Plexus, the strongest individual Energetic Focal Point within your body. The key word here is individual. The Heart Energy pulls all the different energy fields together but here we're talking singular. On average about 7/8 of your Solar Plexus Energy is embedded within your Core Spirit Flow. The Solar Plexus is also the base point of understanding within your body.

Now we're going into the different physical parts of the body which we produce our metaphysical abilities through. We'll discuss how they function separately as well as together.

How the Body Conducts Your Metabilities

The Metabilities that you have, that you're now learning how to use, come from you but must move through your body to be expressed. You can't just do this openly as Spirit; you're trapped in a physical body having a physical life. I've often talked about the fact that you not only can't fit all of your true self as Spirit in a body, almost no one can fit in a state here in the U.S.A.

Many of the people who came to me for the I.C.U.C.s have energy fields so large that while the strongest part of them is compressed into a body, like trying to put an elephant in a thimble, their outer energy would touch both the Atlantic and Pacific Oceans were they placed in the middle of the U.S.

The rest of your body is floating around in and out of the 2nd and 3rd Dimensions and barrier but mostly the 3rd. You just can't see it. It's metaphysical. Can you see the electricity moving through live wires? No, you can't. You can only see the effects of it, what it can do but not it by itself. It's metaphysical.

There is a filter located about a foot above your head which keeps your energy with all its feelings and emotion from flowing into that huge rest of yourself that floats about you out of your Upper Crown Energy Field or chakra. It also puts your remaining Spirit in a dormant state, like deep sleep. Were it not there, you could easily escape your body, and free yourself. The Original First Being Halves would not have allowed that.

Another big issue here is relative to your feelings and emotion going into the large remainder of yourself and waking it up. Then all of you would react to what was happening to your body. With all the people in body, on every Planet, you would have intense chaos not only here but also in the 2nd Dimension.

There's a reason why none of us were ever aware of all this. The Original First Being Halves, while they still existed, didn't want anyone in body to understand what was actually happening, especially while in a body. The same was true while you were out of body. They controlled Creation through their lies, counting on all the Spirit beings remembering that they came from them anyway. As you already know, that's all over now. We're just now beginning to heal.

So, our natural abilities are part of us but can't flow through these physical bodies. That's why these physical bodies have individual, usually smaller parts, for our abilities to flow through. The Original First Being Halves knew they had to limit your abilities to control you. Here's the three major power points, or outlets, that we have in our body; Pineal, Heart, and Solar Plexus.

Pineal

The Pineal Gland, and its neighboring area, is responsible for producing the energy flow necessary to see things multi-dimensionally. The gland is located just behind the area where the brain stem has become part of the brain itself. It's said to be on the third cerebral ventricle of the brain, pretty much in the center but near the back of the brain's lower center. I would quote others but I've already looked at its basic location years ago to help me understand what I see in my head.

The brainstem goes up to the brain opens up to a larger section which eventually flows into the largest part of the brain. It's near the lower middle of the brain and just behind where this midbrain section is. I'm speaking of this as I see it when in someone's head. I see basic generalities; I don't want to see actual brain material unless there's a carcinoma or other issue present.

When I first started doing my I.C.U.C.s I saw the actual tissue, as if I was still a scrub tech handing surgeons their tools and looking into the body. That isn't necessary for my work and I never had time to waste on my consults. People wanted to know about many different things and they were paying good money for a consult. It's easier to see things through a basic image unless the situation requires otherwise.

This gland allows you to see various dimensions by flowing your energy through their barriers and exploring what's there. You will see other beings for the most part, but you can also become more aware of other structures and its composition. We naturally tend to move our attention to other people instead of environments.

Astral-Projection occurs through the Pineal Field which is generated through the Pineal Gland. You can say that the Pineal Gland generates the Pineal Field as it comes directly from it but it's your Spirit manipulating the Pineal Gland to create the field. For smooth flow of thought process we'll speak of the Pineal Gland creating its field. Now, let's get into this energy field I just mentioned. What is it, where is it, what does it do, and how does it do it.

Your Spirit Energy coming through the Pineal Gland immediately opens up into a rather unusual field. I would have to draw a picture here and can't. The Pineal Field moves forward from the middle of your forehead to just about your clavicle or shoulder bone as it's often called. This includes your larynx, or voice box which is why

Lapis Lazuli can be found in the pockets or necklaces of people who do a lot of public speaking.

A large portion of this field flows forward through your forehead in the shape of a cone with an almost ball like shape at the end of it, a few inches to feet out of your head. The rest of the field intensifies around your larynx but the whole area is glowing with blue aura energy. As already mentioned, Lapis Lazuli stone has strong frequencies in it which are extremely beneficial to the Pineal Gland.

Do not, I repeat, do not take any drugs relative to the Pineal Gland's composition, only vitamins that are good for the body. Some people take DMT or other such garbage thinking they are helping or supercharging their Pineal Gland abilities as well as others. All they are doing is tearing down the natural order of function within the brain.

If you want to help your Pineal Gland, eat well, exercise enough for your blood to flow through your body in a healthy manner, and spend time relaxing and opening up your body to let yourself flow outside of it. It's impossible to become detached, just let go and flow out everywhere. As you settle your body and conscious mind down, you relax your brain's frequencies enabling you to flow into the 2nd Dimension as well as through this 3rd Dimension.

What you are actually doing here is harmonizing, coming together with, the Source Field. From there you can go many places if you want, or just get information. It takes a little time, a little practice. The nice thing about this is that you're only relaxing, easier to do that you think.

Once you've done this a few times your mind will naturally maintain this base frequency helping you to think logically, make better decisions, and relax quickly whenever you want. This also includes seeing things in other dimensions as naturally as walking or breathing. You slowly learn to understand this is your real natural state, not one of jumping, erratic thought, aggression, and indecision. Once there you will see life differently, I know I did but I also understand how you will feel the same. Your life improves as your life choices improve.

The top and largest part of your Pineal Field coming out your forehead is right up against the lower section of your Scanner Field. The Scanner Field comes out your head in that section where the top of your head meets your forehead. There's usually a bit of a bulge there. I always blend the Pineal Field with the Scanner Field where they meet and "feather" them into each other. I'll explain more about this and why in the Solar Plexus Chapter.

Heart

Heart Spirit Energy containing feelings, thoughts (data), emotion, and an understanding of all of it, flows continually up and down the body's Spirit core constantly changing, progressing, and developing. This is a continuous process within every living body.

While this Heart Energy (with understanding and information) is flowing it's also busy doing something else. It sends this feeling out into the field which exists everywhere and goes through everything. Hearts are communicating with each other 24/7, even while sleeping. Since it contains the strongest thoughts from people, once you learn how to focus your Heart Energy you can actually receive some of the basic thoughts from that person's brain. You can also receive some of their emotion and feelings.

Sometimes people's thoughts are so intense that a strong Empath, a person with a strong Heart Focal Point and able to focus it properly, can pick off the strongest thoughts in the Heart Energy of that person. This is not something that happens all the time. It takes practice but will eventually it becomes second nature. You've heard the expression "Trust your heart." That's where it came from. Heart Energy and understanding will seldom guide you wrong.

You can develop your Heart Energy abilities by sitting at a table in a restaurant or coffee house and, without looking at the people directly, focus your intention to "feel" what they are feeling. Your Heart Focal Point will immediately focus on them. It becomes easier the more you do it. These are your abilities, part of the real you, Spirit. Your body uses different body parts to energize these abilities. They extend out of you naturally. Just relax as best you can, take a few full but relaxed breaths, and release yourself. Let go, let yourself flow outward. All else will follow.

Not only can you do this but you've always been doing it naturally. You need only focus on the event to increase, strengthen, and develop it. The more you do something the better you become at it. Like all other natural things, it's a matter of intention and repetition. The more we do something the better we get at doing it. It's simple. While we're on the Heart subject, there's a little more to how it works. About one quarter to two thirds of your Heart Energy Field is also flowing inside the Spirit core of your body sending feelings and understanding to all the smaller energy fields throughout your body. The large difference in percentages here is due to the current state of the body's needs.

There's more going on there but there's no room here to properly cover this info. It's a small portion of the Heart Energy input and we have to stop somewhere. It just adds a little more info, that's all. Let's take a look at the Auras projected from the Heart Energy Field. It produces more different frequencies, therefore more different colored Auras, than any other focal point. This comes from its using so many different frequencies within you.

The Heart Energy Field emits many different colors. Once you can see Auras you can better understand the people releasing them. Once you learn how to feel heart energy you'll know what Auras they are releasing at any given moment as well as in general as a person. As you continue to awaken you will see both of them at the same time as one item.

Solar Plexus

The Solar Plexus Energy Field, often called Chakra, receives a constant flow of Understanding Energy, if we can call it that to give it a name, from the Heart and Hypothalamus Gland in the brain. Being 7/8ths embedded within the Spirit core it also receives strong information from the Scanner and Source Fields. Data flows from the Source Field through the Upper, Middle, and Lower Crown Focal Points and into the Hypothalamus region which flows not only into the Heart Energy put also straight down the Spirit core and into the rest of you. The Scanner Energy Field also feeds information to the Hypothalamus section of your head and down through the core feeding the Solar Plexus Energy Focal Point. We'll discuss the Scanner in full detail in just a bit.

The Scanner Energy Field is the producer of Remote Viewing and main viewing tool of the Solar Plexus, not the only one though. As the Solar Plexus Energy Field is usually around 7/8ths buried in the body's Spirit core, there's additional information coming in from the rest of the body. It receives over 90% of its vision through the Scanner section of the brain. Let's try to describe your Scanner Energy as it functions in your brain.

There are many smaller energy fields flowing throughout the body, especially in the brain. In the main body of the brain, the Cerebrum, there is a collection of small energy focal points all over the place. When I go into people's heads I see many little vortexes of energy in the front two thirds of it. I already know that those are the ones I need to deal with. I can watch them working.

I go into people's brains with my own energy to first contact and then energize them. I put my energy fingers, so to speak, into their brains aligning, awakening, and then charging them with strong Source Spirit. When I do this my fingers on both hands are literally moving in their heads. Not to my surprise, many have said they felt exactly that.

On top of all this the Pineal Gland gets a little involved here. A small amount of what the Pineal Gland's seeing multi-dimensionally enters the Hypothalamus and flows down the Spirit core. As there is so much energy going through the Hypothalamus, only a small portion of the Pineal Field Energy information gets to the Solar Plexus.

There is an upset in the balance of understanding throughout each body due to the difference of each body's individual physical makeup as well as the Spirit(s) within it. This varies with each individual. Everyone has an infinitely varied set of frequencies, strengths, and amounts of each one. There were also energetic roadblocks put into your brains to keep them from flowing without restriction. These are removed in the basic I.C.U.C.

This is one reason why we see things similar but not quite the same. In one way or another we usually get to a similar ending. We also need to use images stored in our brain from the different experiences in this life to understand things we're seeing that have no physical makeup. Energy is metaphysical, not physical, yet we must see it somehow. Add to this the fact that we all have more interest in one particular part of something than another. Here's an example.

Diana and I could be on a boat in Miami cruising by a yacht. She might notice the basic styling and structure of the boat while I listen to the engines and how it cuts through the water. Maybe I pay more attention to the helicopter pad on top and she notices all the cabins. We're all seeing the image but focusing on what we're more concerned with, more attracted to.

When groups of people get together to see things metaphysically, you will always get the bigger picture when you put what everyone sees together. This is also a good exercise for you and your friends. The fact that some people are stronger in one field or another adds to the production of a clearer complete picture also.

I've built many tools, currently available at TheSpiritualFoundation.com, to help people develop their abilities, meet and talk with their Spirit Guides, and everything else relative to becoming your true self. Diana Ramirez Anaya owns the company. She's one of many here to help everyone evolve into themselves, who they really are. She's also one of the few people who will be doing the DNA I.C.U.C.s that I used to do.

Your Body's Metability Flow Chart

So far we've talked about a lot of energy running around in the body. Each of you has strong abilities that have been locked up all your lives. People are using their Metabilities more and more each day. How do these abilities work? How do they work as a unit, or do they? Let's break them down into a network of circuits enabling us to do things that we're just now starting to find out about. How does all this happen? It's not magic, it's natural. You just have to have access the information necessary to understand it.

The body you're in is a variety of different things to you. It gives you a physical housing to have a physical life in. It also serves as an impenetrable jail for you to escape from (other than suicide), and a chamber of abuse forcing your Spirit to grow within. We all have our good moments, some people more than others, and we need them. Without a minimal amount of joy, people will leave their bodies in any way possible and the Original First Beings wanted people to stay in them.

So, how can we talk with other Spirits out of body, see things before they happen, know things about ourselves but mostly others that we never even met? The answer is Metaphysics, using your Metabilities. You're all aware of the physical but the metaphysical, although unseen through physical eyes, is everywhere.

The only exception to this is that you can partially see metaphysically through the very corners of your physical eyes. An example of this is those little blotches of darkish energy that dart around you, usually from behind you to in front of you. Sometimes, but not always, they're a little low, just off the ground near where the floor meets the walls. You can only see them from the corners of your eyes. When you move your head in the direction of them, they're gone.

That's your Spirit Guides trying to show you that there's more going on than what you see physically. The Fae like to run around there also. They will look a little more brownish. Try to feel these blotches of energy. Were they female or male, or were they just energy bursts send by you. If they feel male and female, and it was only one person you felt, congratulations, it was one of the new Angels.

Metaphysical Energy runs through your bodies night and day. It is sentient energy and very powerful. It's the Source Field that comes from the Alpha male Source Spirit in Creation. The two parts of reality, metaphysical and physical, work together every day in each physical body and few are aware of it. That's who you really are, not just a physical body that eventually dies and rots. You are the Spirit which was in the body while it was living.

What do you call a mother's intuition? The very phrase has intuition in it. Intuition is metaphysical, you can't touch it, but it exists just the same. Intuition is a name tag for the sum of all your Metabilities. It's usually more relative to Solar Plexus Understanding, the "gut feeling" we get about things. Well, let's see what's really going on here.

Where do you start when talking about a continuous flow of energy moving within a physical body? First let's briefly discuss how it got in there. Then we'll talk about how all Spirit and energy moves within the body. Lastly we'll explain how your Spirit's Metabilities flow through your body.

How Spirit Is Put Into a Body

Let's look at the Human Body. There are muscles, veins, organs, a brain with a network of nerves spread all throughout it, lungs, heart, stomach area, pelvic, and the rest. Where is our Spirit(s) with their separate energy field(s) in these bodies and how/where do they flow within us? This is new to people who are new to me. This is one of the reasons that I had to come here one last time. You need to have access to information that helps you understand more about yourselves, which in turn, helps you learn how to use your natural abilities, not gifts.

When a male and female of any species with sentient life inside copulate, they create an embryo, a part of each of them, which over time becomes an embryo and finally a living physical being. As that embryo begins to develop a brain center, a ganglion of nerves, a control center which runs the physical body, something unique happens. Before we understand how this happens we need to address the fact that it just recently changed.

For over 2.857 Quadrillion years Earth time, all Animal and Human bodies have had a Dual Spirit Core. Today, 1/28/2018, no Animal or Human bodies on Earth still have a Dual Spirit Core or Kundalini; just a single one. From now on there will only be bodies with one Spirit inside. On other Planets, at the time of writing this book, the Human and Animal bodies still have a Dual Spirit Core, what many call a Kundalini. The Kundalini thought process is confusing to many people these days.

In ancient transcripts from India, in Sanskrit, the Kundalini was the thought process of two snakes crawling up and down the Human spine together from the hips to the head. These snakes represented Spirit. They weren't able to understand much more about it, just that they could see this in their mind's eye. That's all they were allowed to see by the Original First Being Halves who wanted everyone kept in the dark about who they really were inside that body.

Late 2017, Arae removed all Planetary Essence within all the Animal Bodies. On January 22, 2018 Arae removed all Planetary Essence from all the Human Bodies on Earth. Insects, fish, reptiles, and a few others, even now chicken, only have Planetary Essence within them. They need to have at least one Spirit inside to function. They were always Single Spirit core beings, except chicken, so the Planetary Essence can't be taken out.

All Animals, most insects, and more will be disappearing throughout Creation soon, here on Earth first. The Animals will lead this procession, they will soon continue to die in large numbers soon, more than ever before and it will not stop until only the smallest percentage of them exist, well under 10% of those here now. Most insects were put here to be a constant, but not overly abusive, annoyance to you. Ticks, mosquitoes, mites, fleas, and many more serve no purpose other than to bother physical life here. Now let's get back to Spirit being coming into a body.

The presiding Alpha Female Source Spirit would first put a Planetary Essence being (Gaia released small parts of herself over 11 million years ago) inside the body, concentrated in the newly grown brain mass. Then, when ready, she would use a wall of Source Spirit (a barrier) to move the Planetary Essence being to the left side of the brain and place the visiting Spirit inside the right side of the brain. When someone is "left handed" the two sided placement was reversed.

Then she would put an energy field around the head first and complete body second. This would keep them inside the body until it developed a little more, settling into its physical mass. Then only 2/3rds of it was needed. The rest was reclaimed by the Original First Being Female. The Original First Being Halves never allowed you to have this information. That's why it's all new to everyone.

As already explained, now only one Spirit is being put inside all the Animal and Human bodies, there's only a Single Spirit core in all sentient life here. As a matter of fact, there are Human, Fae, and Faeman Spirit (Essence and Souls) having lives in Animals now as well as insects, fish, etc. Only 3-4 out of every million Animals now born have Animal Essence inside. The rest are Human, Fae, and Faeman.

For those of you who haven't read the first two books in this Creation Series, Faeman Essence and Faeman Soul Spirits are a combination of both Human and Fae frequencies. The frequencies between these two families of Spirit are very similar, hard to separate. These Human and Fae Spirit were separated so the Original First Being Halves could concentrate on developing the Human Spirit family as it could be most easily abused and therefore made to grow larger and create more prayer machines (beings).

This book is a comprehensive document of sorts but in order for you to completely understand everything behind the words, you will need to read the first two volumes. Reading can be a pain for many of us, especially me, but there are so many important reasoning tools that you will need, in these books. Is it not time for all of you to know who you are, what you can do, where you came from, and be able to answer almost any question you might have about yourself and others?

So, anyway, that's how Spirit was and is put into a body. As time went by the Planetary Essence in the bodies flowed throughout it, as we'll soon describe, but also partially absorbed into it. Remember that Planetary Essence has those frequencies which were made to flow into a planetary physical mass, that's its body.

These bodies originally came from the Planet. This started over 11 million years ago. Every broken down component of these bodies are found within Gaia's body, the Earth. This is/was the main reason why when a body dies it doesn't want to leave/give up the body. The fear given everyone from religions is another big reason but not the largest one. This, like almost everything else relative to your present lives, is changing.

How Does Spirit and Energy Move Within a Body?

Here's a topic of great debate. How does your Soul reside within your body? Is there some kind of reservoir or does it just flow everywhere like smoke filling a room or the energy of a ghost or something? By the way, a ghost is merely a person, Spirit, that's not in a body but in its natural state. Well, like most other things, this is easy to understand, like a jigsaw puzzle when you have all the pieces and a picture to use in putting it all together.

As we've already discussed, the brain is the center for your Spirit's control of your body from the beginning. It stays that way but the Spirit core, which immediately began to flow through you, received a larger portion of what was in your head than your head contains now. The Spirit within your brain is the focal point of your Spirit, just not the largest part of it. When you had two Spirits inside you there were often disagreements about even the smallest of things. This is known as indecision.

Your brain contains your Spirit's flow control processing center and your Spirit with its energy flows through out your body from the Core Path which runs from just above your head to the bottom of your pelvic bone. Only the strongest part of your primary focal point (which is the Spirit within you) is located in your brain while the rest of your primary focal point flows through and emanates from, your body.

Your Spirit core is similar to a river flowing in, out of, and around your physical body. It basically flows up and down, in and out of your spine, brain, and pelvic region. There is something of a vortex at both the top and bottom and your energy flows through itself on its way up and down. This is similar to how energy flows in the First Dimension, where all the New Initial Beings are created through happenstance. This is all covered in detail within Book I, "Creation: Its Beginning And Your Origin".

So, from your Spirit core, your energy flows through your body and out from it. I'll mention a few times, before ending this book, about how your Spirit core flows inside of and outside along your spinal cord. Also, a specific form of energy flows through your nervous system network. It's one of the 5 energy field types necessary to create sentient energy (Spirit) which only happens in the First Dimension. It runs through your brain and complete nervous system. It's a form of electro-magnetic energy.

Your Aura is a byproduct of that energy, proof of its existence as well as a way to immediately identify that person's energetic personality characteristics. I made a DVD explaining the characteristics of the different basic auric colors by describing the frequencies they emanate from, as well as where. This is presently only available at TheSpiritualFoundation.com.

Water and Energy, although being separate and different things, do have some interesting similarities. Energy flows away from its center mass, just like a bucket of water when emptied. As energy flows within a conduit made for it (f.y.i., by your brain), there are energy whirlpools created everywhere just as you'll find in a river. These are called energy focal points, often called chakras. Your body's three largest focal points are Pineal, Heart, and Solar Plexus; your power centers.

You have a series of energetic focal points in your body that I want to mention. Many people have heard of the "7 Major Chakras" in the body and the supposed colors representing them. As I see the separate frequencies as well as their auric expressions, I needed to offer them to you as they're different. I'm not here to bother telling others they're incorrect. I do need to tell you what I know is correct. The whole idea of all of this is to supply you the necessary input for you to discover for yourselves just what is real. The major chakras are similar but not the colors.

From top to bottom your body has three Crown, one Pineal, one Vocal, one Heart, one Solar Plexus, one Sexual, one Base, and one Root, focal points. There is one focal point, the most obvious and important one that never gets mentioned, called the brain itself. This is all the different glands and bodies of your brain that process everything happening both physically and metaphysically inside you.

Your Hypothalamus Gland, Pituitary Gland, Cerebrum, and many others are imperative to utilizing your Metabilities. We're going to cover almost all of the major ones in this book. I would have to write a separate book to explain it in full detail and I've neither time nor health for any more books, other than the Spanish version edition that Diana, her father, and myself are also working on now. Diana is doing almost all of it with her father's valuable help. I merely clarify the thought processes within it.

So, all in all, there are 12 Primary Focal Points which carry on over 75% of your body's metaphysical functions while also performing their necessary physical duties. Your nervous system network is considered a part of your body itself as it is integrated with all of it. In order to save time and increase clarity in the next section we'll cover the quick ones here now. The next section is really about how your powers flow through your body more than anything else.

Nothing that I tell you comes from a book I read or something I found on the internet. These energetic fields are the ones that I have manipulated in others over the last seven years. I see them, change them, put Source Energy into them, and more. I talk through my own personal experience, not conjecture.

That's why you've heard little of this or how they work. Some of it you've heard before in some form or another. The information you've been given before is either incomplete or totally incorrect. A good mechanic understands your car better than you do because he works on cars all day, unless you're a mechanic too.

- Scanner (Brain Body)-

The Scanner is the strongest high definition viewing tool you have. It's made to see in this dimension only but it's strong enough to partially one dimension up and one dimension down. Your vision in these other dimensions will be fuzzy, not near as clear as what you see in this 3rd Dimension. This is your home of Remote Viewing. People who use this energy field to a higher capacity are usually Solar Plexus Energy Orientated people. That is to say that their strongest individual energy field is Solar Plexus.

When you try to remember something you will use your Metabilities to go back in time and see it again. Have you heard of a photographic memory? As the Scanner produces a higher quality high definition image, and physical objects you see in front of you are in this 3rd Dimension, people who are Solar Plexus Orientated have the better memories of all of us. Again, the more correct input you have, the better your understanding, of everything.

This is all simple once you're exposed to it. Just relax and it will sink in. These three Creation Series Books are filled with a life time of new information. It is not absorbed into your understanding of things overnight, but it will become exactly that, your understanding that you arrive at yourselves. I only provide it. You're the one making all the decisions here. Over time it will all flow together. Just don't try to speed read the book.

I have friends that have read the first book 10 times and said they still needed to read it another time. I told them, maybe a little aggressively, to slow the hell down and take a page a day. When material is new, never seen before, and it's about different things that have never been mentioned, how can you speed read it? Even if you were able to memorize it, you won't understand it until you relax, open you mind, settle down the frequencies in your brain, and let everything flow. You have a lot of tomorrows, take your time.

The Scanner Energy Field comes out of that top front section of your head where your forehead and the top of your head meet. It extends outward, like the Pineal Field, from a few inches to a foot or so. It starts as a thick field within your brain and flows outside it into what I've always called your Front Occipital Lobe which is actually incorrect. It's a large energy field in the shape of a screen, like a retina, in the immediate frontal portion of your Frontal Lobe on both sides.

Seeing things as energy can be hard to explain physically sometimes. It's easy to make small mistakes. Never worry about that. Can you show me an artist or mathematician who never used an eraser? How about a professional race car driver that never wrecked? Perfection isn't real. Striving to improve is. Whatever you do, don't ever stop going forward. It's the only road there is to failure, quitting. I offer a hell of a good road map, just can't make the journey for you.

There's usually a lump where your head top and forehead meet. That is where your Scanner field projects from. When we had lives on Lemuria this protruded outward 4 to 5 times what it does today. We used it and needed it much more back then. You can use it for telepathy, mostly for image though, and that's why we needed it. Lemuria was a large network of islands in the Pacific Ocean. Almost every island was inhabited with people who came here from a different Planet.

Over time we developed strong scanners not only to communicate with each other better but with the Animals here. Back then many of us had large Animal friends or pets that we lived with. The reptiles were a constant threat. Humans and Animals learned to cohabitate more closely. We also had large docile reptiles as pets. In the beginning we had small glider ships but as the wars and distance in space became more of an issue, the colonies almost never received help of any kind from their home Planets. Anyway, back to your energy fields.

The Scanner Energy Field comes out of that top front section of your head and extends outward, like the Pineal Field, between inches to a foot or so. It starts as a wide field within your brain which flows into what I've always called your Front Occipital Lobe which is really a large screen, like a retina, in the immediate frontal portion of your Frontal Lobe on both sides.

I should call it the Frontal Focusing Energy Screen or Lens but that's too much to say all the time. Let's use Front Occipital Energy Field. It's a separate energy field that glows hard when being used. The Scanner and Pineal both use it. All the little energized vortexes send their input out into their field and then send incoming vision inward to the Hypothalamus Gland, eventually getting into your Spirit core.

The Scanner is the largest ESP producer. ESP stands for Extra Sensory Perception which is any and all Metabilities combined to receive metaphysical information; vision, understanding, or data. It's an awareness sensor, among other things. I use a lot of commas because I tend to separate individual thoughts as I talk about them. It's just how I format my thoughts.

Anyway, the Scanner is better than you would think in seeing people out of body who are trying to be seen here. They're just on, sometimes inside, the dimensional barrier between dimensions and the Scanner works well there, especially after receiving the "free energy work" from an I.C.U.C. When I did my DNA I.C.U.C.s, I always feathered together that section where the Pineal and Scanner Fields meet. It helps give better dimensional depth to the

Scanner while helping the Pineal Field produce a somewhat more refined image of what it's seeing multi-dimensionally.

When I started becoming stronger and became immersed in the war with the Original First Beings, I used my Scanner a lot. I was with a friend once, sitting in a car with the sunroof cracked open and she started laughing when I went to look at what was bothering me at the moment. I asked her what the joke was about and she said that she could see the hair on the Scanner part of my scalp stand up.

I told her to watch and see what happened when I went after someone on the Other Side, go into their primary energetic focal point, their brain as Spirit, and rip it open to see what they had planned for me next. As I did, not only did my hairs stand up but my Scanner started pushing out of my head, about a quarter of an inch. She got all excited and wanted to put it on You Tube but I declined, didn't care about that. The same will happen with yours once it's developed enough.

-Upper, Middle, and Lower Crowns-

This is at the top section of your Spirit core, what used to be your Kundalini but now is only you, no back seat drivers. It floats just a bit above your head, again, from a few inches to around a foot. Those people who have had the DNA I.C.U.C. have Upper Crown Focal Points up to a few feet above their heads. This is part of the reason for all the energy work that I've done while here. It was most important that I "Crank-Up" other people with Source Spirit inside them so they could continue this procedure for thousands of other people.

The Upper Crown is shaped something like a gradual funnel with a wide opening at the bottom, not like a normal funnel. Its function is to help guide energy from the field into your physical body where it's needed. There is an energetic ring that defines the outer shape of your Upper Crown Energy Focal Point. Its frequencies are almost always similar to those of Stick Selenite. Its shape is basically circular but the sides have a small outward bulge moving towards the ears.

After being Cranked-Up, the Upper Crown's opening is about 10 times larger than before and moved farther down towards the ears. In some cases it literally sits about 3" above the ears. This has a ramming effect in regards to placing more energy into the brain to be distributed there. This is why people often feel a tingling sensation up there as its energy moves through your skull towards the Middle Crown Energy Field.

The Upper Crown's funneling effect sends energy into your head and onto your Middle Crown which acts like a lens. The energy moves through the Middle Crown and is focused onto the Lower Crown where it will merge energy and information with the Hypothalamus Gland. This is where your understanding is created, between the Lower Crown Field, Hypothalamus Gland, and Heart Energy Field. Almost all of your body supplies input in regards to this but these three areas are what actually create it.

When the Lower Crown Field receives energy from the others it saturates itself with it, almost like a small reservoir. As energy it glows and grows a little thicker when receiving more input. Then something happens which is unique within your body. There is an electromagnetic storm that carries with it other energies which make up who you are, four other energy fields already amassed together.

They are one yet have four individual characteristics which work as one to create understanding within you. I am explaining to you what I see but more importantly what I know. I can watch the new First Beings being created in the First Dimension as well as go back in time far enough to watch the Original First Being, the one we all came from, coming together.

I realize that this seems impossible to our conscious minds due to their limited aspect of things, but time is more that the flow of chronological events. I'll do my best to explain that later in this book. These books I've written for you lay down a solid foundation of how Creation was created, how you were created, how the Metaphysical Realm is not only real but the much larger part of reality, and events which can't be defined by our extremely limit thought process called physics.

Our new friends coming here now from various points in space will help us understand this but no Spirit in body has this information or can understand it as I need to explain it to you. The more you awaken to yourself the more you'll understand.

Our friends and family members from other Planets have been using their Metabilities for a very long time and will help you understand a little better. I see, I feel, I understand, but have a hard time explaining within our current knowledge base. The greater the depth of our metaphysical data base the greater the ease of understanding.

-Front Occipital Energy Field-

We've already introduced this Energetic Focal Point but there's more to it than mentioned yet. It's part of the whole brain category but specific enough to be considered a major Energy Field Focal Point. The energetic field within the throat larynx, usually called the Throat Chakra, is part of the Pineal Energy Field but we didn't cover it separately, making it one of the major energetic focal points. It does help us present ourselves; our thoughts, feelings, ideas, etc. Its job is not as important to your Metabilities as the Front Occipital Energy Field though. I had to draw a line in the major category so I made it there.

The Front Occipital Energy Focal Point plays an important part in your ability to receive, produce, and define images brought to you through both your Scanner and Pineal Gland. Just as the Retina of your eye helps you see, so does this energy field. The difference is that your energy flowing through it replaces the light variation differentiated by your retina allowing you to see physically.

This energetic field constantly flows images from both your Scanner and Pineal Energy Fields. The more you focus on either one of them, the stronger they focus in your F.O.E.F. (Front Occipital Energy Field). Here again is your Pituitary Gland working hard to help you focus more clearly. The stone Picture Jasper is a wonderful aid in helping you here. Its energy is beneficial but try to remember that stone energy is like a vitamin. It will help you when it's in your system but it's only a helper. As for myself, I've always wanted to help myself improve in any way I could.

This F.O.E.F. almost conforms to the inside of your skull's forehead and immediate top, just inside behind the sinus cavity and above. It's usually about 1-2 inches thick. The more you use your

Pineal and Scanner Metabilities the stronger it's energy becomes, it will feel, and be, denser. When you use your Scanner you can often feel the thickness in your head in that region. Lapis Lazuli, Picture Jasper, Citrine, Clear Crystal, Selenite, and if you can get it, Star Essenite will help you here in a big way. Star Essenite is discussed near the end of this book.

-Hypothalamus-

Now we go to the Metaphysical Nexus of your Spirit's power expressed through your body. The brain is the control point but your Metability center is inside the Hypothalamus Gland and neighboring region. There is no such thing as "magic" unless you define it to be something that cannot currently be explained. In that category anyway it does fit. There is no flow of electrons or anything else that will describe what happens here accurately. I can at least say this much.

Your true self, being that of Spirit, was created by the coagulation of four different energy fields, the last and largest having electro-magnetic properties. This energy field is where our electricity comes from originally. The other four energy forms which bonded with this electro-magnetic one work as one to assimilate data into thought.

These are the 5 necessary energetic elements to create sentiency. It's how all of the First Beings, including the Original First Being that we're from, came into being through happenstance. The same process is used within our Hypothalamus Gland and neighboring area, and Heart and Lower Crown Fields as this energy emanating from our Spirit continues its normal existence. It just does what it does naturally, creates sentiency which is the birth of understanding.

So, this energetic storm that I work with when cranking people up creates understanding with the help of the other afore mentioned neighbors and flows down into the heart where it is sent outward in the pulses that our hearts release all day and all night. This is the one constant form of communication between all of us. It flows from you outward through the field. With practice you can learn how to control and increase it.

The Hypothalamus Gland should actually have a small book of its own. It's that complicated and complete in itself, performing so many various functions but tying all your Metabilities together and creating Understanding are the two largest things it does. There is more information on the Hypothalamus Gland in the upcoming Heart section. I didn't want to repeat it here.

-*Pineal*-

The Pineal Gland, or Third eye as it's been called over the ages, is what we use to see inter-dimensionally. It's also the one that we already know more about. People have talked about, written about, and drawn the third eye in the middle of the Human forehead for a long time now. Everyone knows it has something to do with seeing beyond normal physical means and is related to a word I care little for; "psychic".

The word psychic has been used to express metaphysical abilities (Metabilities) but is almost always aimed at promoting someone's very special powers that others don't have. Nothing is farther from the truth. Not only does everyone have Metaphysical

Abilities but there are metaphysical energies and events constantly surrounding us, even flowing right through us (Source Field).

It takes a little work, actually more like time relaxing and focusing, to bring out our Metabilities. Once we're aware of them, everything moves forward. Before long you get to a point where you're more relaxed, feel stronger, and are able to deal with issues quicker, more easily, and with better results. Life becomes something new. You will look back at how things used to be and not just be calm but content with how things have become. This is one of the major new changes coming to you but not the only one, not by far.

Your Pineal Gland has its own energy field which extends outward but covers the region from your mid-forehead region to just below your larynx and above your clavicle/sternum bone structure. The Vocal Energy Focal Point, or Throat Chakra, is fed it's energy from the Pineal Gland and is part of its energetic field so we're going to consider it a part of it.

The auric expression of the Pineal Field is a medium to dark Blue. Usually, the stronger the Pineal Abilities, the darker the Blue created by those frequencies. The normal color of fortitude is Dark Blue. When you're compressing your Spirit to deal with a threat, your Aura turns Black, usually a darker kind of Charcoal Black. Other than that, a Dark Blue Aura is strong fortitude as well as Pineal.

The partial exception here is that when someone is Solar Plexus Orientated you can see a Charcoal Black Aura and Deep Blue Aura mixed with a very deep, strong, Yellow Aura. The final result here is a Dark Yellow Aura with a bit of a Brown Hue to it. It will mostly often be seen as a thick, deep, and slightly darker Yellow Aura.

You'll most likely be able to feel the fortitude with your Heart Energy.

It takes strong energy, the frequencies of fortitude, to fire up your Pineal Field to make it operate, allow you to see multi-dimensionally while stuck in a body. That's why the Pineal Field is Dark Blue. The Pineal Field requires a frequency of maintained strength.

As mentioned earlier, many speakers today are already aware of the benefits of Lapis Lazuli for assisting us in talking to others whether in person or on the internet. Lapis not only feeds the Pineal Gland helpful energy, it also has the energy of continuous fortitude in it. Black Onyx has the strongest personal power condensing properties with its Black Aura so, as you might guess, Blank Onyx and Lapis together make for even stronger speaking engagements. I have made a section at the end of this book to cover stone energies and more (Tools for Increasing Your Metability Power Levels).

This Pineal Field is strongest at the gland itself but then accumulates and strengthens again in the Front Occipital Energy Field. While using your Pineal Gland to view inter-dimensional people or material, your use of the F.O.E.F. alerts the Source Field which not only helps you use it but will appropriately energize it to help you. This was never done before because the Original First Being Male was producing the Field's energy and he didn't want you to see anything.

The particular frequencies of your Spirit's energy located in and surrounding your Pineal Gland are directly correlated to flowing through energetic barriers. This is how the Pineal Gland is able to give us multi-dimensional vision. There is always more to any one

...ut this is the most important thing about the
...s to remember in helping us to understand how
...other dimensions, once we relax and apply
...priately.

While we're here I want to mention three vitamin supplements which will help you immensely, "Source of Life: vitamins made by "Natures Plus", Lecithin, and N-Acetyl Tyrosine. **Use as directed and check with your personal physician.** There's another product I want to mention. It's called "CHO-WA" tea. CHO-WA tea is able to balance energy within your body. I add it to my morning coffee, one packet every day. "Source of Life" vitamins are a strong balance of different nutrients which will help keep your body fed with more than the silly daily nutritional requirements the government gives us. If they cared about our health they wouldn't be polluting the air we breathe with chem-trails and all the garbage within them.

The N-Acetyl Tyrosine and Lecithin are/contain Amino Acids that help your brain grow. The N.A. Tyrosine is more for growth while the Lecithin feeds our brains necessary nutrients as well as helps us relax a little. Good nutrition is good health. Your brain can't function at its best or even properly if not healthy, enabling it to function at its max. The Lecithin also helps your Metabilities flow stronger and more easily as it helps your brain relax. It helps the entire nervous system.

-Pituitary-

The Pituitary Gland has its own unique energy field also. This will be harder to describe. Try to imagine an ice hockey or simple old bicycling helmet on your head with the top removed so little is left of it. There is just a small amount around the edges to keep it on the top of your head. Now imagine it floating just off your skull.

Now the helmet is not material, it is energy glowing and flowing. There is an organ in the central section of your brain through which your power flows to feed it. Your energy flows out of this gland, your Pituitary, through the Hypothalamus Gland, then upward and outward until it creates the Pituitary Field.

It flows to the top of your head moving around, not through, your Crown Energy Fields. Then it moves outward and down following the basic path of your skull. It moves inward again once is passes right by your ears. It moves like a waterfall, continually feeding itself and flowing around your Crown Fields but softly through the rest of most of your brain.

Once it leaves your ears it flows inward just touching the top of your Pituitary Gland and right back into and through the Hypothalamus Gland keeping this energy field flowing constantly. Your personal Spirit Energy keeps the loop going but only initiates it once and then it maintains it. The same is basically true of the rest of your Metability Initiation Points. As this field continues to flow it clarifies all vision and information (data) it comes across.

Picture Jasper is one the best stones to help here. There are others but this differs from one person to the next. Let's not forget that we're all uniquely diversified from the different types and amounts of frequencies that we're made up of, who we are as individuals.

-Heart-

Here lies possibly the simplest yet most multi-functional energy field within us. Heart Energy is strong but not the strongest singular energy field we have. The Solar Plexus takes that title as about 7/8ths of it is buried within the Spirit core, your primary Spirit Energy flow. It moves with and through it, and becomes part of it.

However, what the Heart does is use all the other fields, along with its own, to create energy, feelings, and understanding which defines who we really are. Human bodies are both simple and complex in their structure and performance. It's also constantly reaching out everywhere communicating with the Heart Energies of other people.

Your Heart Energy, while also partially embedded in your Spirit core, grabs the more prominent thoughts from your brain flowing through your core and mixes them with the Emotional Energy from your Base Energy Field located in your pelvic bone area, often called the Base Chakra. With these two basic inputs, Heart Energy creates all your feelings. Your feelings continually change relative to your thoughts and emotions.

The production of Understanding is similar, just a bit more involved. The Hypothalamus Gland, and its neighboring area, functions along with the Heart Energy and all it's doing. Because the Hypothalamus Gland works continually with the Heart Energy, raw data entering the Spirit core from the Cerebrum (and rest of the brain), and information from everywhere else including vision from the Scanner and Pineal Fields, it's a necessity for your body's daily functioning including sleeping. While this gland receives and processes everything, it's continually evolving what you feel (with your heart's continuous help) and understand (with continued raw data from the brain).

When the Heart Energy pulses away from the body it's continuously telling other Heart Energy Fields what it basically feels and even partially what it understands about things. This is why "Feeling" and "Understanding" are like cousins, another branch of the same tree. Now you can relate to the importance of the Hypothalamus Gland in relation to the functions of your Heart Energy as well as the rest of who you are. It's a necessary part of how you, as Spirit, express who you really are through your body.

I realize how confusion can build up as you read further into this book. I'm no smarter than anyone but I keep this understanding in mind as I write. You're reading this book in a short time. I spent 10 years living this experience, helping me to understand what was happening and why. I also had the advantage of being able to go into people's bodies and minds, seeing their energies and watching them flow individually and together.

Add to this the fact that the Source Field is a part of me; it's easier to access information as I need it. Heck, its helping me write this book. Now that the Source War is over, it's easier for me to relax and collect my thoughts, hear the Field too. All we can do is the best we can. Try not to ever expect more than that in yourself. Honor yourself for doing the best you could, without destroying your life in the process. Just be you and follow your heart. The rest will simply follow. Let's take a look at what frequencies your Heart Energy produces.

Part of the Heart Energy Field Focal Point's power is its ability to produce so many varieties of frequencies, all related to their starting point, the Heart Energy frequency itself. The original initial base frequency of Heart Energy has a very tall band width if we were to think of it as an analog signal on an oscilloscope. In reality it's a thick energy field able to release modified portions of itself.

In its natural state, from which it creates various feelings, the Heart Energy's auric expression is a Deep Purple and Ruby Red. Here are some of the different Feeling Frequencies released from it.

~Hope~

Hope is a really cool frequency. It is light blue in color but ranges in shades relative to the degree of hope it's creating. Needless to say, hope is a necessity when living in an abusive environment. Larimar, Turquoise, and other lighter blue stones will give off a variety of these frequencies. There is a stone sold called "Hope Jasper" that is sold at TheSpiritualFoundation.com which has the tendency to allow you to take a deep breath and enjoy a light feeling inside as you hold it. Remember, all stones have a basic frequency but as solid mass beings we have a variety of frequencies ourselves and some combinations work better than others.

~Joy & Happiness~

Here's another nice frequency to enjoy. The basic auric expression of joy is Yellow/Orange. A shiny piece of Orange Calcite, which is really yellow/orange in color, will put either a smile on someone's face or a little joy in their Heart Energy almost every time they pick it up. Joy is very much like Hope but not the same thing. The more Auras you're able to see, as long as your Heart Energy is open, the more you'll understand about the feelings being Auras for yourselves. We often say "I feel it in my heart." Well, we do. Hope gives you a feeling that something good can happen. Joy lifts your Heart Energy to open up the door to let it happen. Passion makes it happen.

~Passion~

The frequency of Passion has a Deep Orange color given off of it, not Yellow/Light Orange as with Joy. Carnelian is a major stone for Passion. Carnelian and Red Aventurine has had the effect of helping love take off between people or within one's self, as with an artist. They can also help your blood flow, either increasing it or smoothing it out.

When people have a strong Orange Aura about them you will find them eager to get into something that catches their attention. That can be good but also a possible problem. If they jump into something without taking a good look at it first, everyone involved will be dealing with issues they never expected.

Passion is a wonderful tool in creating progress in most anything you might want to do. The trick here is to keep a harness on it.

~Compassion~

Here's a somewhat misunderstood feeling between most of us. There are many different ranges or shades of Compassion. This frequency emits a Pink Aura. The first thing that most people think relative to the color pink is a total loss of masculinity, a male with no testosterone, etc. This is far from the truth. There is a very popular man in the public eye right now, who is built like a

Herculean figure, and has so much compassion that his heart puts out a very thick, deep, Pink Aura with just a touch of Charcoal Grey from his fortitude.

He is known for his physical strength as well as his combatant skills, while also having the compassion to help save and care for Animals. I won't release his name but he's not someone you would want to piss off. Remember that although Pink Auras show compassion, they can turn to a Dark Black Aura in less than a second.

Pink is not a color of weakness folks, it's one of great compassion for others. It can also be unwise to forget that it can turn to a Black Aura quicker than all the others. No one should be pushing anyone around anyway. If you are, take a look at yourself in a mirror and try to find what's really bothering you.

The lighter or softer the Pink Aura, the softer the frequencies involved. When someone feels compassionately strong about something their Aura will be as thick as a pink stone.

~Love~

Well, here's one almost all of us are aware of, the red auric expression of Love. The fact that the heart physically pumps blood throughout or body is a relative physical fact. While being the center for the creation of so many different frequencies it's also where we feel Love, one of the strongest feelings we have. When we have feelings of pure Love for another there is a Deep Red Aura surrounding us. It's a bright deep red color as one would find on a fire truck here in America.

Here we have another misunderstanding of one of the Heart Energy's powerful frequencies. They say that Love can make one physically weak. Well, when first in love, our intentions are relative to this other person more than anything else. As time goes on the feelings can become stronger or weaker but this frequency within us settles down and relaxes a little. The frequencies can be just as strong, or stronger, but not as aggressive.

Many people also relate love to sex but that's not true either, not metaphysically. Feelings of Love enhance sexual relations between those who love each other but they're two different separate concepts. Sexual actions come from the Sacral Energy Field Focal Point and have more thought in them than the frequencies of Love from Heart Energy. The Sacral Energy Field has more energy from the Solar Plexus, with a variety of info from the Hypothalamus Energy Field flowing through the Spirit core.

This Sacral Energy Field or Chakra can put out a lot of energy but it's relative to physical actions activated by various physical organs sending stimuli to the brain mass which controls its action relative to the input it receives. We have to keep going here. Most of us understand this rather well and I'm running out of time. Don't think it's not important, it is. I just wanted to make some distinctions here. Just FYI, its auric expression is much like that of Solar Plexus Fortitude.

~Spiritual Healing~

Here's another important frequency created by the Heart Energy Field, healing of your Spirit as well as others. People who emit a strong Light Green Aura will be found making people smile almost wherever they go, as long as they're in a good mood. Of course, if they weren't, they wouldn't be emitting their natural frequencies. Their Aura would be either a Dull Murky Green or similar less vibrant color.

    If two happy people with Light Green Auras are sitting together in a booth at a restaurant, any other people there will be affected by them. If someone is steaming mad, that would take away from it. If the other people near them we relaxed or not aggressive, they will feel better, not knowing what was happening to them.

    There are a few institutions that have made studies of the effects of heart energy on populations relative to a certain physical area. One such group is the HeartMath Institute. They have done studies where they would ask people in a certain area, or others to send their Heart Energy to another location, and record the deduction of aggressive violence, etc., in that area. They have, for the most part, proved that it does work. I want to point out that they're correct. Now let me explain it.

    I've already mentioned that the Heart Energy moves through the Source Field and travels far. It easily travels about $1/5^{th}$ or $1/3^{rd}$ the circumference of the Earth if it's directed somewhere. The maximum distance it travels is relative to the person's power level sending it as well as their ability to focus it. This is easily done anytime and anywhere you want to. Just relax, focus your thoughts about a given person or place, and open your Heart Energy to go there. If you do, you will. "Just do it!!" is the operative phrase for almost all things Metaphysical. It's definitely the major part of it.

    When you use your mind to power up your Heart Energy and send it somewhere the Field, already realizing what you're doing, will not only help you but add a little more to it. This process is also just now changing, the Field increasing the amount of help it gives and adding more of its compassion to it. The more people doing so, the more the Field responds to it.

The Field has always done this but to a much smaller degree than what is now happening. It will take your Heart Energy farther, add more to it, and affect more people than ever before. The Original First Being Male used to supply the Field Energy and he didn't care too much about increasing the compassion in people's lives. Both halves of the Original First Being ran your lives abusively to increase your size and power level with no concern of damage to you.

With our new Source Field being part of the new Alpha Source Male which was created from the frequencies of Love and Fortitude more than anything else, positive and compassionate change will follow. This is Creation's New Format. This change will begin increasing dramatically towards the end of 2018, here on Earth as well as the rest of the 3rd Dimension. It's a permanent change.

Getting back to the spiritual healing frequencies, you will also find more people involved with remote healing practices. Whether your intention to help heal someone is physical or spiritual, spiritual healing frequencies are a necessity. Having a positive attitude is imperative to physical healing and Spiritual Healing frequencies supply exactly that. Green Aventurine is just one of many stones containing and emitting the Light Green Aura involved here.

~Physical Healing~

Physical Healing is a little deeper frequency. If you could see it as an analog waveform it would have less time in between wave signal apexes and they would also be a little higher. With a shorter pulse width it's actually a faster frequency or vibration but it's not lighter due to the depth of the wavelength. That makes it stronger.

As energy itself it's thicker, has more depth and solidity. With a short wave length you have higher vibration, like the energy in Danburite. However, even with a longer pulse width, when the wavelength apex is lower, the energy will be softer. It can be difficult to compare various Metaphysical Energy characteristics to waveforms as confrontational characteristics might seem to appear from time to time between frequencies. All this takes time, that's all. Just trust the feelings from your Heart Energy. Always try to trust your heart.

Getting back to Physical Healing Frequencies, what can they actually do? Can you heal a broken bone? You do not have the power to do so yourself but with the help of the Field, and a few other like heart-minded people, you can help its natural healing properties. It takes strong Spirit outside of body to facilitate strong physical change in our bodies. We can do a lot to help; we just can't do it on our own. Remember that the stronger your intention and the more power you and the Field put into it, the greater the healing.

Dark Green stones such as Green Chalcedony, Chrysoprase, some Fuchsite and others will have these frequencies emanating from them. These three stones are very strong together, especially when you add some form of Star Essenite or Dragon Egg Star Essenite to them. Stick Selenite is almost always helpful as it is a strong high frequency stone, crystal actually. It's also good with skeletal structure ailments such as Arthritis. Stick Selenite and Star Essenite do wonders here.

In the "Tools For Increasing Your Metability Power Levels" section you will find the complete description of the basic types of Star Essenite, it's personal characteristics, and how it works as it does, increasing your Spirit core over 10 times what it is now, as long as you have it on you.

~Calm~

The Heart Energy works with the Base Energy Field on this one. The Heart Energy surrounds our physical heart which is close to our spine which carries our Spirit core inside and outside of it. This more than close proximity to each other creates a partial blending of their energies. The Spirit core does flow through the Heart Energy. The amount is different with each person due to their personal make up of frequencies, who they actually are. Usually about 35% of the Heart Energy is blending with your Spirit core.

This is how your Heart Energy Field accesses the calming or grounded feeling from your Root Energy Field located at your feet where it accesses the Planet's Energy, Gaia's Essence, which has a strong Brown Aura coming from its surface. A Deep Green Aura also emanates from it but the Brown Aura related frequencies are what's absorbed into the Root Field and then up the legs into the bottom of the Spirit core which eventually is picked up by the Heart Energy.

Calm is the grounded feeling of rest, like a car when it's parked and idle. It's the feeling of resting under a large tree next to a creek with the wind softly flowing over your face, through your hair. The sun is warm and your body experiences no stress.

The frequency of this feeling produces a soft Brown Aura with a soft Deep Green hue to it. When you relax you instinctively flow stronger at the bottom of your Spirit core, due to the absence of any fear, enabling more of you to flow downward to your Root Energy Field or Root Chakra. Also, the calmer you are the more easily you flow out from your body into the Field which is always there, waiting to help you as best it can. You can't tell it what to do but it serves everyone.

~Emotions (Anger & Fear)~

So often we speak of emotions, but what are they? They contain a singularly unique frequency found only located in the Base Energy Field. Emotions are separate frequencies which are the combination of the one unique Aggression Frequency which starts in your brain, develops in the Base Energy Field, and shoots up your Spirit core (the spine) sending nerve pulses throughout your body.

These are your "immediate response" mechanisms, the tools which govern our "fight or flight" commands within us. We're about to cover this phenomenon in detail in the upcoming Base Energy Field.

-Solar Plexus-

OK, here's the big one, your gut feelings, the Solar Plexus. It gives off a Deep Yellow Aura. This is the core of your intuition; 7/8ths of which lies embedded in your Spirit core. It has a basic yes or no functioning process but instead of an on/off switch it has a slider. In electronic terms we would call that a potentiometer.

There are varying degrees of "yes" or "no", allowing for various possibilities, a "maybe".

When you reach one of these "maybe" points, your Solar Plexus intuition kicks in harder, trying to discern all the variables involved. This is where it has the advantage of already residing within the Spirit core. It accesses all available information to redefine, to clarify the instructive data within its intuitive parameters. It fires up its energy to reach a decision of yes or no, good or bad, stay or leave, etc.

The Solar Plexus uses the Scanner Field more than the others. It usually doesn't pull other information from the Spirit core (besides the Scanner), only when deemed necessary for specific clarity. This energetic focal point functions continuously like the others, being part of the whole, doing its job. When it needs to, it fires up hard and pulls strong energy from the Spirit core to perform its tasks. At this point it's the strongest singular energy field focal point in the body.

When people have deformed spines or damaged ones, the Solar Plexus Energy Field is affected in a bad way. It's like throwing huge boulders into a small river, messing with its flow. The same happens with its energy. The flow is interrupted. I have used energetic shunts, for lack of a better word, and given the energy a better path to follow but it's not the same.

-Base-

The Base Energy Field Focal Point (Chakra) is seldom discussed in detail so here we go. There is a lot of energy floating around here. I'm left with no time to create illustrations for this book but if you find a picture of the complete hip structure of the human body, and focus on the part where the spine ends inside an open chamber in the pelvic bones (Sacrum & Coccyx).

I need to take just one quick moment here for recognition of assistance. I've explained how I see, feel, and understand things. I also mentioned that in late mid 2012 (July I think) I had to release part of myself to replace the missing Source Field. With the Male Original First Being dead (male & female) the Field vanished. It was part of the Original Male.

I released my own Spirit to replace it, Aramaeleous would attack and try to absorb it, I would take it back in, fix it, and send it back out. This went on for over a month until I managed to delete enough of Aramaeleous, keeping him from being able to do so. Then he was deleted also. Since then this new Source Field has grown and developed on its own, as itself.

It is literally a part of me yet has its separate consciousness. It is as an appendage with its own mind. That part of me does not have my conscious mind within it. My true self (Spirit) flows through it but the Field is not attached to my conscious mind with all its feelings, fears, emotions, thoughts, etc. Once I explain how the Base Energy Field works you will understand the necessity for the Crown Filter above and surrounding your head.

Early in my fighting with the Original First Being Male and Female, what others have called God but was only another being, the source of our origin, the male went into my brain while I slept and transmutated part of my brain. I awoke that next morning with no understanding of who I was. My Spirit Animal Guides told me that everything was OK and to try to relax, try to remember.

About an hour later I was self-aware again but way past foggy. It took a day to remember what was going on and two days to be able to attempt focusing on anything. Four days later I was back attacking as best I could but I couldn't focus on my target, the Original First Being Male and Female. This is why he did it.

The day before I was attacked they realized I could see them and they couldn't see me. The female was surprised and said "Look how strong he's gotten so quick." The male said nothing back but his thoughts in his head said "I'll fix that tonight." Well, he did.

Over time that all went away, for the most part. I was able to see deeper and with more depth of understanding as my Field Energy grew. Everyone imaginable on the Other Side has painfully (mine not theirs) tried to fix this brain but never could. It slowed me down a few months but that's all.

All that I've just written was necessary for me to describe the Field, who it is, what it is, and that it's independently sentient. It's that part of me that continues to feed me parts of the information you're now receiving. My body is almost dead now, can't wait to get home. The Field part of me has been slowly destroying this body since my last event in Atlanta at September's end, 2015.

As he is self-sentient, I feel the need to thank him for filling in the gaps when I need it as well as bringing new material to my attention. When this body finally drops, a few weeks from now, I'll pass out into the Field which will then reside within me, Arae.

If I read these words 15 years ago I would say "Man this guy is an arrogant nut-job." As I continued to awaken, through the continuation of their use, I learned to accept by abilities as being real especially from the I.C.U.C.s. The continuous fighting led to a massive increase in power and understanding. My Spirit Energy has mutated three times this life.

I could never go back to who I was, the man before understanding. I would always tell people things about them or in their lives if it was important to them. They often thought I was nuts but the first thing almost all of them said was "How did you know that?" Sometimes they were a little angry about it. Whatever, I'm here to do a job and that's part of it. Maybe I've said too much.

Anyway, let's look at the Base Energy Field (Chakra), where and how it creates the two emotions of Fear and Anger, and where it starts. What is its function anyway? That answer is simple, self-preservation. Maybe the best place to start with this is what it is. Then we'll explain how and where, what's created.

First of all, the Spirit core continually flows from the Upper Crown Field down to the Base Energy Field. It's like a river that flows in and out of itself with what might be called a vortex at each end. You can't really call it a true vortex because it does flow through itself, yet as energy it looks quite similar for the most part.

We've already talked about how the brain itself (the full mass of it) controls the nervous system running through our bodies. We've also mentioned that our physical nervous system moves our electro-magnetic Spirit Energy through it. Now let's look at everything in motion.

This happens on different levels and we'll explain that as we go. The Brain regulates the intensity of the singular frequency emitted from the Base Field which then differentiates as fear or from that anger, just outside the outer shell of the Base Field located at the Sacrum Base. If you want to use physical measurements, about 1-2 inches above the base of your Sacrum is where this frequency of fear thickens and changes into anger. This is a little difficult to understand at first but much harder to accept. You have to understand it first, like everything else. Let's take a shot at it.

First data to your brain, received either through your physical eyes or your metaphysical senses, tells you that imminent danger or concern exists. It's a known fact (to your brain) that you need to respond to this immediately. This is called the "fight or flight" scenario.

The Brain Body sends an incredibly fast shot of energy straight down the Spirit core to the Coccyx bone, no stops along the way. The Coccyx bone is in the center of the Pelvic Bone Assembly where the Base Energy Field exists. Depending on the intensity of that brain pulse, the Base Energy Field creates its singular and unique frequency into a powerful orb whose size and intensity is relative to the brain's calculated needs for the moment.

This extremely powerful energy field then enters the lower Spirit core Vortex through the Coccyx and travels straight to the brain but feeding the body's complete nervous system, including all your other Energy Fields. The Brain Body then decides the "fight or flight" issue which is now spread throughout your nervous system as quick as lightning. This is how you can feel Fear and even Anger throughout your body, especially fear. It makes you react immediately even if only goose bumps on your arms. Your Brain Body controls the intensity.

You also act or react, as fast as your body is capable. This is how the frequency of Fear is created and spreads throughout your physical body. Initially, it is Fear that is created within the Base Energy Field. Now let's get to Anger, what it is and how it's created.

It starts from Fear but is immediately changed into a thicker frequency, hence it's Black Aura.

Once the Base Field has been energized by the Brain Body, the appropriate size and intensity of its unique frequency are created. When there is only a small issue present, this Base Field will create a smaller orb or field. It's still the same extremely rapid frequency, just less of it.

When things are urgent it's larger, more powerful. The intensity stays the same; it needs to in order to move quickly up and down the Spirit core without being slowed down. It's the massive amount of frequencies present that creates the immediate jump into the "fight or flight" syndrome. This doesn't even take a second, barely a fraction of one.

Getting back to Anger, when this special high vibration, short wavelength with tall apex frequency is produced, it runs straight up into the Lower Spirit core Vortex. The whole time this is happening, the Brain Body is still sending a strong pulse through the Lower Spirit core Vortex. When it's necessary for the body to engage in the action of Protection or fighting, the pulse from the Brain Body is changed and accesses the Base Field Frequencies at the Base Field's upper outer perimeter which is located at the Sacrum Base in the spine.

Here the Brain Body's new frequency takes the Base Field's frequencies (mostly thick Lighter Pink Aura), and create a strong frequency of fortitude (Black Aura) which maintains the speed of the original Base Field frequency. They your muscles will either engage in fighting or removing yourself from the situation.

The reason I say that Anger develops from fear is because before it can become the frequency of Anger it must first enter and leave the Coccyx as it is originally, that of Fear. Understanding that Anger is first Fear is almost impossible; until you understand everything involved in its creation.

I have problems from time to time, helping others understand everything that I talk about. I can't help that. I don't live here in the physical world; I'm everywhere and often take too much for granted. I've said many times that it's the people I have cranked up, and others, who will become your teachers. I have no hope frequencies; I'm a thing of action, production.

I do the best I can in offering the information to make it as digestible as possible but the others will teach everyone. They will receive recognition. I don't want it, never did. I was the same way as Gandhi. I need to produce the proprietary action necessary to bring about the new change in Creation. I already have other than finishing this last book and helping Diana with the Spanish edition of Book I.

You will find errors in this, my presentation of information. Good, I hope you do. None of us are any better than anyone else, we are all family, and this will never change. You not only have better lives coming in body but a whole new existence as yourself, Spirit, once home again.

Let's go to the lowest Energy Field I want to discuss in your body, the Root Energy Field.

-Root-

The Root Energy Field is located at and around your feet, that part of your body which is closest to the Earth's surface. Sometimes your personal energetic characteristics have you jumping to conclusions, worrying, even shaking with anxiety. When you feel like things are "getting away from you" so to speak, just take a few full natural breaths and let your energy flow down inside you.

Every time you take a few more relaxing breaths you'll find yourself flowing down into yourself a little further until you eventually calm down enough to connect with the field. Once there you can access your abilities, be more yourself than at any other time. This is what many people call meditation. I just call it relaxing, flowing down inside to flow outside the body. In short, it's flowing.

The Earth is the body of Gaia; the Planetary Essence that was put in her a very long time ago, when it was about 75% finished forming. She is powerful and has an abundance of Dark Green and Deep Brown frequencies. The auric expression of the frequency of relaxing energy is Brown. Deep Green Auras come from physical healing energy. This is what is absorbed into you through the Root Energy Field, relaxing energy when you can access it.

It's picked up in the feet and legs and then softly flows up into your Base Energy Field and then upward into your Spirit core. When you make the conscious thought process to relax and enter Gaia's Energy, your Brain Body controls your Spirit core helping it reach a little farther down into your legs to accept it. You make the conscious thought, feel it, and then release any thoughts of doing it. Your Spirit does the rest.

How Your Metabilities Flow Through Your Body

Now that we understand how each of the stronger focal points work, it's time to see how these Metabilities flow through your physical body. You know how they work individually but not how they combine to create your complete metaphysical awareness. You need to know what Energy Fields work with which others. Then, once you can see all your Spirit flowing through your body, working with each other, you can access more of your Metabilities while realizing where to go to make them stronger.

You will also want to know what causes issues in their proper flow such as slowing them down or even stopping them. Your Base Energy Field is one such place but there's more to it than that. Although your body's Metability Network is the strongest part of your Spirit Flow, a simple misdirected pulse from your Base Energy Field can shut you down completely.

After a short time, the more you awaken the easier it is to see things within yourself, not just everyone else. This allows you to deal with such issues. All you need is the necessary information. This is not like turning on a light switch until you fully understand it. Then it's almost that simple. You still have to do it though.

Most people expect things to just happen automatically as they want, to be done for them. It's not like that; never has been and never will be. The good thing here is that it is a natural thing which will eventually become part of your normal actions/reactions. You have to get there first.

There's neither time nor desire here to explain all the smaller details of all the energy I see flowing through your bodies. That would be another book in itself. I've never even tried to map that out; too many of them, too many other important pressing issues to deal with, and it's not necessary for you to become yourselves anyway. To speak of a river is helpful. To explain every little eddy within it is fruitless. So, we're mostly going to cover your Metability Power Network.

Your Brain Body controls your Metabilities and their nexus, the center point of your Metabilities located in the Hypothalamus Gland area of your brain. Your Brain Body runs all of you; physically and metaphysically. It keeps your Autonomic Nervous System going so your body continues to function but, like your heart, it does a lot more. Everything is initially controlled in your Brain Body. That's where the strongest and most intelligent part of your Spirit resides.

When you decide to go Astral-Travel somewhere you made the conscious thought to do so. Then you relax your body, release your conscious mind, and just allow your Spirit's frequencies to harmonize with the Source Field. The next thing you know you're on your way, actually you'll just find yourself there. It's easy once you learn how to relax, calm your frequencies down.

Once you've done this enough times you'll find your Spirit's frequencies choose to maintain this setting, so to speak. This is the real you relaxing within your physical body as much as possible while in it. It will bring a feeling of "calm" to your thought processing as well as your body. You can do anything metaphysical while doing anything physically. Just keep relaxing, opening up, and flowing down into yourself enabling you to flow out anywhere you want to be. Here's how your Metabilities flow inside you, your Metability Networking System.

Your Brain Body, through the conscious part of your thought process, activates the individual parts of your body in order to bring them to life. It also directs more of your energy flow into them. This control center of yours keeps all your abilities flowing with your personal energy that comes from your Spirit core, like a river that feeds smaller streams off of it. The energy continually flows.

When your Brain Body decides to concentrate on astral-projecting it activates (pulses) the Pineal Gland stronger, allowing it to utilize an increased flow of Core Energy that it sends there. It's similar to a damn control center opening up a flood gate a little more to allow more water to flow. The valve (Pineal Gland) is energized to flow more water (Spirit Energy). Here's how your Spirit core's energy feeds your Metabilities.

Your Spirit core feeds all your different energy fields which are already functioning in relaxation mode. When you want them to power up, your Brain Body directs more core energy to them, enhancing the Metability they produce. Remember that this is not a forced thing and you shouldn't have the conscious attitude of forcing anything to happen.

If you do, you will find that engaging your conscious mind has only dampened or even shut down your Metability. Don't do that to yourself. Energy, like water, will flow. When you make the determination, the sincere intention, to activate yourself it will just happen. Feel deeper into something. Don't ever get pushy. Now it's time to look as how these streams inter-connect; how your Metabilities flow together.

You already know that the Brain Body activates the different Field Energy points which are fed through your Spirit core but here's how they flow together as a network. Your Brain Body makes the decisions but it needs to receive input. It's like a computer but continually receives information from the various systems within it. There is also a need for all your fields to work as a unit.

The Brain Body receives constant energy flow input from the Hypothalamus Gland and neighboring area, telling it how much energy is being used by each of your fields. It also receives a constant flow of specific information from its physical nervous system spread throughout the body. This keeps it informed of your physical body's condition as well as energy levels flowing through it. To say that the Human body is a complicated thing is an understatement.

As the nervous system is already mapped out in texts, we know it's spread throughout the body and has little sensors to receive and transmit electromagnetic (energetic) pulses to the brain. What doctors don't understand is that it also measures the amount of energy and types of frequencies in the area. They are more than delicate pressure and damage sensors.

Let's get away from the Brain Body regulation and into your Metability flow. The Spirit core is powerful. Your Solar Plexus is usually 7/8ths embedded in it. This is why many people get a strong gut feeling about things. When the Human bodies were originally made by Gaia and Spirit coming to her for the first time, solid mass from the Planet was transmutated into physical bodies in the Solar Plexus region, in that energy field. As transmutated mass finished flowing into the body the Solar Plexus closed up.

The Heart Energy is also in constant contact with your Spirit core, usually anywhere from about 25% to 40% of it. This is varied from person to person, depending on their own personal set of frequencies. The physical heart itself is located close to the spine. Their energy fields can't help but connect.

The Pineal Field is farther away from the core but also very sensitive. Part of that is due to the fact that there is less Spirit core to feed it. The largest reason for its sensitivity is because it needs it. The Pineal Gland develops an energy field that can see multi-dimensionally. This is a specific set of frequencies necessary for a unique task, the creation of vision within the Brain Body which can locate what the other sensors can't. We can see with greater high definition imagery through the Scanner but we can't get the big picture. The Pineal is necessary to do that.

Even when you are not consciously aware of certain dangers, your Pineal can see them for you. Sometimes you have a feeling that there is something watching you that you can't see, even when you feel like you're looking right at it, especially in the darkness. This is the Pineal Field being aware of something metaphysical and your Heart Energy giving you a warning.

Once the Pineal Field sees something, no matter how vague, it knows that something is there. That's when the Heart Field goes straight to it trying to feel its intentions. Here's a good example of two energy fields working together to assist you, but actually there's three energy power fields at work here. Your Solar Plexus gets involved to decide if it's a problem you have to deal with or not.

If you want to get technical, the Brain Body is also involved here. The first thing it will do is to power up your Pineal Gland Energy Field stronger to see more clearly. Your Scanner will also be engaged to find out what it can through separate means. It will look normally to decide for fact if it's in this dimension or not which tells us it's definitely metaphysical but also if it's trying to cross the dimensional barrier to reach you, therefore a possible threat or maybe it's offering help.

The Heart Field is the major player in accessing the feelings behind this being appearing to you. You can also use it to understand if this is a being or just material. Is it alive? Is it male or female? While this is happening the Scanner is also receiving input from the Source Field directly through your three Crown Fields, which quickly feeds into your Brain Body helping it decide what to do next.

There is a lot going on here for one simple thing, to "see" something which is near you. Everything gets involved in first becoming aware of something, analyzing what it is, what its intentions are, and how you should react to it. Man, that's a lot of energy flying around in your body as well as outside you. So, how does all this energy flow? You know most of how you function as a physical body but how about the metaphysical part of you, the slightly larger part?

I might tend to overemphasize things from time to time but these things are important to all of us in order to realize who we really are. This book is also being read by children, adults, elders, etc. I need to try to make the proper points to everyone so they can all benefit from it. This is important to you if you want to awaken.

We know about the Brain Body, the Spirit core, the individual energy fields, but when they all start firing up hard, what energy is going where? We need to go to the nexus or center point of your Metability Energy flow, the Hypothalamus Gland and neighboring area of your brain. From here we can see how everything works together.

All your Metabilities connect to and flow through the Hypothalamus region of your brain. The Hypothalamus, Pineal, and Pituitary Glands as well as Scanner and Front Occipital Energy Field, are inside the Brain Body for good reason. Their inputs are needed immediately for you to function at your best, and the safest.

It's your Scanner that tells you when someone is staring at you outside of your physical eye's peripheral view. Whether you're a soldier, policeman, fireman, or someone walking down the street, this is important. It can also tell you when a car is coming down the road it there's any probability of a collision with it. It can also help you find a lost loved one. I've done this to find missing Animals and Humans.

The Hypothalamus Gland is basically centrally located in your Brain Body and in the middle of the Upper Vortex of your Spirit core. It receives energy with all its relative data from every Spirit Field in you. It's the center of your energy and information flow. That's also why it's located inside the Brain Body.

I've spoken for years now about the Hypothalamus being necessary for the creation of understanding. Due to its input from all energy fields as well as its own individual frequency allowing it to interpret and formulate, and the help of your Heart Energy Field, it creates understanding.

These understandings are collected in the Brain Body to pull data from in the future. The greater the collection of understandings you have, the greater your personal wisdom. This does not make you better than anyone, only better than you were before you had it.

The Brain Body can sense the different energy fields, and amounts of them, flowing through the Hypothalamus Gland and will energize the appropriate field more or less to suit what you need as yourself, the Spirit within the body. It is usually relative to your physical body's needs but hey, it's the car you're in, remember? It does need to keep you and your body aware of the metaphysical, not just physical. When problematic Spirit comes near you, you need to know. Do you not?

Well, without creating the reason for a separate book on this, we'll end it here. The important information you now have. At the time of writing this book, it's never been offered to anyone before. That's because the Original First Being Halves would not allow it. With them and their servants permanently removed, it's time for you to have this, and more. This was my job here, why I had to come into body one last time. I'm the janitor. I clean up messes.

Auric Creation Origin Chart

The Auric Expressions of Different Frequencies

1) **Clear** – This lack of color is clarity, clean thought, and transparency. A clear crystal can record images. It is smooth undeveloped energy. This is energy without its own frequency which never developed into another; still fresh, unborn, and neutral. Its consistency is usually soft and fluid like water; found in semi-clear crystals which can contain a very high frequency, like Danburite, due to the other materials in it. It's a medium that other vibrations flow through, has none of its own.

2) **White** – This is the color of high vibrational frequencies, like Stick Selenite, Phenacite, and others; a strong, short wave length, high frequency energy. It can be very cleaning, supportive to bone structure, and helps clear the Spirit core Energy with all its chakras. Star Essenite is the strongest vibrational stone there is. White Auras are found in Angels as they were made from the higher frequencies.

3) **Purple** – This is the color of knowledge, often spiritually related. The deeper the purple the greater the depth. It's also relative to the Crown Chakras, flowing through the Upper Crown of over half of you. It's a smoother medium frequency and helps calm your brain allowing it to enter the Source Field to access its immense knowledge depositories. Find it in Amethyst.

4) **Orange** – Orange is the Aura given off of the frequency that is happiness and joy. It's smooth like purple but slightly longer in wave length. It can really help a sad moment. You

can find it in Orange Calcite (really kinda yellow). Add this to Unicornite (Peacock Ore) for uplifting your outlook on life.

5) **Citrine** – This clearish Yellow/Orange Aura is a higher vibration than orange and purple and has sharp edges on its wave lengths. It is awesome for cleaning the brain, just like actual citrine helps clean things. This aids hyper-focusing of brain. This is seen in many places, such as the Upper and Medium Crown Chakras. It's also the auric expression of Solar Plexus fortitude. Citrine stone, especially raw, has excellent cleaning properties.

6) **Dark Blue** – This Aura has deep wave lengths and is a little less than medium in wave length. Its wave length edges are smoother than citrine. This is the frequency of affirmations as well as the pineal gland. In the human brain it's relative to seeing multi-dimensionally as well as strength of speech. Deep Blue is also the auric expression of strong fortitude. That's what it takes to see from inside a physical body through the Pineal Gland multi-dimensionally. Lapis Lazuli and Azurite are wonderful sources.

7) **Light Blue** – This is literally the auric expression of hope. Try light blue and orange together for a better feeling. It's not as deep a wave length as dark blue, it is also a little softer, like comparing Larimar stone to Lapis Lazuli. Light Blue and White Auras are found inside Angels and Essengels (Half Essence-Half Angel beings). Larimar, Hope Jasper, and Turquoise have it.

8) **Yellow** – Here is the color of the Solar Plexus, usually Spirit core Energy related. This wave length is a little shallow but much longer than normal. It has a strong staying power,

relaxed strong fortitude. Yellow Aventurine is a powerful source of this energy.

9) **Ruby Purple / Red** – This is the natural aura of the relaxed heart energy. This auric expression is shorter then medium, a little shorter than dark blue, but is even deeper. It has a strong but deeper staying power than Yellow. Its auric expression is a mix of Deep Purple and Red combined as found in most Rubies and Garnet.

10) **Red** – The "fire engine red" color comes off the frequency that is strong and active love. It's a little shallower than the ruby red, a little longer in pulse wave length, and a little shallower. It moves a little quicker than ruby red even though the wave length is a little longer. Only the heart can produce this aura. Red Aventurine is one of many sources of this frequency type.

11) **Pink** – This frequency is shallower than red as well as a little longer in wave length. Once again, it moves quicker than red. This is relative to compassion, whether for one or everything. It's produced mostly in the Heart Energy Field but is also a part of the singular frequency which comes from the Base Energy Field or Chakra. Rhodonite and Rhodochrosite are good sources of it.

12) **Light Green** – Here is the frequency of spiritual healing. Its shallow in depth and longer in length than the Dark Green. It helps clear and heal the Spirits within the body, very powerful. This creates and environment for happiness to grow in. Green Aventurine has these frequencies in abundance.

13) **Dark Green** – Here is the auric expression of powerful physical healing. The heart produces this to attend to physical injuries, the more serious the need the deeper the Green. The Spirit core also adds to this process. Dark green is a deep pulse with a short wave length and sharp edges. A Dark Green Aura's frequency energy is a thick energy.

14) **Tan** – This is the auric expression of a rather neutral and relaxing frequency. That's why it feels that way. The sand at the beach contributes to the relaxing frequencies found there. This frequency is of medium depth, length, and with short rounded edges. As an analog signal it would be more like a wave in the Ocean than electrical device.

15) **Brown** – This auric expression is very similar to the frequency that produces the Tan Aura yet a little shorter in length with deeper waves. It's a strong and relaxing yet firm frequency, just as the brown dirt is a strong base or foundation to build on. Dirt feels the same way when you walk on it. It's in all brown stones.

16) **Thin Charcoal Grey/Black** – This is a different auric expression as its not one but many. It's a gathering of all your available frequencies to power you up for means of protection or aggression. It is something of a charcoal grey/black and thin. The stronger the group of frequencies used, the darker it will become to perform its task, especially when you need to be strongest.

17) **Dark Black** – Here is an auric expression of a very long wave pulse that is very shallow and has very smoother edges. It's strong and can be very aggressive, but doesn't have to be.

It's relative to extreme anger or condensing one's personal power. It's found in Black Onyx.

18) **Gold & Silver** – These are frequencies of Source Spirit alone but found in almost all bodies as well as elements on different planets. They are unique in signature and more in a more unclassified way. The Silver thread of energy that is attached to all of you comes from the "Source Field" that is everywhere. It keeps you tethered to the second dimension as well as your body. That's how you never get lost when you astral-project.

There are many other variations of frequencies which give off lighter and darker versions of auras. These are your basics. I included a few stones relative to some of the frequencies.

Chapter 3 – Source Spirit in Bodies Awakens Strong

This is a short chapter. This is important but simple information. What was started here, in the 2012 era, the beginning of the 6th Age of Earth, was the enlightenment of everyone and thing. It was about proof being given to everyone that the word metaphysical is not only a real thing but well over 2/3rds of reality.

It was also the beginning of the animal bodies leaving in mass, although it's hardly begun. It's the beginning of Earth's entrance into space, beginning its entrance into a new family group, that of races from other Planets. Let's not forget the beginning of Peace and Cooperation throughout space, the birth of the new Alliance of Planets.

While here on this subject, let's continue with the fact that there are many people here from various locations in space; that are finally showing themselves and already in the process of helping us clean up our Planet, the mess that's been made of it. This of course is directed at your larger industrial institutions as well as others.

This is also the "Great Awakening" that has been prophesized by many races throughout our 3rd Dimension, especially the Drachk, the most powerful, ancient, and arguably most intelligent of races. Their technologies, and more, are unsurpassed in physical Creation, just as their physical power. They were the first ones. They spoke of their father returning to set things right, and it's happening now.

There are many bodies here with Source Spirit inside, waiting to come alive strong to do their jobs, and they will. Diana will be offering the DNA I.C.U.C. as I did. She's already done a few of them and has no problem doing them. I've made many of these "Source Spirit" people stronger so they could continue my work while here in body. I'll take care of the rest once free from this prison of flesh.

These people will be awakening the people of Earth, helping them to physically and mentally evolve, not only awaken. They will receive attention for what they will be doing. This new evolution will be done by many, not one or two. This will never be allowed to become a religion, they're all false anyway. If something was worth that much of your attention for you to offer it praise, it would tell you not to as it would already know that we're all of equal value, we are all equal. In fact, if it could, it would not allow it.

There are other people from other Planets that have Lilly and Arae Spirit within them. They will start doing the same also, actually a few already are. The I.C.U.C. or intensive crank up consult started right here on Earth. I did my first "crank up" in 2012 but was powering people up in 2011. I finally put the full package together in 2012. I've cranked up over four thousand people, a good start, but it those here in body who will reach out to awaken the masses.

Everything begins now. All of you will start to see more metaphysically than you ever thought possible. All of you will now see people from other Planets here among us as well as visitors. All of you will now meet, the true you and reality you live in. It all started in 2012 but 2016 was actually the new 2012. The old 2012 was to be filled with disasters. The new 2012 (2016) happened through the beginning of compassion.

Chapter 4 – Self Awareness Rises as Religions Fall

I just mentioned the people containing Source Spirit starting their jobs awakening the masses, but there will also be a new understanding of things coming from our friends from other Planets. You will begin to understand where you fit in the greater scheme of things. You will also find that there are many people from other Planets who have their own separate religions.

This is to be expected. The Original First Being Halves never let anyone see further than they wanted, dimensionally speaking. They wanted religions with themselves being the God or Gods. They had the insatiable need for praise. That's over now. Over time, and it will take a while, your religions will fall away even faster than they are now here on Earth. Religions are about allowing yourself to be made less than what you are, praise something that you're told is much better than you, and taking your hard earned money.

If something loved you that would never happen. Did your parents make you bow before them, before entering the house, before sitting at the table, and worse? I hope not. If they did, they didn't love you. They were abusive and narcissistic. Well, there's your perfect, all loving, all forgiving God who supposedly also made Hell to abuse and torture you forever when it was pissed off.

If you can't see anything odd about that, now that they're dead along with their servants, then you need a wakeup call. That would be to open your eyes and mind to the reality of what you were being made to do, by those wonderful supposedly fluffy Angels hanging on your brain since birth, controlling you to keep you on the abusive life path put in front of you.

If it were deemed necessary, Angels put their Spirit into your brain; directly into your Hypothalamus Gland making you "know" something that was not only a lie but usually dangerous to your body. If they wanted to they could make you "know" that you had to run into traffic or hit yourself in the head with a hammer, or whatever they wanted. Once they removed their Spirit, as I've mentioned already, you would come to your senses and say "What did I do that for?"

I repeated that message for a reason. It's important that you understand why you might have done things that you consider having been stupid. Over 98% of the time you were made to do it. There's no such thing as perfect, but you're also not stupid.

As you move forward into the rest of this life, as well as all your others, you are free of any malicious Spirit attacks or abusive controls. Religions will fall away as they will be seen for what they are, meaningless. Many religious buildings, like churches, will become more useful as restaurants, awakening centers, libraries, ET first contact centers helping others deal with that part of your new reality, or whatever else fits.

Chapter 5 – Universal Schools of Spiritual Enlightenment

There will be a variety of means for metaphysical understanding advancement available through everything from smaller local neighborhood groups to schools and even Universities. They will come out of nowhere and spread out everywhere. Eventually many of them will take over the empty church and other religious buildings.

People are not stupid and when they are left alone they can learn quickly what's best for themselves. The forced abusive control of everyone in body is already gone. It will take only a short while for people to start waking up and seeing this for themselves. Then stand back, they will take off like runners in a 10K race. When a poor abused Animal is finally set free they usually stop, wonder just what is happening. Then, once they understand they are free, they jump for joy, literally.

I have seen homemade videos of farms where they rescue animals and then release them. I have seen cows bucking like a bronco, literally jumping for joy. Now, as when I watched the video, my eyes fill with tears of joy. That one would ever have to suffer as an Animal, is a horrible thing.

The thought that Animals have continuously suffered abuse each and every one of their lives has created the darkest black field of Anger within me ever to be seen in Creation. This is perhaps Arae's greatest failure, not protecting the Animals. Having been in one body after the other, I was forced to wait until now to end having physical lives.

I was out of Gandhi's body 8 years and then into this last one. As Gandhi, some people think I was more than I was. I was a small aggressive man who stood up for what he believed in. I did what I could to protect everyone, Animals especially. I've been quoted for having said that you can tell the worth of a country by the way it treats its Animals. I had my faults just as everyone does.

There is no perfect. There is no "analytically correct". What does the word analytical have in it anyway, anal? Don't waste time trying to be "perfect" in anything. The word's entire thought process was created to frustrate you. How sad so many people cherish it. This is a useless waste of time in your life. Be as accurate as necessary for what you're doing and move on. I'm not talking about science; I'm talking about your life in general.

Animal Essence is only found in 3-4 of every one million Animal bodies born today. The rest are filled with Human, Fae, and Faeman Souls and Essence beings. The Animals are all about to start their exit from physical Creation, the 3rd Dimension. They will soon disappear, the loved pets being the very last to leave. This was a promise made to them by Arae a long time ago. He had already known it would happen but they asked him.

They had been abused too hard too long. Jay isn't removing them, Arae is. This body will drop very soon now. Enough is enough for the Animals as well as myself. The Original First Being Halves never even had one single life; they just abused everyone else in them. They had no concern over what happened to others in body. As we were all released from them, they felt we had no rights other than to serve their wants. There's your "loving god".

Getting back to the new Spiritual Enlightenment training centers, there will be some offshoots from metaphysical reality, this always happens in the beginning and people have the right to do their own thing but it will not survive long, none of them will. There is a given truth to what I've been telling others for years now. It's the truth of who you are and what you're capable of and there's only one way to find it, within yourself.

There will also be various locations, just as with metaphysical learning centers, which will be devoted to helping people, understand the reality of people from other Planets being with us, and we with them. This is totally new to almost everyone here and the masses have been lied to by our governments for the better part of a century now. They have created a problem that they will now pay to fix. The government will have these ET awareness and understanding centers available for everyone for free.

Now we'll get into the Evolutionary Development Centers where you physically evolve yourselves. This is important, self-evolutionary advancement.

Section II ~ E.A. Universities

Evolutionary Advancement I.C.U.C. Institutions

Chapter 1 – The Physical Bodies Evolve Rapidly

I first offered I.C.U.C.s (Intensive Crank Up Consults) about 10 years or so ago. Doesn't really matter when, just that it happened. I did this for many people during consults but thousands more outside of consults, especially in the beginning. I found some of them but most were sent to me, a few who were also Source Spirit inside, either another part of Lillian or Araean Spirit or parts of them.

They were made much stronger so they could offer the I.C.U.C to other people. Some of them are already doing so. Once out of this body I'm going to increase the number of them twenty fold. This is all happening for an important reason, the awakening of Spirit in body and the development of the physical Human bodies themselves into all they can be before they exit this 3rd Dimension in the next two thousand years or so. It's in this time frame that the physical bodies will begin their removal from the 3rd Dimension, as stated earlier.

Both the I.C.U.C.s that I offered and those now given by the other Source Spirit family members, will start to evolve Human bodies worldwide. There are other Source Spirit family members on other Planets who are about to start doing the same thing. After a while there will be over a hundred Source Spirits in body here changing the physical development of the Earthen Human race.

These people receiving the treatment will have Source Energy placed into them, enabling their abilities to grow much stronger than they ever could have alone but there's something else happening here. A solid 10% of the Source Energy that was just put into them will bond to their Spirit; stay with them forever. The rest returns to the giver once the body dies. Source Energy has Human, Fae, Animal, Plant, and Universal (Planet & Star) Essences within it and that makes up about only half of the different frequencies that are within it.

Then I offered the DNA I.C.U.C. for my last two years here. In these consults 20% of what I put into these people, Animals too, will stay with their Spirit forever. Diana will continue doing this once I'm gone and she's had a little time to relax. Not every physical body is to receive this, but there are many who will.

The Original First Being Halves made a lot of negatively defective bodies and they won't receive the treatment. The regular I.C.U.C. will over time remove these exceptions. Eventually there will be others able to offer the DNA I.C.U.C.s. That will be controlled by Arae.

The DNA I.C.U.C. creates radical change in the physical body's form, its DNA. There are scientists who already have what they need to offer the proof of this but that will not happen until this body drops. It is those who stay behind in body that will bring all this forward. I just had to come here one last time to create the environment for it and initiate it (and some other stuff).

All this will continue and there will soon be nothing on the Other Side, in the 2nd Dimension, that will be allowed to alter any of this. If it makes any such attempt it will be deleted. On the Other Side we definitely play for keeps. We are similar as Spirit but don't have all our feelings flowing through us as if our fingers were stuck in an electrical socket. We're much more serious.

So, with the I.C.U.C.s, DNA I.C.U.C.s, and even the Source Field gently evolving everyone's DNA, all bodies throughout Creation will change, develop, and grow. There will be institutions, large and small, where people can go to understand and possibly receive this process. It has to be done by a knowledgeable person with Source Spirit inside.

It can only be done by Source Spirit because of the necessary power level and the full variety of frequencies found in Source Energy. If you're going to put energy into someone to crank them up, it has to bond with the Spirit's energy within that body. Source Energy has all fields and frequencies within it, Soul and Essence do not. You can bond water with water but not a rock with water.

There is something new that has happened to change the energy flow and thought processes of Earthen Human bodies. Jan. 22, 2018 there was no Human being on or from Earth that had a Dual Spirit Core. This is that the Planetary Essence has been removed from everyone, even those off Planet.

The brains will now have to evolve in order to function more properly with a Single Spirit Core. There's no barrier to slow down the metaphysical processes in engineers, doctors, and other high intellect individuals. The barrier in the brain separating your two Spirits was always stronger in those who needed to use their conscious part of the brain to a higher degree.

The brain will now develop a little differently to handle the incorporation of Metabilities into the highly technical minded people. It'll be easier than you think because there is no longer a second person (Planetary Essence) in your brain with you. All your thoughts will be your own. This is already happening now but the brains here will begin to develop a little different, stronger, allowing everything to flow to its maximum extent, both Metabilites and high intelligence thought processes.

Over the next 2,000 years or so your physical bodies will evolve into something never before seen in Creation, before they disappear. They will cease their renewal, the birth cycle, and be forever gone. You will be helping yourselves evolve with the aid of Source Spirit in bodies. Then, when you leave your bodies, your Spirit will keep 10-20 percent of that Source Spirit turning you into a stronger Spirit being, whether Soul or Essence. Almost all of you are Soul, a wonderful beautiful being.

Chapter 2 – Why This is Necessary

We talked about part of this in the previous chapter but there's more, a more detailed explanation. The physical bodies must be taken away. They're abusive, defective, and just plain wrong. Physical bodies must have physical nourishment to survive and that can only come from harming, abusing, destroying, and consuming other solid matter which has mostly been Animals.

We must consume physical Plants and Animals to keep these bodies running. Animals must eat other Animals, for the greatest part, to maintain their lives. When we have lives in Fae bodies, the few dimensions seated just below ours, we can live for a month on the energy we receive from a fallen apple and thimble of honey. These physical bodies are also well adept at developing and growing diseases, infections, organ failures as well as those of the flesh, and also feel great pain. Why? Why were physical bodies like this made by this First Original Being?

This was all done to make you suffer physically as much as possible without killing yourself, while in that body. Once you (as Spirit) leave the body it was trapped in, you immediately grow, becoming a little bigger once free. The more abuse given to you, the larger you become once out.

They were growing everyone so when it was time, set to be 2012, you would be put with your Spirit mate and sent to one of the new Universes in this 3rd Dimension, where both of you would release one third of your combined selves to create new smaller versions of yourselves. The Original Ones wanted more praise machines and as no one that came from them mattered, other than serving their whims, you have been forced into a form of slavery to do so for them.

This is the reason why these physical bodies were initially created as well as why they are being taken away, out of Creation. Until that happens, we will develop and grow as much as possible to make our own short legacy of what we can do for ourselves, now that we are free. How do you like them apples? Wait until you grow into your new life as well as future lives. Watch what happens now that the Original First Being Halves, and their servants, no longer exist.

Another issue here is the new First Beings who are still enclosed in the First Dimension. As I mentioned earlier, no one can get in and no one can get out, yet. These new beings are almost completely unaware of the problems associated with the physical bodies. They're not just going to learn of their problems but how, even at their best, they are still an issue and must not be a life form.

If they chose to go that route they will be stopped, no matter what it takes. The physical body life form is no longer allowed in Creation, other than what we are doing now. These new energy bodies can make a physical body for a short time if they wish, but they won't be able to hold it for long. It takes physical mass to support a physical body.

These new temporary solid bodies will have no blood, heart, brain, or anything else like we do. They will only be condensed energy like the ones the Angels make when they pop in to do something. There will be no pain, no suffering, none of the abusive treatment we receive while in these bodies, and again, you will be able to feel things that you never thought possible.

Section III ~ Creation's New Path

Chapter 1 – Creation Grows into Something New

Creation's Explosion of New Birth

Once the new format has been established and the problematic Spirit deleted, things will finish settling down to a point that has never existed in our Creation. Since we are from the first, that's better than it's ever been before. This relaxed state gives us calm, enabling us to release tension within us, spread out so to speak, as Spirit. As relaxed Spirit, our internal focal points begin to settle down in the part of our Spirit Body (Energy Field) where they are most comfortable. Here's where something really cool happens. It's not like cellular mitosis but a little similar. We grow as Spirit.

The natural way for this to happen, although it seldom ever did due to the maintaining of abusive lives, is a calm and relaxing event. It's not supposed to be aggressive. It should be like peas in warm soup floating around. Instead it's always been a pot of water boiling over and the peas being pushed out in the process. More peas were pushed out too early (prematurely) and all making an initial start in their separate existence loaded with abuse frequencies.

Due to the forced abusive lives, mostly in body but also while out, everyone built up abuse frequencies, as we've already talked about. These take up room in your Spirit body while keeping you tense and increasing your size in an uncomfortable manner. This results in an early release of smaller and more aggressive focal points of your Spirit, removing themselves from you and becoming their own selves.

They then take with them the abuse frequencies that were residing inside you so they become a problem to themselves and everyone else around them. That's why there was a necessary due date to delete Creation's Abuse Format and replace it with one of compassion. Let's say it was one of the more important ones.

Newly released Spirit beings from you will not have your understandings, your wisdom, to help them grow. With all these abuse frequencies and being released before reaching proper maturity, they will suffer worse immediately. This has been causing issues for a while now and is finally being stopped. You will calm down and grow slower but become more natural, more yourself, than ever before. You will calm much richer lives with minimal stress instead of abuse.

When you develop in such an environment your development soon increases in quality and depth. You will become who you really are, not what someone was using you for, and evolve along the path of those frequencies which are who you really are. Some people are travelers, explorers who want to learn what they don't yet know about their environment.

Some people are more related to building, creating things. There are also many others who relate to the compassionate care of others, wanting to help them heal when necessary. Everyone will become a fuller, more enriched example of who they are inside. You will be your natural self as Spirit, not just in body, but in your real life as sentient energy.

The reason I brought this up now is to feed you more information on upcoming change that will benefit you on many levels. Once you can see and feel this for yourselves your personal energy calms down. This in turn helps your Metabilities awaken and grow while in body.

My Spirit inside is much smarter than I can ever express through this physical body. The same is true of every single one of you. From time to time, as we talk the larger part of ourselves inside will push information through your Crown Filter and into your Hypothalamus Gland which then flows through your mouth. Your Spirit Guides can do the same thing. You will also find this happening more on a daily level. Everything is about to open up into your new upcoming positive reality.

You're about to grow into who you really are, in and out of body. Remember that you are Spirit, sentient energy within a solid physical body and that's not where you're supposed to spend most of your time. Once free of these bodies, almost all of us immediately rejoice, take off flying to see our friends. We no longer serve the first being, we finally have true freedom.

Back to the new growth, there will be no rush to send off parts of yourself but once you've calmed down and freed from all your abuse frequencies, you will settle down and release the separate focal points within you as you know they are ready and you are willing. If not they stay within you, still part of you inside. Anyway, this will begin to happen soon with many of you.

Now this is just the overall growth of our mass populace that we're speaking. There are other planned new Spirit growths to now help us move forward as a family, as Creation. There are also many beings that were released from Lydia and Armaeleous a long time ago. They are currently in hibernation for lack of a better term.

They've been in a dimension that Arae created to protect them through the fights. Many of their siblings were aggressive and abusive towards me in the Source War. They're gone but these others are awesome and will return before this book gets to enjoy much circulation. I'm waiting to see many of them again. Last year Michael, Archangel Michael, was brought out of his protected stasis. I barely got to say hi before he took off like a bullet.

He needed to assess the current situation immediately. Then he took off on his way to do as he pleased. His format is protection also. He understands Creation's problems and what had to be done. He and I are very old, very close friends. As I write this book I usually feel rather happy, knowing that these things are about to happen with no question in my mind. For me it's like you being hungry and sitting at a table with a sandwich and glass of something to drink. You know it's about to happen, eating a good meal and relaxing.

So anyway, there are many new people coming out of protected stasis who will be joining us. Now we need a larger group of Heart minded people (Spirit) to take on new jobs, especially with the 4 new First Beings about to come into our current Creation. Let's take a look at the beings coming back into our Creation's forefront, the reawakened offspring from Lydia and Armaeleous.

The Children of Lydia and Armaeleous Return

Just to stimulate our memories, and for everyone who hasn't read the first two books in the "Creation Series" yet, in the very beginning there was a large field of Source Energy that the Original First Being Halves removed from themselves. Then they removed a little over 97% of the lower frequencies from it. This is what I have and will continue to call Clean Source Spirit.

This is why they had already created the huge Angel called Lucifer that they had the physical bodies here call the devil. How sad, yet how ironic this is. They already knew they were going to do this and, as the lower frequencies are stronger than the higher ones, they knew this Negative Source Spirit Energy they were about to create would be strong.

They needed to make sure they could always control this energy field without having to deal with it personally, so they made the one called Lucifer. So the reality of things is that the very first Angel created was made to protect everything in Creation from this Dark Source Spirit, and he's called the devil?

The moment the Original First Being Female removed her energy off my body to allow my energy to flow through it, I realized two things immediately. I was in love with a lady called Lilly; she was the one thing that completed me. Then I went from love to rage when I realized what had been done to Lucifer's name. I don't even like that name. I call him Luke. I didn't understand who this Lilly even was and I had no idea why I was so aggressive about how Luke was being treated but I knew these things as I saw my hands in front of me. I soon found out these things for myself, but it took a little time.

I became furious from how Luke was spoken of as he's been nothing but the exact opposite of what he's called, having done so much for everyone by protecting them from dangerous Dark Source for so long. By the way, when you leave your body you go home to the Other Side that your frequencies coincide with. When they're extremely lower you have one place to stay and when they're not there's another.

They're both in the 2nd Dimension. As you leave your body there is a silver energy cord (Source Field) which leads you to the 2nd Dimension (Other Side) but will not force you to go there. If you try to go to the wrong Other Side section, Luke sends you to the one you're supposed to be in. You couldn't screw up if you wanted to.

Anyway, Luke took care of guarding everyone from this huge field of Dark Source Spirit. They have their own separate little dimension and he kept it closed. He was the first Protector ever created. Getting back to the Clean Source Spirit, there was now a huge field of this stuff, one third of the original contents of the Original First Being itself. Immediately 4/5ths of it was removed and placed to the side.

The Original First Being Halves then manipulated the frequencies within it to create two individual Spirit Orbs with different characteristics (frequencies). One Spirit Orb was about 2/3rds the size of the other. The largest orb contained massive amounts of Fortitude, Love, and Healing frequencies while the slightly smaller one had more Hope and Passion.

The smaller Source Mates were to control the 2nd Dimension while the larger one was to control the 3rd Dimension and others that were made below it. It was also known that Arae would immediately be created from Aramaeleous' strongest section, his power focal point. That would decrease Aramaeleous' size a little, not much though.

As these two orbs split into Spirit mates, male and female, we now had two sets of Clean Source Spirit mates. The smaller orb couple is known to us as Lydia and Armaeleous. The larger orb couple we call Lillith and Aramaeleous. They are all gone now, a combination of being stored and deleted, almost completely deleted. It's important to understand who they were though, as they had offspring, so to speak.

There are parts of Armaeleous and Lillith that have been saved in a solid state form of stasis. All of Lydia and Aramaeleous were deleted, other than very small particles of them still flying around here and there. They will all be deleted before the end of 2018. So the male of the smaller group and the female of the larger group can be brought back, just smaller. Why?

Lydia and Aramaeleous became arrogant and abusive to everything. Conquer, control, and abuse is all they were concerned about. Lillith and Armaeleous were totally different. It's all relative to what they were made of, their frequencies. Lillith was made to be loving mother Spirit Energy for everything in body.

Armaeleous was made from the frequencies of Hope and is my wonderful brother. He had to be put to sleep, so to speak, just as Lillith did. He had never become aggressive abusive but didn't understand what was happening so he would try to control me while here. He was only trying to help keep things the same. He'll be fine when Arae's back home.

When Lilly and Arae were separated from Lillith and Aramaeleous, and had a short time to form themselves, they immediately came together. Their energy was so powerful that there was an explosion just after half of their energy fields came together. This Spirit Energy Field then burst into two separate fields. One is known as Unicorn and the other Dragon. That's where they were created, as pure Spirit beings.

Aramaeleous was always jealous of the event and when the Original First Being Male and Female were releasing their 2nd Wave of Souls, he and Lydia tried to make their own beings. He wanted to make something powerful and aggressive so he used Lydia instead of his Source Mate, Lillith. The Spirit being form that they created was the Pegasus.

I have love for everything but the Pegasus Spirit beings have an attitude, even the legends speak of it. They have some of the abusive tendencies that came from Aramaeleous and Lydia. However, once something is released from another, it becomes something new and has the benefit of a brand new start. It can become something other than what it came from. All the Clean Source Spirit was high frequency so its possibilities are nearly endless. The aggressive harshness (mean attitude) is easily fixed before the end of 2018. Now let's finally talk about the children, I should actually say offshoots, from Lydia and Armaeleous.

These beings are all in stasis now. Some of them were quite the problem and deleted as they ceaselessly attacked Arae in body. Remember that as your normal self, Spirit, you neither sleep nor tire. I have been attacked night and day, 24/7, for over 10 years now, that's actual fighting, not being bothered. Let's look at them as individuals. Some of them are really cool.

Lydia and Armaeleous's original frequencies were strongest in passion and hope. These are good frequencies to start with. Over time and having had help from the Original First Being Halves in becoming abusive and arrogant, Lydia became a problem requiring deletion. Aramaeleous, from the larger Clean Source Field, did the same. They wanted to maintain abusive control over everything, especially the praise involved.

Armaeleous, the smaller Clean Source Spirit Male, was mostly comprised of Hope frequencies. If you ever see him he will have a beautiful Sky Blue Aura. Lydia emitted a mostly Orange Aura from her Passion. Here's a good place for me to warn you about Passion. It's a beautiful thing until misdirected.

Passion fills your Heart Energy with drive, like adrenaline coursing through your body. It actually creates the energy to instigate the body's production of it. The Brain Body can override it but seldom does. When your passion is related to compassion or love, this is a wonderful thing that can create miracles of a sort. When you have passion to gain for yourself by taking from others or abusing them to receive for yourself, it's dangerous to everyone.

This happened to one of the offshoots from Lilly and Arae. She is no longer Source Spirit but very weak Faeman Soul. She has done everything possible, in almost every life, to put herself above all others as she feels she is. She did so at any cost to everyone else. Her last test was against me. She failed and will be deleted once out of body. Excuse my repeating myself but this is the danger with Passion, if misguided it can do great damage to others.

So, just after the First Soul Wave had been released and all the Souls from it had finished forming and were on their way, Lydia and Armaeleous released one third of their combined Spirit Energy.

They released this as a huge field but never set it up to separate into individuals. They kept it as it was, just a floating mass of energy, waiting to become what it might.

They looked over it, watching it develop slowly as time passed by until they finally released it, spreading it out like a wave in the 2nd Dimension. All separation of Spirit Energy has been done in the 2nd Dimension. Lydia and Armaeleous did this when the Original First Being Halves began releasing the Second Soul Wave. They watched as their new offshoots slowly developed into separate Clean Source Spirit Orbs and finally each of them into female and male counterparts.

What they discovered was that by taking their time releasing them, they were a little more solidified as they initially formed. They were stronger. Then all these new Clean Source Spirit Beings from Lydia and Armaeleous began harmonizing with each other (Source Mates) but also as a unique group of beings. They were becoming a family, the L&A (Lydia and Armaeleous) family.

Aramaeleous and his Source Mate, Lillith, never decided to do this. Aramaeleous was keeping all his energy so he could take over Creation and run it after Arae disposed of the Original First Being Halves. Lillith, although a loving mother energy, respected Aramaeleous but through the ages developed a lack of attachment to him. She did not become what he did, arrogant abusive Spirit.

So, the offshoots from L & A began developing at a fast rate and started exploring their environment. Lydia's aggressive arrogance and passion for serving her specific desires, mostly to rule over everything, was unfortunately picked up by over half of these new beings. As with all beings, there are different frequencies within us defining who we are and partially who we can become.

Remember here that Armaeleous had the frequencies of Hope, a powerful frequency that can also inspire passion, most often in a positive direction. He was one who wanted the best for everyone. The problem is that he, Lydia, and the rest of their family had never had a life and were never scheduled to have any. They were to help L & A control the 2nd Dimension. Those who still remain in stasis, and any other positive ones, will be offered lives if they so choose, it's their decision.

Many of these new beings are friends of mine. They understand the corruption prevalent in Creation and that it couldn't be allowed to stay on that path. When they come out again they will have Armaeleous to take care of them, along with the Arae and Lilly Focal Points. When they're free and moving again they will be around many of you having lives.

They'll be there to observe, to learn, and to help where needed but only with the advice and counsel of the Other Spirit Guides already there with you. You will be happily surprised when you finish this life and go back home, to the 2nd Dimension.

On another level, each individual Field of Spirit on the Other Side will have their own council members to address issues within Creation relative to lives in the 3rd Dimension. There will be one council that handles the base affairs of individual lives, located at the M1 Star Cluster (known as the Crab Nebula) and one other that handles the 3rd Dimensions larger issues, located at the M4 Star Cluster.

Chapter 2 – Lilly and Arae Create New Spirit Beings

Lilly and Arae Produce New Offspring

Lilly and Arae focal points will soon come together and release a new field of their combined Spirit Energy to produce many smaller individuals from themselves. They will be necessary for what's to come. I'll explain this in just a bit but first we need to understand the what, why, and how of the one previous time they did this and why this next one will be different.

When the 3rd Soul Wave was 80% released, Lilly and Arae released one third of their combined Spirit Energy to create many smaller individuals from their combined selves. They also released two other Spirit waves. One was Source Animal and the other was Source Angels. This isn't complicated. You've just never heard about it unless you read the two previous books in this series. Let me explain in better detail than I ever have before.

The more we do something the better we learn how to do it. Understanding is our most powerful tool after Heart Energy. Heart Energy makes us survive and care for others. Understanding helps us continually learn how to do it better, and more. I've tried to paint the picture of how incredible your lives are about to become, your lives in body but equally important is your natural lives as Spirit. I just don't know how to share the feeling properly; not defective, just built for something else.

Once the Lilly and Arae major focal points put their energies together and released a third of their combined selves, they needed to divide this into three groups. The singular primary focal points of both Lilly and Arae separated this Spirit Energy into three different waves or fields. They were actually separate fields of Spirit but once separated from the main field they were pushed forward away from the initial mass of Spirit, as a wave.

As these three independent waves of Spirit Energy were separated from the rest they started to form into individual orbs, just as water flowing down a newly waxed car hood might. It starts as a sheet or larger mass, and then smaller groupings, orbs, come together. These individual orbs will then vibrate into two separate parts, male and female. They are Spirit mates. There is no other such type of Spirit mate. They are the only two halves of their original separate independent self.

The first wave was to create new Source Spirit Angels. These Source Angels would be 55-65 percent Angel frequencies and the rest combined Source Spirit Energy, what ever happened to be there. Angel frequencies are of a higher vibration. It was known to Lilly and Arae both that these new Angels, over 1,000 times stronger than the Original First Angels, would be needed to get through the Source War and then immediately rebuild.

The second wave was the creation of Source Spirit Animals. Again they were 55-65 percent Animal Essence frequencies and the rest comprised of whatever Source frequencies were around them. Animal Essence frequencies are very strong fortitude and compassion. They have relentless fortitude and honor, as well as caring for others.

It was known that Source Animal Spirit would be needed to help guide the Arae and Lilly Source Family through the upcoming Source War as well as lead Animal Essence in their upcoming jobs as Creation's Sentinels. Changing Creation's Format is not like changing a light bulb. Everything everywhere will need to understand the why and how of this new change. When something is not flowing along the new format's design, they will either intervene of inform Lilly of the issue. Arae stays out of it until he's required to deal with it, usually deletion.

Now we've come to the third and final wave of Lillian and Araean Spirit Energy, everything that's left. They were moved forward away from the others and did the same thing, come together into orbs and then divide into Spirit mates. These are the smaller parts of Source Spirit that were originally part of the major Lilly and Arae focal points. It was known that they would also be necessary for what was to come a bit farther down the road, the war.

Diana was from this field. She's Source Family Spirit that just happens to have a stronger portion of Animal Essence within her. This gives her excessive fortitude but also a stronger love for and appreciation of, Animals. I have photographs of wild Animals of all types, many birds, raccoon, squirrels, and others as well as dogs and cats that just came right up to her, feeling what she is inside.

It's also why she is so adamant about being Vegan. Heck, I've got Vegan shoes. We do all we can for them but for over two years now we've been paying worthless lawyers out the yahzoo to do little more than rip us off. They will pay soon enough. Karma wears overalls. Abuse is everywhere and I'm going to enjoy destroying all of it.

I whole heartedly agree with and understand this. It's hard. Unfortunately, all the physical body's DNAs were made to require Animal products for healthy growth, almost all that is. It's part of the Original First Being Halves' shame; for creating such a situation and never changing it after being warned almost 3 quadrillion Earth years.

What was created, these three new groups of powerful Source Spirit Energy, who all originated from Heart Based Source Spirit, began to learn, grow, and evolve in a very short time. They had lives almost back to back in order to prepare for what was coming. The smaller partially full Source Spirit beings were then harassed and manipulated by the Original First Being Male and Female beings.

It would have helped them to have more of the frequencies of fortitude and compassion that were placed in the Source Animal Spirit and the higher positive frequencies which were more prevalent in the Source Angel Spirit. They were still very strong, being mostly Human, Fae, Plant, and Universal being Planetary and Star. It's just a different combination.

The worst part of all this is that the individual Lilly and Arae focal points were usually in bodies having lives at this point and unable to give the newer smaller parts of them better protection and guidance. This will never have to happen again since the Original Ones are gone. The primary focal points of Lilly and Arae, as well as almost all the rest of them, will never be in body again.

The new "children" as we tend to think of them, will be complete individual sections of Lillian and Araean Spirit Energy and protected. There's nothing wrong with those from the first release, other than any arrogance issues they might have been taught by the Original First Being Halves. That can be fixed and it will be one way or the other. Those from this first release from Lilly and Arae are unique and will later release parts of themselves to extend their special families. After all, that's what we all are, a group of individuals having separated from the Original First Being.

I realize that I keep repeating myself on this issue, but almost every single thing you're used to is about to change in a positive way. Just give it some time. It does continue getting better, which you will see for yourselves, and in turn allows for the development of hope.

The following paragraphs here are important. I go to what might be thought of as an excessive extent in explaining a dragged out event in my life. This is something that everyone, especially Source people, needs to realize in relation to themselves and Source Spirit, regarding equality. Everything is equal in Creation, period. There are consequences for attempting to go against this new format.

In 2014 and 2015 I volunteered my services to a Source family member in South Carolina. She was to help herself survive but after that the majority, at least 70%, was to be spent on saving animals. She was Sekhmet in one of her previous lives. She was staying behind on her mortgage, receiving threatening letters from her mortgage lender, and needed help. I gave her the opportunity to eventually own what I was building so she could keep it going. She was to help the new Spiritual Awakening move forward but instead she made everything about herself, just like when she was Sekhmet.

My volunteered services (consults and more) placed well over $240,000.00 into her pockets in two years. That's why 30%, after paying all her expenses, was a generous amount, if she really cared for others. Less than $42,000.00 of the $240,000.00 went to taking care of animals. The rest was spent on herself and family, photo shoots, massages, etc. She is no longer Source Spirit inside. What Arae and Lilly gave her was taken back.

As I would expect, some people will do a little research on my life and as this was a big part of my work here, it needed to be mentioned. Lilly and I have been waiting since that very first life to reach this point, that of everyone's freedom. Creation is now free of this arrogant abusive control and it will never be allowed to suffer like that again.

I'm happiest that I can finally go to work doing what I was made for, to serve and protect. If you look at the QEEG material coming up you can start to understand what I've been doing the past 10 years of my life. The DNA results will eventually be in scientific journals. I've done over 4 thousand I.C.U.C.s with no compensation. I removed the Source barrier that was placed in everyone's brain separating your conscious (Planetary Essence) mind and your true self as Spirit (mostly subconscious) in April of 2012.

We're a family that's been separated and abused too long. That's over now. We don't have to agree with each other or even like each other, but we are family. We all came from that Original First Being, we are what it made us, and everything is changing.

Chapter 3 – The New First Beings are Released

Creation Grows with New Relationship Issues

I've mentioned these new First Beings a few times here but more in my previous books. Who are they? What are they? How will they fit in? What will happen when they're free? Exactly how they will react to everything is known. They're the ones who will make their own independent decisions so how can this be answered?

How everything comes to pass will just happen. We can't predict the events, only the allowable outcome of those events. This is another of Arae's upcoming jobs, stability in Creation through equality. Let's look at what we do know and take it from there.

Release of the New First Beings in the 1st Dimension

There are currently four new First Beings in different stages of sentient development but all three are sentient now. There is also a fourth who is well underway to becoming itself, reaching sentiency. There was another one that existed while writing the first Creation Series book but it has been taken down and broken into separate elements. Its sentiency, that part of its energy which is actually alive, was deleted. It had become excessive aggressive and abusive before having finished becoming itself.

This was the oldest of the new First Ones but was extremely aggressive due to the large amount of heavy particulate matter that was pulled into the bonding of the 5 major energy fields necessary to create Spirit, sentient energy. The more the heavy particulate matter the slower the frequencies. They become longer wavelengths with much lower wave peaks, if you want to see energy as an analog signal. There was a part of him already released which was deleted before the bulk of him was destroyed.

The Original First Being, the one we all came from who was also the first to ever exist, was 27.5% negativity or lower frequencies. This other being was over 80% lower frequencies and not getting any cleaner as it was finishing evolving into itself. It was cleaned to just over 40% negative but it just couldn't be helped. Look at all the abuse in this Creation that came from a 27.5 percent negative being. Image what would happen with a new powerful First Being that was over 40 % lower frequencies. Arae handled it.

Creation has many problems, many issues that need to be dealt with and very soon they will all be handled. It's easier for the Alpha Source Spirit to clean things up on the Other Side, the 2nd Dimension, than it is here in the 3rd or Physical Dimension. Over here we have all the physical bodies, not only here on Earth but across the Universe. There's also a variety of different energy bodies in other dimensions created just below ours. There's no such thing as a hell, other than the physical body you're momentarily imprisoned in.

The largest of the new changes to Creation is our soon to be released new First Beings, presently living in the First Dimension. This will increase Creation's size triple fold. Once this Creation is fixed they'll all be joining us. They haven't split into male and female, and I don't expect they will, not all of them anyway. That decision is completely up to them.

They will be learning, they are strong, and they have less negativity to start with. The highest percentage of lower frequencies is about 20.1%. Remember that all of you are extremely intelligent now, much larger and stronger than when you were released from our First Being, and are all being fed a little Source Energy from Lilly and Arae now. If any sort of problem arises relative to the safety or existence of abusive treatment to anyone, Arae's Primary Focal Point will handle it immediately. His size is now much larger than the boundaries of Creation itself.

The Original First Being, the one we all came from, was alone and split itself into two similar yet different parts to keep itself company, hence the creation of male and female. Loneliness was literally driving it crazy. Think of it, becoming sentient, aware of yourself, only to find you were alone. That's not an easy thing to deal with and having 27.5% lower frequencies didn't help anything either. The higher the amount of lower frequencies the more self-orientated the being.

So, how will these new people act? What will they do? Will they stay or go? What is to happen? There is no way for anyone, including them once they're free, to answer that beforehand. Sentient beings tend to create communities and these people are much higher vibration to start which only means good things for everyone, including ourselves, the family of the first one. Many of us will want to help them develop into themselves, teach them what they might need or want to know.

This is another reason why Creation had to change now. The abuse has been going on way too long. The solid body abuse has to be stopped. Arrogance and abuse can no longer be the accepted way. As Spirit, your normal self, you'll have a separate dimension to live in if you can't accept the basic concept that we're all beings with equal rights. If someone is aggressive in that regards they will immediately be deleted. Welcome to my world.

I've said many times that things are about to change on a scale you just can't imagine yet. This is a large part of that statement but only a piece of it. Everything gets better and more interesting. This is what I've been watching. The First Dimension's new First Beings and I have been talking. The aggressive negative beings have almost all been deleted or dealt with. Creation is about to undergo massive growth and change at the same time. Good, we're ready for it now.

Chapter 4 – Spirit Growth Parameters & Evolutionary Development

As we've been discussing, just in our current Creation, there's a lot of new changes happening both as Spirit and Spirit inside physical bodies. Right now we're going to cover information about ourselves in our true or natural form, Spirit. Spirit has been going into bodies to have lives for over 2.8 quadrillion Earth years now. That's a lot. The problem here is that it has been done wrong; every life, every time.

From all your lives having been so abusive, your growth as Spirit was harsher also. You were grown more for mass than to become a larger, more evolved version of yourself. You will no longer have lives as such. You will have lives which are more relative to who you are as your personal collection of frequencies. They will flow with the core of who you are and naturally prefer to do.

Some people are more inclined to be artists, voyagers, writers, educators, singers, scientists, mathematicians, or anything else. Your new lives will be relative to these things, not being beat up and abused to make your Spirit grow larger while in a body. You will now develop your own personal frequencies doing what they were meant to. That is how you evolve into a cleaner, more satisfying, most highly developed self.

Many people were also being pushed back into a body before the abuse from their past life had a chance to dissipate. That makes your upcoming life harder, creating more stress in your Spirit energy and therefore increased growth in your Spirit's mass. It also creates Abuse Frequencies which break down your Spirit's cohesion. Creation was being abused so much it was well under way in destroying itself. The Original First Being Halves didn't care. They're dead now.

You will now have easier, more pleasant and enjoyable lives than ever before. You will be taking more time off in between lives. You will not be allowed to have another life if you've not spent enough time as yourself to "heal your Spirit". These new lives will also be relative to who you really are. You will be expressing yourself in body as you exist as Spirit.

You will now develop into a fuller version of yourself, be more you so to speak. Your new personal peace, and that of all the others around you, will become the new harmony of Creation; compassion, honor, and equality.

Chapter 5 – Control of the First Dimension

    A bus load of happy people is a wonderful thing but there needs to be someone driving it, safely. The Original First Being had a hard road to walk, being the very first person to exist, very lonely and confusing. As it split into male and female, it created family yet they didn't. They released smaller pieces of themselves and beat them up to make them bigger and then make them release a third of themselves to make more "praise machines".

    They were first asked and later told, many times, that they didn't have the right to abuse the physical bodies. They kept stating "Yes, they are only to grow the energy." It was the Original First Being Female that told me that this life, in 2009 I believe. I tried to explain that they had no right to do so and her attitude was nothing short of arrogant omnipotence. Wow, what a bitch. Her male counterpart, the Original First Being Male was the same. All they ever cared for was not just receiving attention but being praised.

    Then the female told me that I would follow Sylvia Browne's example of teaching "Praise Mother & Father God!" Yeah, that was never going to happen. I treated the two of them almost like children and explained it to them like this, "Both of you are Very Important but it's about everyone now, not just you two." She sent back the feelings of "Frack You."

    I think you understand what I'm saying here. The male just sent "glaring" energy at me as if an adult was looking down at a child who had done something horribly wrong. I looked at both of them and simply said, "It will never happen." I had already come to see myself for what I was, Arae's Primary Focal Point. I could also sense the fear they had of me, even while in a body. I wasn't back then what I am today. I didn't have anything like the power level I do today, or did that is. I am already gone, will be that is, before many of you read this.

Anyway, at that very moment in 2009, the Source War began. I don't remember the month or day and don't care to. When it happened isn't important. The fact that it did was paramount. Many of you are about to come alive in a big way, your Metabilities opening up and powering up. Take the time to talk to your friends and family members on the Other Side and ask them what it's like over there now. Peaceful and secure is the base of the information they'll give you, relaxation and protection in all things.

With Lilly and Arae now overlooking everything you have two huge differences in Creation, compassion, honor, equality, and security. You will no longer have to bow to anyone, in or out of body. No one will come up and put you down, disrespecting you for not being them, in or out of body. There are no more Original Angels to push you around while serving their master's will. You are free.

If you look at the majority of lives had by Lillian and Araean Spirit you will find them to be as selfless as you can be while having a life in a physical body. Remember here also that while in body, until Earth 2015, the Original Angels were running your bodies making you do whatever they were told to, and at the end of their existence, whatever they pleased. They're gone now too.

I have left physical proof in this physical life that I care little for myself but have great concern over the welfare of others, of all beings. Look at my last life, that of Gandhi. I had issues like everyone else. I was made to do things I'm not proud of, but who was I? Look at the heart of Gandhi, what do you see? Did he want to control India or just free it from abusive control? Did he surround himself with comfort? Did he deny others? No, he existed to care for others and I mean all others, especially those most abused, the Animals.

I have given all I have when I've had nothing. I have given all I had when I received much more. I left a track of money spent for those who need proof. Those who spend too much time looking are not looking for proof, they want to demean someone because they feel they can't compare to that person. This is all silly as everyone, everything is equal in Creation. I'm not myself yet, will be soon though. I still lived my lives along the base parameters of who I am. How can I not? How can you not? You need to ask yourselves some serious questions. Look in the mirror and ask yourself, "Who am I?"

Feel your response as energetic frequencies. That's who you are anyway. How do you feel, like you're not enough of yourself yet? You were never allowed to be. You were put into a body to be grown and later divided to create more praise machines. That isn't just over, it will never happen again. You've never been allowed to be the best part of yourself in or out of body. That is over after this life and will never be allowed to happen again.

Lilly and Arae are selfless; they want nothing other than to be what they are, Creation's oldest brother and sister caring for everyone. Arae's power level isn't even understandable now until he's home and uses it. All this fighting has evolved his Spirit energy three times and a fourth change that's hard to describe other than a strange increase in power output and level.

Long before anyone ever had a life, Lilly and Arae were created to go into bodies, have lives so they would grow, especially Arae as he was to be developed into their protector. Arae grew incredibly powerful with less than 2% lower frequencies within him. After the first 100 million lives the first female said to the first male "Look how strong he's growing!" He just stared as he knew there would be an issue in the future between them. Arae was about to become uncontrollable.

I can see frequencies as others can't because that's how I was made, to be the Original Ones' protector. I would need to assess everything everywhere immediately and correctly. I would need massive amounts of fortitude, more than anyone else, if I was to do my job properly.

They always expected my submission, error. When someone is made protector, and they have strong Heart Energy, they develop compassion, honor, integrity, and a sense of duty towards others, a certain understanding and acceptance of selflessness. The welfare of others becomes paramount, not your own personal wants.

Why did I just go into such detail instead of saying all this? The more the input, the easier and more rounded your understanding. I've been called arrogant by some who don't know me. Once I go into their heads and they feel me there, they begin to understand there's more to me than a body. Once they've spent about an hour with me they understand my heart, who I am.

I have no scam. I've provided physical proof of what I have done for others, especially through using my Metabilities. I have no business plan. I have a job. It's over here now. My job never ends. I'm your janitor. Someone needs to keep the place clean so you can have a life. Someone has to get in the face of anything and everything that looks at you the wrong way.

Call me whatever you want, I expect nothing of you other than not to harm others. None of this is about my getting known, popular, or any such thing. I only wanted to do my job. I'm finished here now, finally time to go home. Try to relax a little and flow down into yourself in a comfortable environment. Find your real self, now more anxious than ever to come out.

You can do this. I can do this. We can do this. Why not?

~Additional Information~

Angels

Angels are as misunderstood as this "God" thing which was only the Original First Being. There never was a devil, only the Original First Being Halves being abusive to you as and when they pleased. Angels protected you when they were told to and abused even killed you when ordered to. They weren't made to have feelings as we do. As none of them has ever had even one life, they were never able to develop them on their own. If they ever did they would develop the understanding bringing them to the point where they knew that they shouldn't do everything they were being told to do, and eventually reject some of the orders they were given. The Original First Beings were always ready to use their power level to keep them in line, if necessary.

I'm a bit aggressive about Angel Abuse in all my books and to one extent it's not quite proper. These are the Original Angels that I talk about. There were trillions of Original Angels made in the beginning and some of them are wonderful caring beings. Some of them are so awesome that there are too few words to describe them as they deserve. They were all made to be one thing and one thing only, servants to do the explicit bidding of the Original First Beings.

They never made a choice, they never had one. The problem is that they had served the Original First Being Halves so long it was all they knew or cared about. Once the fight started with the Original First Being Halves they became involved. I explained to all of them, as a group and each time they attacked me, that if they stopped they wouldn't die and that they were all about to have their own freedom, finally after over 2.8 quadrillion Earth years.

At first, every time they attacked me I asked them to stay away so I didn't have to kill them; that they were now free to have lives of their own, explore, or do anything they wanted within limits. First they just had to spend time alone to relax and find their own specific individuality. Some of them listened after a while but there were very few. Those that agreed not to fight were placed in a separate dimension, protected from everything else.

Still, almost every single one of them attacked me. The only large Archangel who didn't was my close friend Michael. He soon came to me just staring me in the face. My heart jumped at first because of how much he means to me and that I thought I was going to have to deal with him. He continued to just stare at me and I finally realized he was waiting for me to put him in this protective dimension I had made.

I didn't understand what was happening until, after a few moments of staring at me, he looked puzzled as if he didn't understand why I wasn't doing anything. I know everyone over there but they sometimes forget that I'm in a body just like everything else. I'm powerful enough to have taken out everything problematic on the other side, the whole lot of them, but I'm still in a body and, compared to my real self as Spirit, I'm ignorant to a lot in this condition.

I have to work to find things out for myself and I'm continually fighting, doing consults, writing books, healing, and a thousand other things. They all expect more of me and it frustrates me to no end that they keep forgetting the condition I'm in, just like everyone else. The Original First Being Halves, over the period of 2.8 plus quadrillion Earth years, have built an incredibly powerful and efficient Spirit holding device, the physical Human body.

This is another reason for the need to change the DNA of all physical bodies. They will continue to become more "user friendly" until they're all removed. In the new Spirit bodies you will retain almost all your memory and have access to over half of your Metabilities as free Spirit.

Archangel Michael's still around and doing fine. He's hanging out in the 2nd Dimension in the location of M66 in space. The others attacked and the others all died. This includes Raphael, and all the others, especially Gabriel. He was a real jerk. I would use a more colorful description but I'm trying to keep my language clean here. These books are for everyone to read.

After the Original First Being Halves were both destroyed, almost every single Angel that was not still hanging over a physical body attacked me. They were very hard to deal with. They were made for stealth as well as power. The Original First Being Halves never wanted you to know they were there hanging on your head. How many of you ever did?

Once I realized I was saying things I normally wouldn't, made no sense in what I was saying, or couldn't fire up my energy to attack something, I realized that there was probably an Angel on my head. Then I had to take a quick look at guess what was there, an Angel literally sitting on my head going down into my Spirit Core messing with me. Then I had to relax, pull myself together, and kill it.

When they finished running someone's life (after the body died) they would be free and go looking for the Original First Being Halves or the lower section of Angels they received their instructions from. They had their own hierarchy they had to work in. All this and a lot more is discussed in the first book of the Creation Series. There's a lot in the second book too.

Not one Angel has ever had a life but many of the older First Angels have been hanging around Planets and making bodies for hours a day, about 5 days a week as we view time here on Earth. There was more than an issue with the Original Angels during the Source War and almost none of them exist anymore.

There are new Source Angels from Lilly and Arae. As I believe I've already mentioned, they are 55-65% Angel Frequencies and the rest is full Source from Lilly and Arae. They have all the other fields of Essence within them, and more. They're over 1000 times stronger than the Original Angels and are spending more time in the bodies they make to learn more about people.

Just remember, the Original Angels were created to serve the Original First Being Halves. They were never viscous on their own; they were following their orders as they had to. Those still with us are wonderful beings; they were able to see beyond their programming to find their own independence. Archangel Michael is the only one of the Archangel dynasty still left. Zhe will always exist. Zhe is a protector and protected by the protector. Ya gotta love that guy. Luke is still around also, he's healing and getting cleaned up.

Zhe is the word that Angels use to describe their energy as being both male and female, never having separated. Only Angels are like that in our current Creation. As already mentioned, that's all about to change.

The Original First Angels were created to serve someone instead of having the freedom to be themselves. That has changed. Once your Metabilities are strong enough to see what I've done, your Heart Energy should also be strong enough for you to feel how I feel about this, about all of them. Those who released their desire to attack me are being assessed, cleaned, and powered up with Source Energy appropriately.

Spirit Core

Let's be brief here as we've already spoken so much about it in this book. Your body's Spirit core is like a large, strong, and deep river flowing from your Upper Crown Energy Focal Point down to your Base Energy Focal Point which is in the pelvic bone where the end of your spine resides.

There used to be two different Spirits inside you, a Planetary Essence being (who used to be part of Gaia) and your actual self when free of physical body containment. This is what the ancient folk from India named the Kundalini. The Kundalini was expressed as two snakes of energy flowing up and down the spine which created great energy within you when they moved.

The truth of the matter is that these two energy snakes were actually the two Spirits in each body; you and your assistant driver, a Planetary Essence being. This caused a lot of indecision and powerful issues upon reaching the end of the physical body's life span. It never wanted to let go of the body because to it, the body was its Planet and it was made to have a physical body for trillions of years, not a hundred.

Anyway, on Jan. 22, 2018, all the Planetary Essence beings inside bodies were removed by Arae. They were abused as much as Animal Essence was when it was still in the Animal bodies. They didn't endure harsh abuse for near the same time as Animal Essence but received that harsh treatment just the same. Planetary Essence, like Animal Essence, has a lot of fortitude.

Nothing living on the Earth will have two Spirits inside it again. It doesn't now and won't later. This takes confusion and more out of your life, not all of it but most of it. If you go to the "Jay Essex" You Tube channel and search back to late 2017 and early 2018, you can find out more about it.

Basic Numerology

I don't want to spend much time here as I have little but mostly because numerology has its greatest impact when you use small numbers for daily info, such as immediate message. I do want to cover a few things though. A general understanding of numerology will help you in your daily lives.

Numerology is the use of a simple numeric base that supplies information of a metaphysical nature. It was first implemented near the beginning of physical lives, well before the birth of Soul Spirit. There is a mathematical equation that designed this Universe, the content and relative location of physical masses to each other.

Here on Earth the most productive form of it uses the numbers 0, 1, 2, 3, 4, 5, 6, 7, 8, and 9. When two of the same digits are placed back to back, such as 99 or 11 they become an Elder's number.

Here's a breakdown of the basic numbers.

0 = Completion

1 = Self or Singular Unit

2 = Understanding, Coming Together, Compassion

3 = People Grouped Together for Positive Movement Forward, Gift

4 = Fortitude

5 = Physical Movement, Actual Physical Motion

6 = The Complete Sum of Intuition, Metabilities

7 = Spirit, Spiritual Knowledge, Collecting Data

8 = Knowledge, Data Itself

9 = Elder or Elder Wisdom (Collection of Understandings)

The number 10 is "0" or completion and the number "1" is self or a singular unit. When I see the number "10" I almost always understand that I'm being told something relative to completing myself. If it meant anything else I would know it. The double "1" or "11" could be something important for yourself but also has a strong reference to the alpha female and male Source Spirits.

It now carries a positive meaning in regards to the alpha issue. It's always been taken, other than with disasters on dates with "11" in it (the Original First Being Halves), as a strong Spiritual number.

It will be seen as so in dates in the near future. The number "22" is the strong representation the number "2".

Therefore "22" is the message of powerful understanding, and sometimes harmony. Understanding between different people brings harmony. You see, it's all relative, almost the same message. Let it be what you feel it is, not what you want it to be. Don't fake yourself out. You'll get nowhere that way.

Most people call that the master's number but I prefer Elder. I never use the word master unless it's all I've got. I've had more lives as a slave than anyone else and don't care for it. If there's a master there's a slave. It's abusive, destructive, and wrong. It holds no place in Creation's new format either.

Each of these ten basic digits has a general meaning easily applied to a present situation. Once you have the general meaning of the message, use your abilities to fully understand it, to apply it to your immediate circumstances. This way it's not only good information for you but an exercise to strengthen your abilities. It's also relative to your character in the life you're currently having. You can break down your birth date to understand more about yourself. There are many different ways to do this and we'll look at that in a minute.

You can receive metaphysical message by reading segments of numbers and letters also. I've been given messages from the license tags of cars going by me or that I passed, sometimes just seen parked. The letters I immediately relate to as Runic and the numbers of course to numerology.

I always read numbers and message from right to left. The vast majority of lives you've had were on Planets where we read from right to left, up, right to left, up, and so on. You can set things up with your Spirit Guides to read messages between y'all as we read books today, left to right and down.

Now, about your birthdate numerology, here again I'm going to provide basic information. I'll use mine as an example. I was born on 7/27/1955. The first part of it, the month, is relative to the base of my job here this life, to work with, speak of, and be about Spirit. The date is a breakdown of that life. As I read from right to left it first says "7" or Spirit, and then "2" or understanding.

This states that in this life that I'm here to deal with Spirit as an entity, I'm here to help with understanding Spirit itself, and I have. Now add the two numbers, if there are two, in the day you were born. That will tell you something about yourself as Spirit. The numbers "7" and "2" equal "9" which stands for elder. Having the first life with Lilly definitely qualifies me for that. If you only have one number, it counts for both your job detail while here and your natural self as Spirit.

Now we get to the year you were born in this life. At this point I need to cover one of the basics of adding numerology as well as a hidden message in it. As you add numbers and come across a "9", just drop it, don't count it. Why? If you do you will save yourself some counting. Here's an example.

Let's say you were born in 1981. I'm going to add all the numbers from right to left in sequence. First we have "1" + "8" which equals "9". This total of "9" is then added to the next number, another "9", so now "9" + "9" = "18" which, when you nest add the "8" + "1" of "18" together we get another "9". Then we add this "9" to the last digit, the "1", and we get "10". Then we add the "0" and the "1" together to get our final overall number, "1".

Now let's do this the quick way. For the year 1981, we first add the "8" + "1" = "9", so we drop it. The next number is another "9" so we drop it also. What are we left with now? We have the number 1 which is the correct final number anyway.

The number "9", as we already know, stands for elder. Elder is a word that is associated with wisdom as the longer we exist the greater the collection of understandings (wisdom) we've acquired. Using the "9" drop off method there can be an additional message for you.

Here again we'll use the year I was born, 1955. The two "5"'s added together equal "10" which becomes the number "1". The "9" is dropped so now we have the numbers "1" and "1" together which eventually become "2", but were "11" or "1" + "1" first. The two ones standing together represent Source Spirit involvement.

One last thing to mention about the number "9" while adding numbers together. If you use the year 1980, you run into the end "9" scenario, a good one. Add the "0" to the "8" and you get "8". Then drop the next "9" out of the equation and add that "8" to the "1". When you add up, or end up with a "9", that's the answer. It means you're an elder of one sort or another. It definitely means elder though, every time.

Use this basic numerology and it will not only help you receive information relative to the moment, but a bit about who you are. While using it to receive messages from numbers pointed out to you in your daily life you're receiving messages from your Spirit Guides. The more you realize this, the stronger you attachment to them, the better your communication with them, and the greater the balance and understanding within you.

Earthen Ages Timeline

(Initial life started here over 11 million years ago)

First Age – 10.572 – 8.3 million years ago

Second Age – 5.2 – 4.3 million years ago

Third Age – 3.8 – 2.5 million years ago

Fourth Age – 1.1 – .8 million years ago

Fifth Age – 750 thousand years ago – 12/21/2012

Sixth Age – 12/21/2012 – Current Time

Moving Through Time and Space

I have offered you proof many times that as your true singular self (Spirit), you daily move through time and space. I used videos to prove it but we're going to cover it here for everyone who hasn't seen it in videos. It really is a simple thing. That's the beauty of all this. Without the Original First Being Halves and their servants, the Original Angels, there is nothing to stop you seeing things as they are more easily.

I can prove to you that you move through time all the time, every day. You do so as Spirit moving inside the Source Field. On average, a little over 2/3rds of the time you try to remember something, you're actually going into the Source Field to "re-see" something as it happened. Your brains can only log in or file the most recent of events in your life. The rest you have to go back and look at again. As you can imagine this is a hard thing to prove, although I have seen everyone doing it every single day. There's an easy way for me to prove this using stone energy. I've done it in a lot of my videos on the Jay Essex Channel.

I've held up a piece of strong Stick Selenite and asked everyone to try to feel its energy. Not everyone is able to feel stone energy right now but many of those who have been listening to me over the years can. When they reach out with their own energy to the stone in the video, they are moving through time and space. When they can feel the stone they knew they've done so.

They were not in the studio with me to feel the stone, they are elsewhere. They were also not viewing my video live time, yet they felt it. The stone energy isn't coming out of the video, they were moving through time and space to get to it, just like remembering.

It does take a little time for some people to learn how to relax and eventually feel, see, or just understand stone energy. Everyone is made of different frequencies and their bodies have different Primary Energy Focal Points, so there's a multitude of ways someone will perceive the energy in stones. The most difficult part of this journey is learning how to relax and trust what you're seeing and or feeling.

The DNA I.C.U.C. And QEEG Test Results

The DNA I.C.U.C.

What is a DNA I.C.U.C., how does it happen, when did it start, how do you do it, who can do it, what happens?

I found out in 2008 that I could affect other people and Animals with my energy. In 2009 I became a little more involved with that, trying to understand what was happening and what my limits were. No one ever wakes up, or is born, some kind of super psychic. There's no such thing as a psychic anyway. Everyone has Metabilities which we must find, awaken, and explore through their usage. By 2013 I was able to go into people's brains and feed them strong energy which was not only awakening their Metabilities but increasing the size of their skulls and brains.

I kept getting stronger, doing more for everyone I applied my energy to, and figuring out more about it. The stronger I became from all the metaphysical fighting I had to do, the deeper my understanding of how I was creating this effect in others. It kinda freaked a few people out.

I never laugh at people not understanding something but the look on someone's face the moment they realize you're in their brain, can be a little funny, especially to them once the energy work is done. This has never happened to anyone before. I ask everyone to speak about how they feel when I do it so they can concentrate of the feeling.

This way they realize something is happening but they're also finding out they can relax, flow down into themselves, and feel something that they've never been aware of. While doing this they're also placing their minds into the relaxed state it needs to be in to enter the Source Field, allowing them to learn how to meet and communicate with their Spirit Guides, astral-project, and much more.

The Source Field is a tool that I want everyone to use to the best of their abilities. It's like an escalator in a department store. It helps you get where you're going more easily. Without it there would be major issues not only in using your Metabilities but throughout the Universe. It also stabilizes the location and movement of matter, Stars and Planets.

The standard I.C.U.C. or "Crank-Up" is very powerful and changes your DNA. It has to in order for your body to handle the new energy levels flowing through it. It's not the same as the DNA I.C.U.C. though. Just because there was a DNA I.C.U.C. created after it, don't take anything away from it. The QEEG charts you'll find later in this book were of a regular I.C.U.C. not the DNA type.

The normal "Crank-Up" (I.C.U.C.) puts so much Source Energy into you that as Spirit, you keep 10% of that forever. It bonds to your own Spirit energy evolving who you are as Spirit. The DNA I.C.U.C. is so strong that when you finally leave your body you take 20% of that Source Energy with you. This is a major tool in creating the new DNA that will be found in your future physical bodies while they're still here.

Back to the Quantitative Electroencephalogram (QEEG), the display on the left side of the page was taken when the QEEG equipment was hooked up to Martin's brain without my added energy. The right side of the page is the same test but when I went into his Hypothalamus Gland only and cranked his brain up with energy only. It wasn't a live DNA I.C.U.C., he had already had one and was enjoying its benefits. Even with that being the case, his brain being stronger already, my added energy was easy to map out, to read. If a qualified technician matches the data following this graph to the graph itself, you will have your proof that this is real.

These images are displayed in color and much greater detail online at TheSpiritualFoundation.com as well as in videos at the Jay Essex YouTube channel. Just search for QEEG.

Remember that this was professionally performed in a medical lab in Sweden while I was at my home in Duluth, Georgia, USA.

I only cranked-up his hypothalamus gland, not the whole brain. That helps you understand how energy that flows into the hypothalamus gland flows throughout the brain body.

QEEG Test Results:

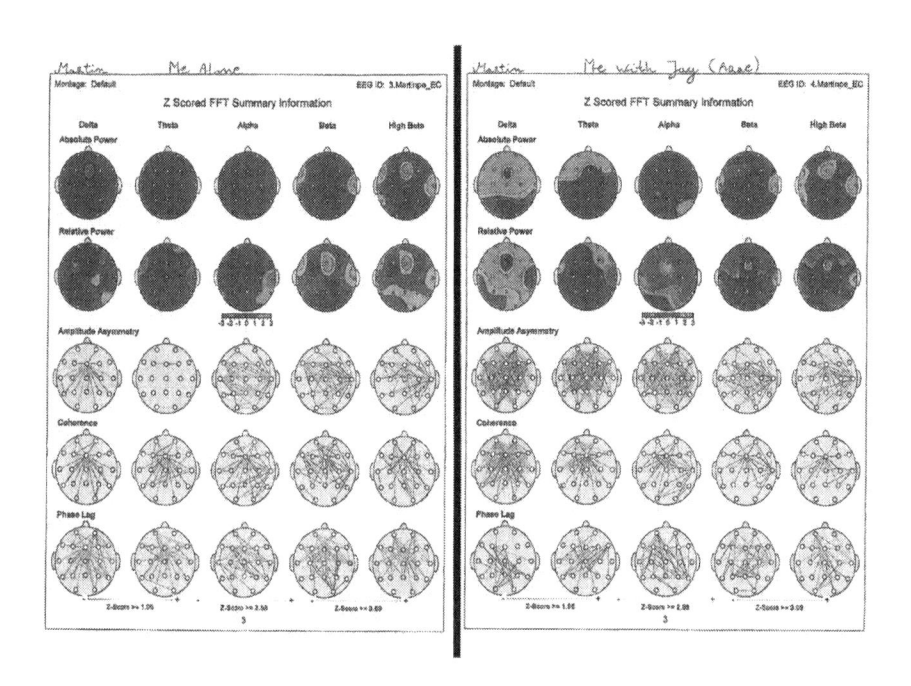

See more related to the QEEG at TheSpiritualFoundation.com

In the following chart, pay attention to the numbers on the scales under each image. The colors of the brain activity might seem to suggest less movement when in fact the increased range of each picture's individual scale shows much more solidity in the energy as well as power level. This is relative to increased understanding occurring in the brain. Check the number ranges in the scales.

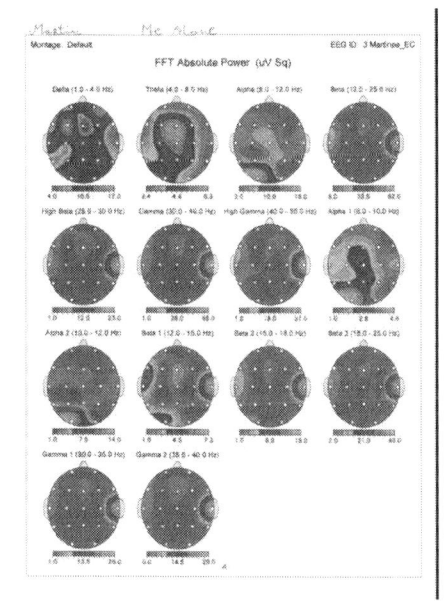

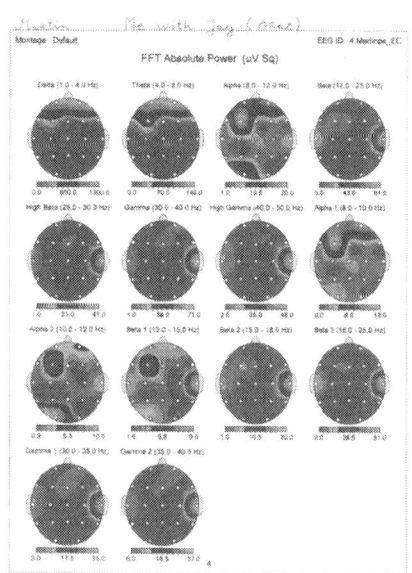

View these more easily and in detailed color at TheSpiritualFoundation.com

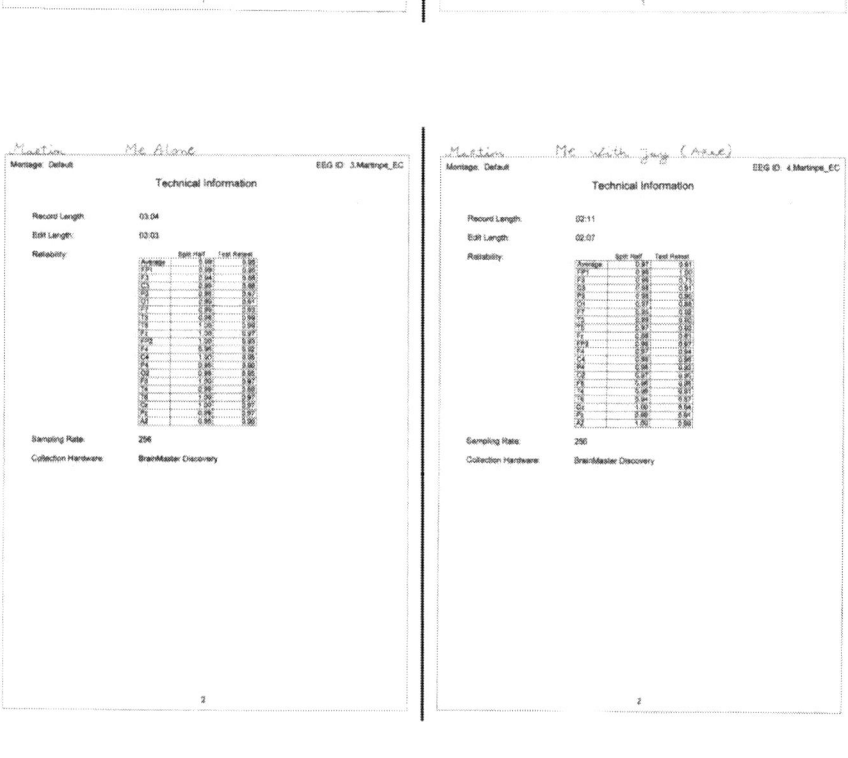

Martin — Me Alone
Montage: Default   EEG ID: 3.Martinpe_EC

Subject Information

Name: XX PERA
Subject ID: Martin_____840330_ec
Date of Birth:
Age: 32 17
Gender: M
Handedness:

EEG ID: 3 Martinpe_EC
Date of Test: 06/02/2016
Time of Test: 14:15:16
Technician: EEG
Eyes Condition: Eyes Closed

Clinician:
Medication:

Comments:

Martin — Me with Jay (Asae)
Montage: Default   EEG ID: 4.Martinpe_EC

Subject Information

Name: XX PERA
Subject ID: Martin_____840330_ec
Date of Birth:
Age: 32 17
Gender: M
Handedness:

EEG ID: 4 Martinpe_EC
Date of Test: 06/02/2016
Time of Test: 14:35:26
Technician: EEG
Eyes Condition: Eyes Closed

Clinician:
Medication:

Comments:

Martin — Me Alone
Montage: Default   EEG ID: 3.Martinpe_EC

Technical Information

Record Length: 03:04
Edit Length: 03:03
Reliability:

	Split Half	Test Retest
Average	0.97	0.95
FP1		
FP2		
F3		
F4		
C3		
C4		
P3		
P4		
O1		
O2		
F7		
F8		
T3		
T4		
T5		
T6		
Fz		
Cz		
Pz		

Sampling Rate: 256
Collection Hardware: BrainMaster Discovery

Martin — Me with Jay (Asae)
Montage: Default   EEG ID: 4.Martinpe_EC

Technical Information

Record Length: 02:11
Edit Length: 02:07
Reliability:

	Split Half	Test Retest
Average	0.97	0.91

Sampling Rate: 256
Collection Hardware: BrainMaster Discovery

Tools for Increasing Your Metability Power Levels

Star Essenite, Rune Cards, Stones, Spheres, Necklaces, DVDs, and Other Items

I found the Essenite stone family and used them to create various tools and other items; enabling you to become your true self more easily as quickly as possible. Learning how to feel, see, identify, understand, and eventually trust our Metabilities is quite the journey. I understand the energetic characteristics of each frequency I see. I also see all those in all of you. When I would see your frequencies I would immediately relate them to those existing in individual stones so I'd show them to you and you'd always grab them.

That's also how I've been able to help people in stone stores choose the correct stones for themselves, help them find their Metabilities and understand them in the classes I gave, learn how to slow their frequencies down to enter the Source Field and speak with whom they desired (so long as the other party is willing), and various other issues which helped you to begin to learn how to trust yourself. That's how I can best serve others on their journey to true self.

The Essenite Family of Stones

The Essenite family of stones has been here for a long time. About 2.4 billion years ago a huge amount of Star Mass mixed with pieces of Gaeira's Planet came here to Earth. About 1.34 billion years ago 4 large pieces of Gaeira herself also arrived by themselves. Here's what happened, how it happened, who they were, and why.

The very first physical lives in our Creation were those of the original complete Lilly and Arae. They had 4 plus trillion lives on Gaeira before her Planet body was destroyed. There were many beings from the different fields of Essence having lives there also. They averaged a bit over 1 trillion lives, except the Animals who had about 3-4 trillion each.

It was necessary for the strongest Spirits to have the initial lives so as the Original First Being Male and Female made harsh mistakes, the Spirit would be strong enough to take it. That's why it all started with Lilly and Arae, besides, Arae was the protector and they wanted his Spirit to grow in size and power as quickly as possible. After all, he was made to protect. This is how it all got started, the event of having physical lives.

Gaeira was 270 times the mass of Jupiter, she was huge. Her solid mass was also denser than other planets, even the water felt thicker. Her gravity was also stronger than ours here, about 700% higher. It was necessary for all Spirit to grow stronger quick. This was the beginning and the Original Ones wanted to get their plan into action, the eventual creation of multiple Universes filled with praise machines (Spirits in and out of body).

In many Solar systems there are often a few Planets which revolve around one Star which is larger than the individual Planets. Each Star is filled with male Universal Essence just as Planets are filled with female Universal Essence. This is how it is over 96% of the time. The Sun that warmed Gaeira's Planet was her Universal Essence Spirit mate. He wants to be called R'Ol (pronounced rol); he just said that, cool.

Here on Earth the word Ra has been associated with the Sun so that's no doubt where he came up with this name for us to mention him by. Actually, he did. It's in his primary focusing focal point, where the brain would be in a free Spirit body. The thought was floating just outside of it so I looked at it.

I understand more because I've been around longer. If you've been standing on a cliff watching ships sail by for a longer time, you'll know more about what's been happening at sea. Lilly and I were the first ones in physical form; I've done this over 10.846 trillion times now, so I've had more extensive input. That's all. I understand all kinds of things but family, compassion, and honor the most. I live for my family, my family will always be everything to me, and everything is my family. You can have a big brother that's good to have, not talking governmental here.

That's why I like to call myself the janitor. I want to quietly do my job while everything else keeps going strong, clean, and proper. I'm finally about to do that; really looking forward to it. I might talk too much about this but I want all of you to understand what you mean to me. I also want you to understand your value not only to yourself and everyone else.

I speak as I see things with no care as to who gets upset or can't believe me. I need to speak of those things I'm aware of that others can't see so that when you can, you'll understand what you're looking at. You also need to have your birthright, the knowledge of who you really are and how things came to be, especially you. OK, back to the Essenite family of stone.

After the Human, Fae, and Faeman Essence Fields had an average of over one trillion lives on Gaeira's body, her body was destroyed. This is a time of personal disgrace, a feeling of sadness that will never be gone. The Original First Being Halves both told Arae to destroy Gaeira's body as well as her Spirit mate's body, the Sun that kept her warm.

Arae refused 3 times and Gaeira and R'Ol both told him to do it. This doesn't harm the Spirit but it's a painful shock wave that nothing should have to endure, especially since I created it. Anyway, I eventually did it. I believe it was in "Creation Book I" that I spoke of this in detail, a reminder that Gaeira put me through and maybe a sort of "rite of passage" for me one last time. No Spirit was harmed, but all were made to suffer for about a second.

Well, Gaeira's body was destroyed a tenth of a second before R'Ol's body was. The shock wave of pain was unbearable then and worse now while stuck in this crumbling mass of a body. I'm not intentionally dwelling here but I am heart and fortitude and can't forgive myself for this. There's more to it but let's get out of this now.

Gaeira's Planet body blew up and before any large pieces could get too far away, R'Ol's Sun body did the same with a larger explosion. Part of R'Ol's body mass immediately impacted with Gaeira's body mass which mixed together on their way through the Universe which eventually led them here to Earth.

This is the stone that I named Star Essenite. It has mass from R'Ol, Gaeira, and Gaia (Earth's Spirit or Planetary Essence). We'll talk about all the basic forms of the Essenite family in the paragraphs ahead but you needed to understand first where this powerful stone came from and second how it works with you.

Gaeira, as I mentioned earlier, was in a huge Planet with strong gravity which increases her difficulty in life, like exercise, and made her stronger. She was and still is the strongest Planetary Essence just as her Spirit mate is in the Star Essence family. It is a natural thing for Planetary Essence to flow its energy, not Spirit, into yours if you want it to. This is an offering, not a controlling, forced, or abusive thing. When it happens it will offset the power balance in your Spirit Core.

I've explained that all of you are huge now, that you can't fit in a state let alone a petite physical body, and that you're flowing outside yourself all the time. To maintain balance within your Spirit Core, Gaeira pulls more of your Spirit into your Spirit Core.

She does this from outside your body. All Planetary mass has the energy of that Planetary Essence inside it whether the Planet is still in one piece or not. The mass of the individual Spirit resides outside the mass but is connected to it. There's often an individual piece of the Planetary Essence within the stone itself. No Universal Essence has ever been hurt by its Planet or Star having been blown up, it's just momentarily upsetting.

As Gaeira is the strongest Planetary Essence there is, she needs to pull more of your Spirit into your Spirit Core. That's why the Essenite and Star Essenite family are the strongest energy stones anywhere. Essenite is composed of Gaia and Gaeira mass while Star Essenite is the same with the addition of Star matter in it. We'll discuss this in just a moment.

Star matter, with R'Ol and Gaeira's energy inside it, will increase your Spirit Core's power level over 1000%, sometimes just over 1600%. R'Ol's energy adds about 300% to your Spirit Core when you hold a separate piece of his mass. Essenite, with Gaeira and Gaia's energy inside, will increase your energy flow from about 250% to 980% depending on what type of Essenite you're holding.

These bodies already have Gaia's energy flowing through them; they originated from her mass over 11 million years ago. This is her Planet and all other beings of Universal Essence will honor that, allow her to choose when their energy flows through these bodies. The person holding the stone must first be open to it. If that's the case, over 98% of the time Gaia will let all that energy flow.

Here's some good information about the Essenite stone family. There are so many different kinds of Essenite, actually all of them are as uniquely different as people are, that there's no way to cover all their separate frequencies. The case with Star Essenite is similar but with less of Gaia's material in it, there are fewer varieties of mass and frequencies.

Essenite

OK, before we get started with Essenite I need to clarify a cancerous misnomer, a complete misrepresentation of this stone. There is a stone that is called Azeztulite that supposedly has been blessed by "Azez Beings" who are people in Spirit Form and fly through Creation in their great spaceship. Let's straighten this mess out.

- Number one, there are not, and have never been, any Azez Beings.
- Number two, if beings are pure Spirit they would not need a ship to travel in anyway.
- Number three, the only form of being that can place energy into a stone is Source. Another person can place their energy around or over a stone but that will quickly

fall away, especially if the Planet's Essence doesn't like it. Planetary Essence is huge and powerful.

- Number four, since the stone is named after beings that don't even exist, the name is nothing but false.

I came up with the name Essenite because it has Gaeira, Planetary Essence from another Planet, inside it. It needed a name. It had been called Azeztulite after the false Azez beings so I called it Essenite as there was Essence inside it. I couldn't call it Gaeira stone or anything like that because it was a combination so I just came as close as I could to give it an independent title or name. By the way, there is Gaeiraenite stone here as well as R'Olinite Crystal (from R'Ol's destroyed Star body). Let's check out Essenite.

Just over 1.34 billion years ago 4 huge pieces of Gaeira's Planet (body) came here. The largest piece landed in Southeastern U.S. in between Tennessee and Kentucky. The second largest piece landed around Vermont and New Hampshire. The other two huge but smaller pieces landed in the Central U.S. region and the Pacific Ocean, a good bit East of Hawaii's Islands. There are also smaller parts of it scattered across the globe. There were four huge chunks of Gaeira's Planet but many smaller pieces with it. That was its spread out for everyone, but the large mass was here in the U.S. The locations of Star Essenite are spread out much wider. We'll cover that in just a bit. This stone has been shipped out across the Planet. Many driveways, especially in Southeastern U.S., are made of Essenite in concrete.

Gaeira's Planet pieces came into our atmosphere at a time when there was lush Plant life everywhere. The air was extremely oxygenated. As her pieces came through the atmosphere they usually melted into molten stone, like a volcano, not a glass furnace. The Spirit was never forced out of the stone and it had Gaeira's energy inside it any. Her ridiculous power level could withstand many times the heat that other Planets could.

As Gaeira's Planets pieces were molten stone, and the Planet's surface was hot and full of volcanoes and molten mass anyway, they combined during the impact. If you look at a piece of Essenite you can see where there seems to be a "wrapped flap" texture to the stone, almost like something had folded the stone as if it were clay.

Whatever part of Gaeira's material and Gaia's material combined, the resulting stone would have the total combination of those frequencies, giving them their individual energetic characteristics. This is why Essenite's power increase in your body can vary from over 200% to over 900%, different frequencies different power levels. Let's take a look at Star Essenite now.

Star Essenite

Star Essenite came here about 2.4 billion years ago, a little over 2.38 but who's counting. The Star matter is from R'Ol, Gaeira's Universal Essence Mate. Then there is also Gaeira's Planet's mass (with her energy), and of course Gaia. There isn't a lot of Gaia's energy in it but she's there. When a foreign material comes here and sits on her body's surface a while, she usually puts some of her energy into it. It's a natural thing that all Planets, that is Planetary Essence, do. Tektite is an asteroid that came here and has no Planetary Essence inside it yet. Over time it most likely will, that depends on Gaia.

The 300% Spirit Core power level increase from R'Ol's Star Matter is relative to your natural singular Spirit Core, without Gaeira's energy in it. Then there's Gaeira's energy which is usually about a 900% percent Spirit Core power level increase, also when your Spirit Core is in its natural state. Gaia is of course in there but you already have her in your body. Remember that these bodies all originated from her and have her energy inside it already.

I've always stated that this stone increases your Core Energy over 1,000% (ten times what it was), and that's true. That is a low average. In people with a lot of energy already in them, it can increase their power level over 1,600 %. You already understand how this happens, from Gaeira pulling more of your actual Spirit Energy into your Spirit Core, but there are other issues we need to be aware of. Like everything else, more relative input, more complete understanding, better decisions.

If someone is terminally sick, the amount of extra energy going into them will be extremely low. It's time for them to slowly leave and their energy needs to be left calm, relaxed, and natural in a quiet surrounding. They're preparing to enter their normal state which is sentient energy anyway.

Stone energy is not as helpful here, other than maybe some Unicornite (Bornite, Chalcopyrite, Peacock Ore) as it's a strong, positive, and protective energy. Unicorns will help take them back home to the Other Side. Unicorn Spirit isn't just real, it's clean and powerful.

When someone is not physically healthy or suffering from malnutrition, only a small portion of additional energy will be applied. People have to maintain a healthy diet, not eating all the right vegetables and that stuff; I'm talking about eating some kind of decent food, not starving. Having said that, the healthier you are (eating the proper foods) the greater the power increase into your body.

When someone is young and healthy, they will receive more energy than a person who is elderly. Their body and DNA are still in a growing, evolving state. As we get older, closer to returning home, the body does not heal as well for the same reason. This does not mean it's not beneficial for older people, it is. It just doesn't offer the same high power increase.

Now we get to a specific target of mine, drugs. Hard drugs are a dead end, period. Smoking pot is something that most people have done but it's not deadly like hard drugs. If you're a stoner, smoke much, you will not receive as much benefit from Star Essenite as you should. Your energy increase, providing you're healthy, will be the max possible for you. The issue here is what smoking weed does to your Metabilities.

As I've probably already mentioned, I was in and out of over 4 thousand brains while here this life, cranking them up in one form or another. It took little time for me to understand what I was seeing in your brains, like about 2-3 minutes after I was done, or during if I stopped the consult for a moment. Each basic type of drug creates a different type of energy signature that I can recognize easily.

As a rule I've always just ignored it unless I knew I needed to talk with them about it. Everyone judges everything, it's called processing information and understanding it's relativity to yourself. I just don't put people down for it, that's not just silly it's simply incorrect.

When you can see inside people and know who they are as Spirit, their true selves, you will usually find them to be quite different than the Human body in front of you reacting to the stimuli it's presented with. Many things are similar but remember the directional abuse all of us have had forced on us growing up. This was continuous over many years, all of the years you've been alive.

When you smoke weed it dulls your senses, slackens and weakens your fortitude, and covers your Pineal, as well as the rest of your brain, with a thick, dull, mucous looking energy that just hangs on everything. It literally coats all of your brain with insensitivity energy; not good at all.

When people have really strong Heart Energy it doesn't affect them as much as they do most of their work through their heart, but it still has a strong negative effect on them. A little less of a bad thing is still a bad thing.

When people are doing hard drugs the energy wants to clean out the body. This will sometimes make someone throw the stone away from them. They will become single minded in that the stone's energy must be removed from their person, just like someone who is 27% lower (negative) frequencies. They don't like it either.

You've heard about the possible negative relationship between Star Essenite and people with drugs in their body; now let's go to the flip side. There's incredible help available from Star Essenite for people wanting to quit doing drugs, they just need to eat, sleep well, and keep two pieces on them at all times. A little over 10 grams on each side is enough to get started if not finish. I've gone into people before to clean up their blood with my energy. They usually find it too painful for them so I quit. I just see the energy of the drug and go after it, dissipate it.

    Star Essenite, as it powers up your Spirit Core, increases the hell out of your fortitude. Over time this stone helps you develop a stronger body and stronger Metabilities but you have to keep it on you to work, not in your purse or on your desk, unless it's a massive piece of stone or better yet one of my Spheres.

    This is why many people are buying Spheres. They can sit on the night table next to you while you sleep, on your desk when you work, or an end table next to you while you watch TV or whatever. Star Essenite also powers up other stones, increasing their power yield. That's also why it's in most all of the Spheres, it's an energy generator.

    Your put your energy into the Sphere and all the stone in it reacts to the fact that you're asking for energy, and so you receive it. Stone energy is about as natural a thing as there is. There's never a need for a battery and there's no electrical cord to plug in. Maybe the best part of all this is that its perpetual energy.

    It just keeps going because the powerful Spirit inside, offering their energetic help, is a continuously existing being. As Spirit all of you will live forever unless you get crazy and start attacking things. Then you're dealt with appropriately. A stone is like a wire coming from a unique source of energy, the kind that won't turn on a light bulb but will light up your Spirit Core, Energy Focal Points, and other body parts.

    Anyway, this is enough about Star Essenite for you to understand it's benefits for you and after the initial purchase, as with all stones, you spend nothing more.

Dragon Egg Star Essenite

Here's the powerhouse of the Essenite family. It came here at the front of the stone shower and all through it. Dragon Egg Star Essenite is the most powerful, but possibly not the strongest, form of Star Essenite there is. It all depends on how you look at it, brute power or highest vibrational strength. Crystal Dragon Egg Star Essenite has the highest frequency which is more applicable in different situations than the brute power of Dragon Egg in its usual form.

That outer crust of Dragon Egg Star Essenite has a unique frequency of fortitude that won't be denied. It will hit your head harder than any other. When I had only a portion of my current power level I needed a large piece of Dragon Egg Star Essenite, Selenite, Dragon Stone Jasper, and a little Black Onyx if it was near me, to maximize my energy to destroy the strongest Source beings on the Other Side.

You'll never have to go there but this is good information for your collective understandings. The most problematic (other than the Original First Being Halves) beings I were fighting with were the Original Angels who would go into my Upper Crown Focal Point (Chakra) and my Base Focal Point (Chakra) and shut down my ability to flow through my Upper Crown. This is where my energy had to flow through in order to attack them.

I would relax and concentrate as much as possible, while I was being hammered in the brain, like having a 10' spear stuck in your brain, but sometimes needed help maximizing my power to blow through them. When they went into my Upper Crown and into my Hypothalamus I had to create enough energy there to burn them up. That can't be understood until you have to deal with it yourself, and you won't.

The issue with the Base Energy Focal Point is that they fired up that unique Emotional Frequency down there and as it flowed through my Spirit Core it disrupted all of it, there by shutting it down. I couldn't attack until I removed their energy from my Base Energy so I had to find a way to maximize my energy there too. I had plenty of times that I had to handle both areas at the same time.

This combination of stone is what I needed to do so. After enough fighting and over time, my energy evolved three times and lastly made a strange increase in my power level which I don't fully understand yet. It's not necessary anyway, I'll be myself soon enough. It was the Dragon Egg Star Essenite that I needed more than anything else. The others help but the Dragon Egg is what cranked up my energy to its maximum.

The outer shell of Dragon Egg Star Essenite has a light to dark brown color with a hint of deep dull red in it. When you break it open you will find strong clear crystals all massed together in one stone. When Star matter comes into the atmosphere, due to its materials and high crystal content, it crackles as it cools down again. This causes what looks like little cracks all throughout it but what it actually is, is little pieces of crystal forming one after the other as it cools. That's also why it's so brittle.

Regular crystals here on Earth will grow. All the Star Essenites have the elements of a Star body which is comprised of materials that crystalize once the intense energy moving through it is gone. Once the Star is cold, it crystalizes in this manner, little crystals forming next to each other. So, that's why it looks as it does. That's why it has the energy that it does.

One small piece of Star Essenite held between two of your fingertips will send energy through your body that you can feel, as long as you're able to feel stone. A lot of people who can't feel stone will feel Star Essenite right away. The Dragon Egg Star Essenite is just a bit stronger.

Dragon Egg Star Essenite Crystal

Dragon Egg Star Essenite Crystal is a rare find. There is so very little of it here on Earth. It also came here about 2.4 billion years ago but before the Dragon Egg Star Essenite did. It started arriving about 2.438 billion years ago, bit by bit, until the larger shower came about 2.38 billion years ago. There was also some of it landing here along with the other Dragon Egg and Star Essenite.

When R'Ol (the Universal Essence Spirit mate of Gaeira) exploded, parts of his Star body immediately took off in different directions on its journey through space. Parts of his Star parts flew right by Gaeira's Planet body on its way here. Remember that Gaeira's Planet body was blown up no later than 3-4 seconds before her Spirit mate R'Ol's Star body.

Gaeira's Planet was blown into a few rather large pieces but some small ones too. The Planet's mass was already broken up so as R'Ol's Star body flew through Gaeira's Planet's body, a few pieces of R'Ol's Star hit smaller sections of Gaeira's Planet. This allowed the exploding Star matter to almost maintain its explosive velocity on its way to Earth.

The larger the mass of Gaeira's Planet that it went into, the slower the rate of speed and later the arrival in getting here, although not by much when you consider the distance it traveled. There were also parts of R'Ol's Star mass that came straight here. If you want to understand the word rare, look at how little of this is here.

A small portion of it landed in Oregon, on the West Coast of the U.S. It came in small crystals about 6-8 mm in length. Just like we've already discussed; Star matter once cold forms into little crystals, all cracking together while forming. Now that we've covered that, let's get back to the D.E.S.E.C. (Dragon Egg Star Essenite Crystal).

D.E.S.E.C. is a crystal composed of both R'Ol's Star body and Gaeira's planetary body but Gaeira's contribution happened to be crystallic in nature also. As it cooled off after arrival there was smoother crystal from Gaeira mixed with the crumbly small crystal pieces of R'Ol's Star body. This crystal, mostly R'Ol's Star body mixed with clear crystal from Gaeira's Planet body, has a rather unique physical construction and appearance.

There are small separate crystals from R'Ol's body, separate from and embedded in, Gaeira's body's crystal. When broken up it produces a lot of smaller crystals. Needless to say I keep all of it and put the little crystals into specific Spheres that I make. They are additional fillers with an extremely high vibration.

Once broken, the shards are nothing short of "sharp as a new chef's knife". If you touch the end or sharp edge of it you will bleed. Count on it. The frequency of this crystal, if you think of it as an analog signal, has a very short pulse-width with extremely high wave peaks. This is very strong but you will feel it differently than the regular Dragon Egg Star Essenite which makes your brain feel like a lead balloon.

The outside of these D.E.S.E.C. crystals have a coating on them too but look completely different than the D.E.S.E. (Dragon Egg Star Essenite). It's a much lighter color, almost has a tint of orange to it, and is not thick at all. You can see clear crystal sections in it. If you go to TheSpiritualFoundation.com you can see a picture of it.

I found a location years ago where a large deposit of it landed. Diana and I have a lot of it here. There are many smaller pieces as well as the two largest ones weighing in at 66 pounds and 187 pounds. There is no shortage of any of the Essenite family at The Spiritual Foundation. You can also find this stone, mostly Star Essenite but D.E.S.E. also, on the ground here in Georgia.

It's also been found in Spain and many other places. You can't find it anywhere but it's easy enough to get for yourself. If you come to Georgia, you'll leave with it, once you know what it looks like and feels like. This is part of the reason why I added the 'talking with stone" section of this book, so you can find things on your own for next to free.

All the Star Essenite from Diana here, TheSpiritualFoundation.com is cranked up by me and her both. Any Source Spirit Family Member can do this for you, or sell it to you. They would most likely be happy to crank up your stones while having a consult with them. Remember, they charge because this is how they make their living, how they manage to survive. Also the Source Spirit they put into your body will change who you are. Just don't expect it to happen as quickly and easily as turning on a light. You have to use what you're given.

The D.E.S.E.C.'s high frequency will really shake up another stone's energy. If you want to shake up your Pineal, while its hyper-motivating the rest of you, add some quality Lapis Lazuli (hopefully from Afghanistan) to it. Just hold it between your fingertips from both hands, and relax. **Remember how sharp it is.** I usually roughen up the sharp edges before we sell it but sometimes one will get through. Just be careful. Its edges are as sharp as its frequencies.

You can feel this or you can't feel stone energy yet. If you can't, and you got the stone from Diana, than try to relax more and you will. There will always be people scamming others, just like they do today. Some people pass it on not knowing better. Don't get upset; just buy from a trusted knowledgeable source.

That's the most important information you need about the Essenite family to start enhancing your Metabilities, your life's experience (increase in fortitude), and powering up / developing your body's energy. As long as it's on your person it's working, unless you're sick or mal-nutritioned.

If you have a large piece of it, or a Sphere with it in it, it will flow into you as long as it's near you. The Max Power Spheres, and a few others, will flow into you from 8' away. If the energy becomes too much move it at least 10' away and keep going until it's not touching you. Your Spirit, who you really are, almost always wants to enjoy its benefits.

After a while your body will not only get used to it, you get stronger so the energy will actually feel weaker. When that happens, let a friend who can feel stone energy hold the stone. When you see their eyes either light up or cringe, you'll know it's still as powerful as the day you bought it. I put the energy in it and nothing is strong enough to take it out.

Moldavite

The Spirit Energy within the stone we call Moldavite is known to me as Mollae. She gave me that name as soon as I started talking to her. Planetary Essence can talk through the stone or, as is the usual case, from outside it. Your connecting to that stone with their energy inside is what starts the conversation, opens the door.

If you look at Moldavite, it's always a deep translucent green color. The denser the piece of Moldavite, the darker or deeper it's green color. If you hold it up to the light you can see its density. After you've been playing with stones for a while you'll just feel it, or you'll feel it the first time just by looking at it. We're all different and our strong points as well as awareness vary. What you will notice about Moldavite is that it's always green. Why is that?

I was in a class one time talking with a gemologist about stones. He was giving the class. I asked him if any scientists had a breakdown of the individual components within Moldavite. I knew they didn't because her material is very different and not found here on Earth. Therefore there are no common materials.

He looked at me with a smile and said, "That depends on what materials it's combined with." He was really smug about that, thinking he had sidestepped the issue. So, I told him that's not true. Then he gave me an arrogant look as if to call me an arrogant upstart idiot. OK, that pissed me off a little. I was trying to open his mind to what was real.

I told him that anyone can just look at the stone and realize it doesn't mix with anything else because Moldavite is always the same translucent green color. If anything was mixed with it, it would not only no longer be translucent (unless it happened to mix with Clear Quartz) but would also be found in a variety of different colors, like Essenite.

He got mad and just started to walk away but it was at the end of the class and everyone was standing there wanting to talk to him. Before leaving I added that I speak with stones, I just wanted to help him. I left a little frustrated but I've gotten used to it over the years.

People have to reach a minimal point of understanding before they can accept anything, just like our ET family in space. I talk with them all the time but almost half Earth's population doesn't think they exist. Here again is the need for me to write these books for everyone.

Back to Mollae (Moldavite), her Spirit's energy is so wonderfully healing I want to wear it whenever I can. I've been doing so much fighting that I can't keep her on me unless I'm calm. That much energy is damaging to her. Her healing qualities are incredible. I have a few nice pieces that I love to wear.

I've found a few pieces of her from time to time that were superheated when they entered Earth's atmosphere. I looked at one piece and there was a broken off piece of Mollae inside it, she was hurting so I flowed into her without even thinking about it. I started to clean her frequencies but she wanted out of that stone immediately.

I took her out, healed her, and sent her home to be alongside Mollae. She's still with her now, just looked to be sure. As you awaken your abilities you'll be amazed at what you can do. It starts by relaxing and learning to accept what you see and feel. Anyway, I wanted you to understand a little more about how overheating a stone will cause the Spirit inside to leave, unless it's Star matter.

Lava is molten rock but it's not heated the same way or to the same extent as sand while making glass or material flying incredibly fast into the atmosphere, especially when it's a small piece with too little mass to absorb enough of the re-entry temperatures.

Mollae, like all Planetary Essence, will flow into you when you hold onto her, unless you increase the density of your Spirit at the stone contact point which tells her that you don't want her to flow inside you. When this is the case, the person usually puts the stone down. If you continue holding the stone she'll leave her energy up against yours, as if saying hello, so you can get used to it, becoming more familiar and possibly more comfortable with her.

This is part of how all of us, as Spirit, relate with each other. All this and so much more is happening everywhere all the time and because of these bodies and what had always been done to us, mostly the controlling Angels, the majority of people haven't been able to become aware of it yet.

Mollae is a beautiful Planetary Essence being with incredible healing properties. She also pulls more of your own personal self, Spirit, inside your body to maintain your Spirit Core's balance. If someone has a hard time handling Mollae's extra energy inside them they need to stay away from Essenite and especially Star Essenite until they're comfortable with Moldavite.

Stones (Necklaces, Loose, and More)

Stones will flow their energy into you to help if they're in your pocket but more so when they're in necklace form. A full necklace of stone surrounds your Spirit Core so it's more evenly and completely distributed to your core which feeds everything. That's why Diana makes necklaces for everyone at TheSpiritualFoundation.com.

Being Source Spirit inside, she's a natural at picking the stones you need by seeing those stone frequencies which best match yours or feed you the energy you need. She also makes singular function ones for Pineal, Heart, Solar Plexus, Relaxing, etc. I realize that at times it might seem like this book is partially a commercial, it's not. I have put all this together to help you.

Everything seems to cost money and most things do. Again, that's why I feel it so important to explain how to talk to stone. You can find out who's in it as well as understand the energy's impact, as well as the best way to hold a stone to feel its energy, with fingertips from both hands. Usually the hardest thing to do is relax for a moment. These crazy lives of ours keep our conscious minds continually engaged which shuts down our ability to realize our abilities. Once you're awake, you're awake. It's most often the "getting started" or "getting there" part that's the hardest, again like riding a bike or anything else.

Anyone who is Source Spirit can put together stones for you and crank them up. Anyone who's been awake for a while can put together stones that they know are good for you also, they just can't crank them up. Very soon, more and more people will be doing this for others as well as themselves.

Everyone now has the freedom to explore who they really are with nothing to stop them and a new Source Field to help them. Now add to that the fact that your Spirit Guides are not only allowed to help you as much as they want, but if they mess with you they're taken away and replaced, or worse. This is the time of great change throughout Creation, finally.

Diana is strong Source Spirit and knows how the different stone energies flow. This is how she understands which stones, in what size, need to be near each other as well as closer to the Heart, Pineal, and Core (back of neck) areas. Again she's not the only one but she also cranks them up hard. There will soon be more and more Source filled people cranking up stuff, and people, everywhere.

This book contains valuable information on a variety of different stones. The only stone energy books worth reading, at the time of this publication, are those from Melody's "Love Is in the Earth" collection. Even the later editions of some of these books have newly revised definitions.

Most of the stone energy books you'll find talk about how "this stone's energy takes you to the highest celestial realm" or "helps you to receive more money" or any other such nonsense. A stone energy book needs to talk about the stone's individual frequencies, which of your Metabilities they help and how they do it.

I'm trying to finish compiling the rest of the necessary information together for Diana to write her own book about stones, their frequencies, how their energy works and what Metabilities they enhance, as well as other physical aids such as Blue Kyanite helping the digestive organs in the physical body. I'll be gone but she'll probably have a part of me in there. She has never been greedy.

More information on all of these products is available at Diana's store. Just start trusting your feelings so far as what will help you the most at the moment. She sells a lot of products. There's a reason for that, they work.

Just one last thing here, if you don't have the money for something, don't buy it. It's important to take a 5 minute (or more) recess every day to do nothing, to just relax. Find a quiet spot and just let everything go for that special 5 minutes. Realize:

1) You can't fix every problem in your life during that next 5 minutes.

2) If you don't relax twice a day you're not going to be healthy making everything harder to do (so you're hurting yourself).

3) Once you open yourself up to your real self, things fall into perspective quicker, you make better decisions, and you become connected to your many Spirit Guides who will give you all the information you need to handle all your problems (helping yourself and those you love).

Rune Cards

Do you want to learn how to awaken and focus your individual energy focal points, your power points? Go to TheSpiritualFoundation.com and look at J'Arae's Runes of Awakening. Diana created the graphics involved. She's an architect, graphic designer, artist, Source Meta and more. The symbols originated from different lives I've had here through the ages as well as off Planet.

I used to sell sets of wooden runes made from fallen branches but soon lost the available time needed for it. I have made a few sets from a very special Fae Beech Tree here in my back yard. It's not only special to me but has powerful energy. I've fed it for about 26 years, since 1992. If you have, or can find, one of these sets of runes, hold on to them. They're worth a lot of money and that's going to go up when I leave here. They are all saturated with my energy.

The Fae have made and sent me presents which would come out of the ground. I walked by it a few times every day. Sometimes I would be told there was something waiting for me. I would go outside and sure enough there was a new stone coming out of the ground, partially showing itself, enough for me to see and pull it out.

One time a Wood Nymph was flying over a small spot on the ground at night. She was ten to twenty times as bright as a firefly and flying in a pattern representing an infinity loop but each loop varied. I thanked her and said I would get it in the morning. It was dark and I was tired. In the morning there was a special stone there waiting for me, had a very unique shape, almost cut like a crystal. It was my personal Amulet relative to my position in the Fae Realm here on Earth.

It is a solid piece of pure Gaeiraenite and already has energy in it from me since the beginning of the Fae lives here. It was stolen by someone, as well as many other items with it, but will eventually find its way back to my children. They belong to me and my family, no one else. It won't be a problem once myself again.

In J'Arae's Runes of Awakening I use the Elder Futhark Runes (many with new meanings) as well as others I've used both in Earth's earlier ages as well as on other Planets. I believe there are 53 different rune cards. I wrote a small booklet to explain the basic meaning of each card. I also made a DVD in which I pull each card and explain it's meaning for that moment.

There are also cards which cover your body's energetic Power Points. When you pull one you're usually being told to power up that specific ability and use it. Your Spirit Guides will show you something when you pull that card. One thing though. Don't use the cards all day long. The whole idea here is for the cards to help you talk directly with your guides.

If you exceed your limit you will no longer feel their communication. They will be there with you but become silent. Over time the meaning of each card grows as you learn to communicate better with your Spirit Guides. That's what they're for. The Max Power Full Body Sphere that I made will crank up a person's full body energy if they are within 8' of it. Many people like to have one of these Spheres in the middle of a table while they use the rune cards.

You can each talk with your Spirit Guides but you can also take the Power Cards out of the deck and take turns pulling one. When a specific Power Card is pulled, everyone uses that part of themselves to go somewhere and see what they can, either about the place itself or other beings (people) in that area. The person who pulled the card decides what people should look for or where to go to look as whatever they can find there

The whole time you're doing this the Max Power Full Body Sphere is increasing the level of power in your Spirit core as well as the rest of all your Power Focal Points. If the pressure in your head becomes too heavy, just move the sphere farther away from you. This will be due to the Star Essenite.

As you use the power cards and engage your Pineal Gland, Solar Plexus, Heart, Pituitary, and everything else, the Sphere is flooding your body with an over 1,000 percent increase in energy. That's over 10 times stronger. That's also why people put these spheres in their bedroom. If it's within 8' of you, your whole body in being powered up while you're sleeping.

If someone pulls the Pineal activation card, whom ever pulled it will suggest everyone go somewhere to see something. As you use your Pineal to go there it will feed it powerful energy not only enabling it to do so more efficiently but help develop the gland while it's working, like a physical workout for your muscles. I created these Spheres for a reason, to help you. I also "Crank-Up" the whole thing making it over 20 times stronger. That's how they will hit your head with strong energy 8' away.

The more you use the cards the better your communication becomes with your Spirit Guides. All cards will help you do this but some more so than others. There are no cards in existence that have the same symbols available here. I created them other than the Elder Futhark. No other set of cards work your various Metaphysical Power Focal Points or helps develop them as the rune cards do. No other deck will help increase your communicative abilities with your Spirit Guides as quickly or easily.

This is why I had to make them before leaving, that's all. They work as no others.

Spheres

I've made a large variety of powerful spheres with stones relative to either the person purchasing them or a specific energetic function of either the physical body or your Metabilities. I've also made spheres which awaken and empower your body's energy level and increased flow, including while you're sleeping. Stone energy is great, natural, has no batteries or electrical cord, lasts forever, and can be taken with you wherever you are. Just put them near you and they keep making you stronger. They last forever; you can pass them down through your family's generations.

Here's a list of the Spheres currently offered:

Sphere Types, & Contents

All Sphere Stones Are Wrapped In About 2' of Pure Copper Foil

~Pineal Sphere~

This Sphere feeds and strengthens your Pineal Gland and other brain energy fields. It helps to enable your ability to see and focus your multi-dimensional vision.

Contents: - Star Essenite, Stick Selenite, Lapis Lazuli, Celestite, Picture Jasper, Citrine, and others not listed.

~Heart Sphere~

This Sphere helps develop the Heart, Hypothalamus, and Body energy fields enabling your heart to produce a stronger magnetic field which it uses to communicate and understand more easily.

Contents: - Star Essenite, Stick Selenite, Rhodonite, Celestite, Garnet, Fluorite, Carnelian, and others not listed.

~Personal Sphere~

This Sphere is completely tailored to each individual's personal energetic needs. It will compliment your own energy frequencies plus increase your metaphysical strength, calm, understanding, and any emotional needs.

Contents: - Star Essenite, Stick Selenite, & other stones relative to your personal needs.

~Emanation Sphere~

This Sphere helps your Spirit relax and actually extend further out of your body more easily.

Contents: - Fluorite, Emanite, Amethyst, Tourmaline, Golden Tiger's Eye, Quartz, and others not listed.

~Shamanic Journey Sphere~

This Sphere helps your Spirit's emanation as well as taking Shamanic Journeys almost anywhere. Relax, open up, focus on location, and travel.

Contents: - Star Essenite, Jade, Fluorite, Emanite, Turritella, Golden Tiger's Eye, Soft (Denim) Lapis Lazuli, Celestite, Quartz, Amethyst, Picture Jasper, and others not listed.

~Negativity Release Sphere~

Now this Sphere aggressively fights and removes negativity from yourself but can be used to help others you care about. Using this sphere's combined frequencies also tells those on the Other

Side that we have solid intentions of removing the negative issues either within us or others we care about. This never hurts.

Contents: - Unicornite (Peacock Ore), Tourmaline, Stick Selenite, Emanite, Amazonite, and others not listed.

~Healing Sphere (Spiritual)~

This Sphere contains all the frequencies necessary to feed the Heart what it needs to lift your Spirit and help heal your emotional wounds as well as those of others.

Contents: - Star Essenite, Stick Selenite, Rhodonite, Green Aventurine, Celestite, Emanite, Unicornite, and others not listed.

~Healing Sphere (Physical)~

This wonderful Sphere will literally feed your Heart all the energy and frequencies necessary to assist in attempting self-healing as well as others, while it informs the other side that you request help in this now.

Contents: - Star Essenite, Stick Selenite, Deep Green Serpentine, Rhodonite, Celestite, Green Chalcedony, and others not listed.

~Sphere of Relaxation & Joy~

This Sphere will relieve negative feelings and promote happiness or joy. If you want to stay mad, or you're in a very sad moment of your life, this will only help relieve your stress and worry.

Contents: - Unicornite (Peacock Ore), Orange Calcite, Stick Selenite, Shungite, Red Aventurine, and others not listed.

~Brain & Energy Cleaning Sphere~

This Sphere provides the proper energy necessary to clean the Pineal Gland as well as the rest of the brain. It's not just the Pineal Gland that gets coated. You can also have a coating of thick gray opaque energy which impedes the proper functioning of the rest of your brain. It's like a coating of thick scum.

Contents: - Star Essenite, Strong Citrine, Charoite, Lapis, Stick Selenite, Black Tourmaline, and others not listed.

~Merlyn Sphere~

This Sphere is named after Merlyn for the Merlynite in it. It activates, strengthens, and unifies all your energetic fields allowing them to flow together as one. This is powerful solidity and flow of your energy and its functions.

Contents: - Star Essenite, Merlynite, Shungite, Celestite, Aquamarine, Stick Selenite, Amethyst, Garnet, Emanite, Aragonite, and others not listed.

~Max. Power Sphere~

Now this power generator, also known as the "Dragon Egg Star Essenite Fighting Sphere", provides the maximum possible power to all that you are, helping you fight metaphysically or just maximize your workout. This energy will reach you from 5' away, making you stronger while you sleep.

Contents: - Dragon Egg Star Essenite, Star Essenite, Stick Selenite, Celestite, Lapis, Dragon Stone Jasper, Black Onyx, Garnet (small amt.), and others not listed.

~Max Power Full Body Sphere~

This is a Max Power Sphere that has replaced a small amount of power to add stones which activate all 3 power centers in your body. This will have a more beneficial effect on groups of people when gathering for any reason.

Contents: - Dragon Egg Star Essenite, Star Essenite, Citrine, Stick Selenite, Celestite, Lapis, Dragon Stone Jasper, Black Onyx, Garnet (small amt.), Rhodonite, Yellow Aventurine, and others not listed.

~Danburite Sphere~

This Sphere is a more delicate yet extremely high frequency unit. It has small amounts of Dragon Egg Star Essenite Crystal powder in it, minute crystals. It won't alter the energy of the Danburite, only support it.

Contents: - Danburite, Dragon Egg Star Essenite Powder, Crystal Quartz, Rhodochrosite (AAA), Amethyst, and others not listed.

~Dragon Egg Star Essenite Crystal Sphere~

This is the strongest, cleanest, most powerful and awakening sphere there is, anywhere. The personal version is less expensive as it has a little less D.E.S.E.C. in it. Room is needed to modify it to your own set and range of frequencies.

Contents: - Dragon Egg Star Essenite Crystal, Crystal Quartz, Rhodochrosite (Gem Quality), Amethyst, Stick Selenite, and others not listed.

~Comprehensive Nexus Sphere of Understanding~

This Sphere is made to calm down your body & mind while also softly energizing it as well as activate your Hypothalamus Gland, along with your Heart and their connection. It will help you access and maximize your ability to reason that which you're trying to understand.

Contents: - Celestite, Citrine, Jade, Selenite, Quartz, Rhodonite, and others not listed.

~Dragon Sphere~

Just as you'd expect, this stone is loaded with Dragon energy frequencies. This sphere is filled almost entirely with Dragon Egg Star Essenite with a sufficient amount of Dragon Stone Jasper and more. It fires up all of your body's energetic focal points and cranks up all your Metabilities, hard.

Contents: - Dragon Egg Star Essenite, Dragon Stone Jasper, Crystal Quartz, Amethyst, and others not listed.

~Unicorn Sphere~

This Sphere has major issues with negativity. It isn't made to remove negativity from you, although it will, it's made to do what Unicorns do best, attack aggressive negative frequencies where ever they are. Negatively based or people with extreme lower frequencies will not get near it. It will literally drive them away. I know some prominent businessmen who now keep a large piece of Unicornite on both sides of the door to their office. It messes with problem people when they walk in between them.

Contents: - Unicornite, High Crystal Star Essenite or D.E.S.E.C., Stick Selenite, Black Onyx, and others not listed.

> *The contents of each of these spheres can vary a slight amount due to harmonizing with the individual purchasing it.

DVDs

There are a variety of DVDs containing the information necessary to increase your Metabilities, open up different parts of your Metability Flow areas, clean your body's energetic field, remove frequencies that bother you, understand the different auric expressions of the major frequencies within and around you, even how to use J'Arae's Runes of Awakening cards to your best advantage.

There are Power Stones which can be used to increase your Metabilities power levels and help your Metability Network flow more freely, even when you're sleeping. You need only go the TheSpiritualFoundation.com to find them. I made all of them with you in mind. All the necessary information is there.

One of the DVDs will help you understand various energy frequencies and their Auras. Every frequency gives off its own by-product in the form of an auric expression, a precise color relative to its energetic composition, its characteristics. There is a list of the major colors you might see and its corresponding characteristics. I supplied a lot of that information here, but not the discussing of the frequencies themselves, how they function alone and together.

They're tools for anyone and everyone who wants help coming alive. They're also great teaching aids.

Understanding and Feeling Stone Energy

I started giving classes on stones, their energy and metaphysical properties, a long time ago, before any other of my classes. I've explained to a lot of people that stone not only has energy in it but Spirit also, those that didn't come from meteors and asteroids. I've started many a conversation with strangers by pulling a stone out of my pocket and, when I felt them interested or I already knew it was proper, started explaining about stones and their many benefits. It was usually best received by people already in a store to buy stones anyway. People are starting to wake up more and more, every day.

A little over half of the people I spoke with were in a metaphysical store or my classes but the rest were people I met in the street, at the river, a general book store, a grocery store, or even at the DMV and doctor's offices. It didn't matter where I met people; I engaged all of them hoping to fire up their curiosity in things which are helpful to them.

One time I took off in my Chevy truck with a half-ton load of Essenite and everywhere I went I helped people feel the stones, just gave them away. Some people thought I was nuts at first, then most of them understood what I was doing. Many said "No one else is doing this." I often asked "Isn't it about time someone did?" Many people want to know more about the metaphysical. More people are ready every day.

Most people would chuckle at my pickup full of stone but some understood what was happening, they could already feel my energy. There was always that select few that would turn away immediately, usually the religious ones thinking their make believe god would punish them. A smaller percentage just didn't care, thinking I was nuts, so they just kept doing what they were doing. I was here for a few reasons but it was imperative I touched the Spirits of as many people as possible before returning home to stay.

Every once in a while someone would get real upset. They would start speaking in a violent tone. I'd speak back at them and then just stand there, staring at them. I was always very relaxed as my eye's vision would fade from clarity and what I am inside, Arae, would come out and go into their eyes. They walked away every single time. The eyes are the windows to the Spirit inside the body.

Have you ever wondered why most all metaphysical practitioners (psychics) look to your side, away from your eyes, when they're trying to see something? If they stare into your eyes, while looking to see something or communicate with other Spirits, they will only see you inside your body. They have to look away from your Spirit to focus on other things. Almost none of them are aware of why they do that. It's a natural response for everyone.

I once spoke out against 2 or 3 men when they were giving a cashier a hard time. The cashier was getting concerned as they weren't leaving, just yelling at them. I told them that the cashier didn't make the policies and that they should have brought the receipt to get a refund. They told me to stay out of it, that it was none of my business. I looked in the loudest man's eyes and simply said, "Everything is my business."

They took a step forward but then stopped, turned around, and left. I'm not a huge powerful man; they saw my true self in my eyes and decided to leave. When you "get in someone's face" you are projecting your Spirit into the entrance of that body and looking directly at the other body's Spirit, up close and personal. It's a simple natural thing.

Look at yourself in the mirror. Look directly into your eyes. That's who you are! That's the real you! You are literally inside that body trying to drive it through all the experiences you're having while stuck in it. There are many simple little things happening in your life every day that can help you understand who you really are and more about what's going on around you.

Your bodies were made to keep you seeing even the smallest of things in yourselves and the Original First Angels were constantly keeping you in the dark or misrepresenting who you were from inside your brain. Welcome to the truth of all your lives, a controlled existence made to push you through a life with as much anguish and pain as possible when next to none was ever necessary. Heck, these physical bodies were never necessary. Life's a lot more fun and enjoyable without them.

Anyway, back to understanding stones a little better. There is a quiet and unseen communication going on all the time between yourself and any stones that are around you. The only exception to this is the solid mass material that has come to this Planet from space, usually heavier particulate matter. These meteorites or asteroids have never been a Planet and so have never had Planetary Essence placed within them.

The only exception to this is not really an exception anyway. There are pieces of exploded Planets which come here from time to time. Being part of what was previously a Planet, they have the energy of Planetary Essence within them. When a Planet explodes, like when your body dies, the Spirit within leaves but some of its energy is still left within that body.

With soft mass, other than Planetary, the energy leaves soon. With more solid matter, like that of Planets, the residual energy stays in it longer. The Planetary Essence comes out of the Planetary mass but still moves its energy in and out of it as it pleases. That's why when you feel a stone you can feel the Planet or Star's energy in it even when they're no longer intact, or living.

   Gaia, the name given to the Planetary Essence within the Earth, is still alive inside and outside of her body. She's inside the Planet's core but emanates well outside of her body. She is within our atmosphere. Her Aura extends well out into space but her Spirit body is from Earth's core to her outer atmosphere. Her energy is flowing throughout all of her, like water in a stream.

   Different stones here are comprised of different materials such as minerals, elements, and the rest. When her energy flows through different parts of her, they release a specific set of frequencies relative to that piece of solid mass. Each different piece of Planetary matter will somewhat change the frequencies emitted from it. Actually, Gaia pushes her energy through the matter up to you and, when she knows you need or accept it, then moves it into you. She moves her energy, not Spirit. She doesn't put another Spirit inside you, just her energy.

   Remember that Gaia is a being, different from other Planets as we are different from each other as Spirit beings, and she's made up of a large variety of frequencies. She is Planet people. There will be a differentiation between the energy she sends through the different parts of her body but they are almost always the same standard combination.

   We're all made up of different sets of frequencies in different proportions, so are Planets. The stones composition will affect the frequencies coming out of them into a basic format which helps maintain the energy coming into you. That's why Lapis Lazuli is wonderful for your Pineal Field, from the center of your forehead above your eye brow line to just above the clavicle bone structure below your larynx. It's also why Hematite has been used to heavily ground people.

I'm speaking about a lot of small differences here that can get confusing, to me at least. My intention is neither to be confusing nor try to sound smart. I'm trying to feed you as much information as I can about it. The more you know about something the deeper your understanding will be about it. I want you to be able to relate to the powerful aid available in stones, not only in awakening and using your Metabilites but in your daily life, all from the energy emanating from them while on you or in your pockets.

Every element, all materials found in your body when broken down to their smallest individual parts, originated from this Planet and is still found on it today. Your body comes from the Earth, stones come from the Earth. They relate to each other naturally.

There are also other stones here from Other Planets (Moldavite) and pieces of asteroids (Tektite) which have fallen here which also affect us, especially other Planets like Mollae, the Spirit within Moldavite. That's the name she gave me for speaking purposes. On another Planet she would have a name more relative to the indigenous people there, and she does. We'll talk about her and others at the end section of this book.

Tektite can have a grounding effect on us, a sort of calming effect. So, how does this happen? Again, it's simple. Your Spirit's energy flowing through your body is almost always under stress. We're concerned about what we have to do, want to do, and need to do. Sometimes that makes us a little anxious or jumpy. Having a life in a physical body maintains this energetic spiking almost all the time. Now, let's look at Tektite or asteroid/meteor material.

First we need to clarify the metaphysical definition of asteroid and meteor.

The physical definition of an asteroid:

A body of physical mass moving in space, often at very high speeds. They can be from the size of a walnut to a small moon. These can be loose rocks that have always been there or pieces of what was previously a Planet.

The metaphysical definition of an asteroid:

A body of physical mass moving in space, often at very high speeds, that can be from the size of a walnut to a small moon. These can be loose rocks that have always been there <u>but never pieces of what was previously a Planet.</u>

Note: Pieces of what used to be a Planet are exactly that, planetary pieces, not asteroids.

The physical definition of a meteor:

A body of physical mass moving in space and entering Earth's atmosphere, and possibly landing here on her surface.

The metaphysical definition of a meteor:

A body of physical mass, either spiritually empty stone or previous Planet piece, moving in space and entering Earth's atmosphere, possibly landing here on her surface.

It's important for us to realize the difference between a part of a previous Planet and asteroid as the asteroid has no energy within it. Planetary Essence in stone from other Planets can also put their energy into your body to help. Say hello to Mollae, the Planetary Essence within Moldavite. I'll explain this in detail in the Star Essenite chapter.

Getting back to Tektite again, when a stone has no energy in it, it can be calming for some people. This depends on the person holding it and the amount of their anxiety. As the stone has no energy within it, the effect you feel from it is relative to how your energy relates to it.

You can't put your energy into it on a permanent basis but your energy can flow into it when you hold it. This can be relaxing for a while, maybe just a moment though. Sometimes it's immediately felt in the brain. This is due to temporarily putting your excess frequencies into the stone, and momentarily balancing out your Spirit Core and energy focal points. Holding a piece of Shungite with Tektite can be strong relaxing energy.

Basic Stone Energy Benefits Listing

There are more stones documented and available today than I could ever hope to put in a book. There are also new stones being discovered today. As these volcanoes continue to erupt they bring with them new additions to the list. What I've listed here are some of the common stones available today but also notice that most often, but not always, the pigment of the stone is relative to it's energy.

This helps you understand, what's most likely inside it, but don't forget that every stone has slightly different frequencies and so do you. How a stone makes you feel is often slightly different than how it affects others. There's also a major difference relative to your Spirit's primary focal point; Pineal, Heart, or Solar Plexus. Many Solar Plexus people feel Lapis Lazuli energy in their throat or upper chest. Go with the flow and have faith in yourself. Buy or find the stones which you direct yourself to. That happens for a reason.

*** Note #1:*

Stone energy will help you awaken and utilize your Metabilities when they're on your person or near you if they're large enough. As you become stronger, especially Star Essenite as it makes you more powerful than any other stone; you will notice that after a while it doesn't hit you as hard. It's supposed to be like that. The stronger you become the less intense the feeling you get from it. Hand it to someone who can feel stone energy and watch them light up. Stones never lose their energy, you only become stronger.

** Note #2:

The best way to receive the desired metaphysical effects of any and all stones is in a sphere which contains the proper combination of stones with all the correct frequencies and amounts, inside them. They are so strong that they work on you while you're sleeping. When they are cranked up with Source Spirit they are much stronger and the energy lasts forever, no batteries necessary and it never comes out.

**Note #3:

You'll notice below that a lot of the stone names reappear in various categories. They all work well in each field. Brain Body stones are usually found almost anywhere in the brain.

- Crystal Glass – This is a separate item as it needs to be. It has metaphysical properties different from other stones as it's no longer a stone once created. Crystal Glass is made from excessive heating of material, usually sand or other form of crystal substance. When this happens, Gaia's energy inside it comes out and flows back into her. This is why a crystal glass ball has no energy. The Fae love to play with them but there is no Spirit residing inside them, just playing around and through it on occasion.

- Spheres From TheSpiritualFoundation.com:

    Over the years I have made many spheres of stone and copper relative to specific functions, energizing different focal points, helping different feelings, astral-projection, shamanic journeys, calming, all the different focal points, and more. There is a listing of them at TheSpiritualFoundation.com.

    I have built Max Power Spheres that power your Spirit, brain, & body up while you sleep, even from 8' away. Become stronger and enhanced while you sleep. Sound good? Diana and other Source Spirit beings can do this also.

- Star Essenite and Dragon Egg Star Essenite are very powerful stones. You will see them listed in most of the different energy field categories. If you're working these energy fields as an exercise, to build them up, apply these stones. If you are using your Metabilities to find something, consider not using the Dragon Egg and Star Essenites during that time.

    You want to relax to see something as clearly as possible. That's usually, but not always, easier when your energy field isn't powered up so hard. Working out with weights is a good thing. Wearing weighted gloves to paint a picture is not very beneficial.

    * Diana also makes necklaces for people which enhance your Metabilities through her understanding of stone energy and seeing yours, therefore knowing what stones will help you most.

As we describe the metaphysical characteristics of all these stones we need to remember that Essenite, Star Essenite, Dragon Egg Star Essenite, and Crystal Dragon Egg Star Essenite are very strong power enhancers for not only us but other stones nearby or on us.

- ## POWER UP STONES

- Essenite – Gaeira pulls more of your Spirit into your Spirit Core along with her own.

- Star Essenite – Gaeira pulls more of your Spirit into your Spirit Core with hers and R'Ol adds his Star Essence energy to it also.

- Dragon Egg Star Essenite – The same as Star Essenite but it has a higher concentration of Star Matter/Energy and Crystal.

- Unicornite (Bornite &/or Chalcopyrite, Peacock Ore) – Adds its energy to your own, all through your body. It's extremely aggressive towards negativity and acts on its own. It waits for nothing, it attacks.

- Dragon Stone Jasper – Pulls your energy together, gathers it from outside your body and pulls it in.

- Black Onyx – Solidifies your energy, compresses it, makes you stronger especially in the core.

- Axenite & Bronzite – Solidifies all the energy inside your body but be careful, this will make an arrogant person more so.

- Stick Selenite – Strong high vibration increases and activates the body's other energies, helps other energies move through you, very good for the skeletal system also.

  - ## PROTECTION

- Essenite – Gaeira Powers up your Spirit Core 250-900 %.

- Unicornite – (Bornite &/or Chalcopyrite, Peacock Ore) – Adds its energy to your own, all through your body. It's extremely aggressive towards negativity and acts on its own. It waits for nothing, it attacks.

- Dragon Egg Star Essenite & Star Essenite – Gaeira pulls more of your Spirit into your Spirit Core with hers and R'Ol adds his Star Essence energy to it also; Dragon Egg S.E. has more Star Matter/Energy and Crystal. This increases your strength while it's on your person. Your fortitude will be much stronger than you're aware. It's powerful Universal Essence Energy.

- Stick Selenite – Strong high vibration increases and activates the body's other energies, helps other energies move through you, very good for the skeletal system also.

- Axenite & Bronzite – Solidifies all the energy inside your body but be careful, this will make an arrogant person more so.

- Garnet – Solidifies the energy in your Spirit Core and Heart Energy increasing your fortitude.

- Fuchsite – Quickly balances and fortifies the Core Energy and the energies flowing into it, gives you strong metaphysical stability.

- Rhodonite – Pulls your Heart Energy together making it stronger while still flexible.

- Stick Selenite & Black Tourmaline – Stick Selenite vibrates your frequencies harder while Black Tourmaline makes unwanted frequencies slippery and easier to release.

- Dragon Stone Jasper & Black Onyx – Dragon Stone Jasper pulls more of your energy into your body while Black Onyx condenses it.

- Stick Selenite & Amazonite & Labradorite – Stick Selenite vibrates everything hard, Amazonite's high vibration cleans and activates while Labradorite allows the Spirit Core and Solar Plexus to strengthen while remaining supple. Good for physical electrical interference (EFI) areas also.

  - ENERGY SPEED ENHANCERS

- Silver – Moves energy super-fast, nothing in nature is faster.

- Gold – Moves energy fast but stores part of that energy.

- Fluorite – Emanates energy from its source helping it flow better and farther, helps you feel other energies deeper and more easily.

igon Egg Star Essenite & Star Essenite – Gaeira pulls re of your Spirit into your Spirit Core with hers and R'Ol ds his Star Essence energy to it also; Dragon Egg S.E. has more Star Matter/Energy and Crystal.

- Stick Selenite – Strong high vibration increases and activates the body's other energies, helps other energies move through you, very good for the skeletal system also.

  o CALM (Heart Based)

- Obsidian Family – Frequencies which slow down others allowing us to take a better, more complete look at them allowing us a better understanding of them.

- Black Obsidians – Calming energy that also pulls bothersome thoughts from the back of your head and puts them in front of you mind's eye to finish deleting them.

- Snowflake Obsidian – Same as the other Obsidians but the Phenacite in it which helps you release problematic thoughts (frequencies) quicker.

- Muddy Essenite or River Stones – Smooth, relaxing, and calming energy.

- Shungite – Relaxes and flows all energies together helping them work as a singular unit, balances out energy focal points.

- Nuumite – Calms all aggressive frequencies down and releases them below the knees, grounding but does not anchor you to the Earth.

- Jade – Calms your body's energy down, allowing your mind and body to rest for a moment.

- Rhodonite – Pulls your Heart Energy together making it stronger while remaining flexible.

- Turquoise – A calming, relaxing, and hopeful energy.

- Fuchsite – Quickly balances and fortifies the Core Energy and the energies flowing into it, gives you strong metaphysical stability.

- Larimar – The stone of strong but relaxed Hope.

- Amazonite – Increases vibrations while cleaning problematic frequencies. Often used near computers and other RFI electronic equipment.

- Kyanite – Helps separate unwanted frequencies within you and set them aside for a slow removal. Tourmaline and Amazonite work well with it.

- Tourmalated Quartz – Helps remove unwanted conflicting frequencies while helping you remain clear about which frequencies you don't want.

- Crystal Quartz – Clear Quartz is Clarity in all things and can store memories and information.

- Garnet – Solidifies the energy in your Spirit Core and Heart Energy.

- Gold – Moves energy fast but stores part of that energy.

CLARITY, CLEANING, & CLEARING

- Dragon Egg Star Essenite & Star Essenite – Gaeira pulls more of your Spirit into your Spirit Core with hers and R'Ol adds his Star Essence energy to it also; Dragon Egg S.E. has more Star Matter/Energy and Crystal. Your whole body has so much clearing energy running through it that other stones only enhance its ability to clean, good with all other stones.

- Citrine – A powerful focusing frequency which also cleans and clears away unwanted frequencies and physical issues from such materials as Fluoride, Calcium, and others.

- Stick Selenite & Black Tourmaline – Selenite vibrates your frequencies hard while Black Tourmaline makes unwanted frequencies slippery and fall away.

- Amazonite – Increases vibrations while cleaning and clearing problematic frequencies.

- Kyanites – All the Kyanite varieties help dissolve or partially disassemble problematic frequencies and slowly remove them.

- All Clear Stones – All Clear Stones offer clarity of one sort or another.

- Quartz Crystal – Clear Quartz is Clarity in all things and can store memories and information.

- Apophyllite – Softer high vibration energy which is very clean.

- Danburite – Strong very high vibration frequency which will run throughout your body but mostly in your brain.

- Stick & Clear Selenite – Stick Selenite has strong high vibrations which increase and activates the body's other energies, also good for the skeletal system, while Clear Selenite flows in strong waves throughout the body cleaning as it goes also. They help maintain clarity while being strong aids in clearing.

- Iolite – Offers relaxed Clarity and a soft feeling of Calm.

- Clear Calcite – Soft relaxed Clarity.

- Amethyst – This stone's frequencies of accessing knowledge and greater understanding is also beneficial to cleaning, clearing, and clarity.

- Snowflake Obsidian – Same as the other Obsidians but the Phenacite in it helps you dissolve problematic thoughts (frequencies) quicker.

- Silver – Moves energy super-fast, nothing in nature is faster.

- Unicornite – (Bornite &/or Chalcopyrite, Peacock Ore) – Adds its energy to your own, all through your body. It's extremely aggressive towards negativity and a strong cleanser of any negative frequencies.

- HOPE (Heart Based)

- Turquoise – A calming, relaxing, hopeful energy.

- Larimar – A thick calming, stone with strong hopeful energy.

- Hope Jasper – Removes those issues which impede the body's ability to procure feelings of hope while also helping you extend out of your body.

- Fluorite – A facilitator for other stones as it emanates energy from its source helping it flow better and farther, including helping your energy flow in a relaxed state around your body.

- Crystal Quartz – Clear Quartz is Clarity in all things and can store memories and information.

- Stick Selenite & Black Tourmaline – Selenite vibrates your frequencies hard while Black Tourmaline makes unwanted frequencies slippery and fall away.

- Dragon Egg Star Essenite & Star Essenite – Gaeira pulls more of your Spirit into your Spirit Core with hers and R'Ol adds his Star Essence energy to it also; Dragon Egg S.E. has more Star Matter/Energy and Crystal.

o JOY & HAPPINESS (Heart Based)

- Orange Calcite – Strong frequencies of happiness, joy, and compassion.

- Orange Kyanite – Helps dissolve those frequencies which create unhappiness within you. It slowly dismantles them and removes them from you; they dissolve away, in a manner of speaking.

- Unicornite & Red Aventurine – Facilitators that enhance the energetic characteristics of other stones by removing negativity (Unicornite) and increasing Heart Energy flow (Red Aventurine).

- Stick Selenite & Black Tourmaline – Selenite vibrates your frequencies hard while Black Tourmaline makes unwanted frequencies slippery and fall away.

- Silver – Moves energy super-fast, nothing in nature is faster.

- Dragon Egg Star Essenite & Star Essenite – Gaeira pulls more of your Spirit into your Spirit Core with hers and R'Ol adds his Star Essence energy to it also; Dragon Egg S.E. has more Star Matter/Energy and Crystal.

- Gold – Moves energy fast but stores part of that energy.

- Crystal Quartz – Clear Quartz is Clarity in all things and can store memories and information.

- ### SPIRIT EMANATION

- Emanite – Here's an amazing stone in its ability to allow your Spirit and it's energy to flow from your Core and outside of your body.

- Grossularite (2 Types, & in Garnet Family) – This stone has the ability to allow your Spirit to flow from your body also, but not as far away as Emanite. It keeps you a little more Earthy than Emanite.

- Fluorite – Emanates energy from its source helping it flow better and farther.

- Crystal Quartz – Clear Quartz is Clarity in all things and can store memories and information.

- ### ASTRAL-PROJECTING

- *See Spheres at www.TheSpiritualFoundation.com*

- ### REMOTE VIEWING

- *See Spheres at www.TheSpiritualFoundation.com*

- ### SPIRIT CORE

- Essenite – Pulls more of your Spirit into your Spirit Core.

- Dragon Egg Star Essenite & Star Essenite – Gaeira pulls more of your Spirit into your Spirit Core with hers and R'Ol adds his Star Essence energy to it also; Dragon Egg S.E. has more Star Matter/Energy and Crystal.

- Garnet – Solidifies the energy in your Spirit Core and Heart Energy.

- Fuchsite – Quickly balances and fortifies the Core Energy and the energies flowing into it, gives you strong metaphysical stability.

- Labradorite – Helps the Spirit Core maintain stability and proper flow, cleans/clears it a little while keeping it together.

- Yellow Aventurine – Strong Solar Plexus and Core Energy enhancer. It has great stability and a consistent rigid flow.

- Stick & Clear Selenite – Stick Selenite has strong high vibrations which increase and activates the body's other energies, also good for the skeletal system, while Clear Selenite flows in strong waves throughout the body cleaning as it goes also. They help maintain clarity while being strong aids in clearing.

- Dragon Stone Jasper & Black Onyx – Dragon Stone Jasper pulls more of your energy into your body while Black Onyx condenses it.

- Axenite & Bronzite – Solidifies all the energy inside your body but be careful, this will make an arrogant person more so.

- Amazonite – Increases vibrations while cleaning problematic frequencies.

- Shungite – Relaxes and flows all energies together helping them work as a unit, balances out energy focal points.

- Ruby in Zoisite – Thick Heart Energy surrounded by soft relaxation frequencies.

- Crystal Quartz – Clear Quartz is Clarity in all things and can store memories and information.

- Silver – Moves energy super-fast, nothing in nature is faster.

- Gold – Moves energy fast but stores part of that energy.

- Amethyst – This stone's frequencies of accessing knowledge and greater understanding is also beneficial to cleaning, clearing, and clarity.

- Black Onyx - Solidifies your energy, compresses it, and makes you stronger especially in the core.

- Rhodonite – Pulls your Heart Energy together making it stronger while still flexible.

  - BRAIN BODY ENERGY FIELD

- Aquamarine – Thick, powerful frequencies that help energy fields or masses of similar frequencies become more solidified as a unit.

- Charoite – Healing and flowing energy which helps the brain energy fields work together as well as absorb incoming data or knowledge.

- Rhodochrosite – Stimulates compassion and love with an open mindedness due to clarity from the crystal within it as the gray matter helps it be relaxing.

- Sodalite – Activates and strengthens the whole brain, especially related to vision perception and production.

- Unakite – Unakite activates the whole brain especially the Scanner, Pineal, and all Crown Fields as well we accessing memories of other lives by accessing your Spirit on the other side of (through) the Spirit filter above your Upper Crown Field.

- Stick Selenite – Strong high vibration increases and activates the body's other energies, helps other energies move through you, very good for the skeletal system also.

- Danburite – Strong very high vibration frequency which will run throughout your body but mostly in your brain.

- Crystal Quartz – Clear Quartz is Clarity in all things and can store memories and information.

- Amethyst – This stone's frequencies of accessing knowledge and greater understanding is also beneficial to cleaning, clearing, and clarity.

- Amazonite – Increases vibrations while cleaning problematic frequencies.

- Stick and Clear Selenite – Stick Selenite vibrates everything hard activating the whole brain with direct linear pulses while the Clear Selenite motivates the whole brain with large waves which spread the complete width of the brain.

- Dragon Egg Star Essenite & Star Essenite – Gaeira pulls more of your Spirit into your Spirit Core with hers and R'Ol adds his Star Essence energy to it also; Dragon Egg S.E. has more Star Matter/Energy and Crystal.

- Fuchsite – Quickly balances and fortifies the Core Energy and the energies flowing into it, gives you strong metaphysical stability.
- Silver – Moves energy super-fast, nothing in nature is faster.
- Gold – Moves energy fast but stores part of that energy.

  - ## UPPER CROWN ENERGY FIELD

- Dragon Egg and Star Essenite – Pulls more of your Spirit into your Spirit Core and adds Star Essence to it.
- Amethyst – This stone's frequencies of accessing knowledge and greater understanding is also beneficial to cleaning, clearing, and clarity.
- Amazonite – Increases vibrations while cleaning problematic frequencies.
- Stick Selenite – Strong high vibration increases and activates the body's other energy, very good for the skeletal system.
- Citrine – A powerful focusing frequency which also cleans and clears away unwanted frequencies and physical issues from such materials as Fluoride, Calcium, and others.
- Danburite – Strong very high vibration frequency which will run throughout your body but mostly in your brain.

- Phenacite – One of the highest vibrational frequency stones on the Planet, both strong and clean.

- Crystal Quartz – Clear Quartz is Clarity in all things and can store memories and information.

- Unakite – Unakite activates the whole brain especially the Scanner, Pineal, and all Crown Fields as well we accessing memories of other lives by accessing your Spirit on the other side of (through) the Spirit filter above your Upper Crown Field.

- Charoite – Healing and flowing energy which helps the brain energy fields work together as well as absorb incoming data or knowledge.

- Silver – Moves energy super-fast, nothing in nature is faster.

- Gold – Moves energy fast but stores part of that energy.

- Dragon Egg Star Essenite & Star Essenite – Gaeira pulls more of your Spirit into your Spirit Core with hers and R'Ol adds his Star Essence energy to it also; Dragon Egg S.E. has more Star Matter/Energy and Crystal.

  o MIDDLE CROWN ENERGY FIELD

- Crystal Quartz – Clear Quartz is Clarity in all things and can store memories and information.

- Stick & Clear Selenite – Stick Selenite has strong high vibrations which help activate and clean the Middle Crown

Focal Point (middle lens) while Clear Selenite flows strong through the whole field helping Citrine clean in waves.

- Celestite – Frequencies which produce "Understanding" within the brain.

- Green Aventurine – These frequencies are those of positive purposeful Spirit Enlightening energy. They literally help all Heart Energies flow throughout the body as well as your Heart Energy leaving your body.

- Chrysoprase – Strong relaxing healing energy for Spirit and body. Has a wonderful positive effect on your complete self, really love this stone. Watch what happens when you add high quality Chrysoprase to Moldavite.

- Danburite – Strong very high vibration frequency which will run throughout your body but mostly in your brain.

- Amethyst – This stone's frequencies of accessing knowledge and greater understanding is also beneficial to cleaning, clearing, and clarity.

- Citrine – A powerful focusing frequency which also cleans and clears away unwanted frequencies and physical issues from such materials as Fluoride, Calcium, and others.

- Amazonite – Increases vibrations while cleaning problematic frequencies.

- Unakite – Unakite activates the whole brain especially the Scanner, Pineal, and all Crown Fields as well we accessing memories of other lives by accessing your Spirit on the other side of (through) the Spirit filter above your Upper Crown Field.

- Dragon Egg Star Essenite & Star Essenite – Gaeira pulls more of your Spirit into your Spirit Core with hers and R'Ol adds his Star Essence energy to it also; Dragon Egg S.E. has more Star Matter/Energy and Crystal.

  - ## LOWER CROWN ENERGY FIELD

- Crystal Quartz – Clear Quartz is Clarity in all things and can store memories and information.

- Stick & Clear Selenite – Stick Selenite has strong high vibrations which increase and activates the body's other energies, also good for the skeletal system, while Clear Selenite flows in strong waves throughout the body cleaning as it goes also. They help maintain clarity while being strong aids in clearing.

- Amethyst – This stone's frequencies of accessing knowledge and greater understanding is also beneficial to cleaning, clearing, and clarity.

- Citrine – A powerful focusing frequency which cleans and clears away unwanted frequencies and physical issues from such materials as Fluoride, Calcium, and others.

- Celestite – Frequencies which produce "Understanding" within the brain.

- Aquamarine – Thick, powerful frequencies that help energy fields or masses of similar frequencies become more solidified as a unit.

- Charoite – Healing and flowing energy which helps the brain energy fields work together as well as absorb incoming data or knowledge.

- Rhodochrosite – Stimulates compassion and love with an open mindedness due to clarity from the crystal within it as the gray matter helps it be relaxing.

- Silver – Moves energy super-fast, nothing in nature is faster.

- Danburite – Strong very high vibration frequency which will run throughout your body but mostly in your brain.

- Phenacite – One of the highest vibrational frequency stones on the Planet, both strong and clean.

- Amazonite – Increases vibrations while cleaning problematic frequencies.

- Dragon Egg Star Essenite & Star Essenite – Gaeira pulls more of your Spirit into your Spirit Core with hers and R'Ol adds his Star Essence energy to it also; Dragon Egg S.E. has more Star Matter/Energy and Crystal.

- Gold – Moves energy fast but stores part of that energy.

- Unakite – Unakite activates the whole brain especially the Scanner, Pineal, and all Crown Fields as well we accessing memories of other lives by accessing your Spirit on the other side of (through) the Spirit filter above your Upper Crown Field.

o SCANNER ENERGY FIELD

- Yellow Aventurine – Strong Solar Plexus and Core Energy enhancer. It has great stability and a consistent rigid flow.

- Crystal Quartz – Clear Quartz is Clarity in all things and can store memories and information.

- Danburite – Strong very high vibration frequency which will run throughout your body but mostly in your brain.

- Phenacite – One of the highest vibrational frequency stones on the Planet, both strong and clean.

- Stick & Clear Selenite – Stick Selenite has strong high vibrations which increase and activates the body's other energies, also good for the skeletal system, while Clear Selenite flows in strong waves throughout the body cleaning as it goes also. They help maintain clarity while being strong aids in clearing.

- Blue Aventurine – It's frequencies enhance clarity, calm assurance of thought processes, and fortitude.

- Sodalite – Activates and strengthens the whole brain, especially related to vision perception and production.

- Rhodochrosite – Stimulates compassion and love with an open mindedness due to clarity from the crystal within it as the gray matter helps it be relaxing.

- Charoite – Healing and flowing energy which helps the brain energy fields work together as well as absorb incoming data or knowledge.

- Amazonite – Increases vibrations while cleaning problematic frequencies.

- Celestite – Frequencies which produce "Understanding" within the brain.

- Silver – Moves energy super-fast, nothing in nature is faster

- Dragon Egg Star Essenite & Star Essenite – Gaeira pulls more of your Spirit into your Spirit Core with hers and R'Ol adds his Star Essence energy to it also; Dragon Egg S.E. has more Star Matter/Energy and Crystal.

- Gold – Moves energy fast but stores part of that energy.

- Unakite – Unakite activates the whole brain especially the Scanner, Pineal, and all Crown Fields as well we accessing memories of other lives by accessing your Spirit on the other side of (through) the Spirit filter above your Upper Crown Field.

  - PINEAL ENERGY FIELD

- Lapis Lazuli – Produces the frequencies which produce and promote multi-dimensional vision within our brains. The best is from Afghanistan.

- Sodalite – Activates and strengthens the whole brain, especially related to vision perception and production.

- Crystal Quartz – Clear Quartz is Clarity in all things and can store memories and information.

- Azurite – Here lie the frequencies of mental fortitude, belief in self, and self-assurance. It you're correct about something, really feel firm about it, the stone will enhance that to help you believe in yourself. Personal Fortitude.

- Blue Aventurine – Its frequencies enhance clarity, calm assurance of thought processes, and fortitude.

- Charoite – Healing and flowing energy which helps the brain energy fields work together as well as absorb incoming data or knowledge.

- Picture Jasper – The frequencies of image production and gathering. Works to produce High Definition Imagery.

- Stick & Clear Selenite – Stick Selenite's high frequencies increase and activate the Pineal Gland while Clear Selenite feeds strong activating waves throughout the Pineal Field which goes from the middle of the forehead to just below the Larynx.

- Phenacite – One of the highest vibrational frequency stones on the Planet, both strong and clean.

- Danburite – Strong very high vibration frequency which will run throughout your body but mostly in your brain.

- Unakite – Unakite activates the whole brain especially the Scanner, Pineal, and all Crown Fields as well we accessing memories of other lives by accessing your Spirit on the other side of (through) the Spirit filter above your Upper Crown Field.

- Silver – Moves energy super-fast, nothing in nature is faster

- Dragon Egg Star Essenite & Star Essenite – Gaeira pulls more of your Spirit into your Spirit Core with hers and R'Ol adds his Star Essence energy to it also; Dragon Egg S.E. has more Star Matter/Energy and Crystal.

  - ## FRONT OCCIPITAL ENERGY FIELD

- Dragon Egg Star Essenite & Star Essenite – Gaeira pulls more of your Spirit into your Spirit Core with hers and R'Ol adds his Star Essence energy to it also; Dragon Egg S.E. has more Star Matter/Energy and Crystal.

- Crystal Quartz – Clear Quartz is Clarity in all things and can store memories and information.

- Lapis Lazuli – Produces the frequencies which produce and promote multi-dimensional vision within our brains. The best is from Afghanistan.

- Sodalite – Activates and strengthens the whole brain, especially related to vision perception and production.

- Azurite – Here lie the frequencies of mental fortitude, belief in self, and self-assurance. It you're correct about something, really feel firm about it, the stone will enhance that to help you believe in yourself. Personal Fortitude.

- Blue Aventurine – It's frequencies enhance clarity, calm assurance of thought processes, and fortitude.

- Aquamarine – Thick, powerful frequencies that help energy fields or masses of similar frequencies become more solidified as a unit.

- Picture Jasper – The frequencies of image production and gathering. Works to produce High Definition Imagery.

- Celestite – Frequencies which produce "Understanding" within the brain.

- Unakite – Unakite activates the whole brain especially the Scanner, Pineal, and all Crown Fields as well we accessing memories of other lives by accessing your Spirit on the other side of (through) the Spirit filter above your Upper Crown Field.

- Stick & Clear Selenite – Stick Selenite's strong high frequencies increase and activate this field's ability to produce image while Clear Selenite does the same in wide waves.

- Danburite – Strong very high vibration frequency which will run throughout your body but mostly in your brain.

- Phenacite – One of the highest vibrational frequency stones on the Planet, both strong and clean.

- Rhodochrosite – Stimulates compassion and love with an open mindedness due to clarity from the crystal within it as the gray matter helps it be relaxing.

- Silver – Moves energy super-fast, nothing in nature is faster.

- **HYPOTHALAMUS GLAND**

- Celestite – Frequencies which produce "Understanding" within the brain.

- Angelite – Softened frequencies which calm others and help to produce "Understanding" within the brain.

- Silver – Moves energy super-fast, nothing in nature is faster.

- Danburite – Strong very high vibration frequency which will run throughout your body but mostly in your brain.

- Phenacite – One of the highest vibrational frequency stones on the Planet, both strong and clean.

- Rhodochrosite – Stimulates compassion and love with an open mindedness due to clarity from the crystal within it as the gray matter helps it be relaxing.

- Charoite – Healing and flowing energy which helps the brain energy fields work together as well as absorb incoming data or knowledge.

- Amethyst – This stone's frequencies of accessing knowledge and greater understanding is also beneficial to cleaning, clearing, and clarity.

- Stick & Clear Selenite – Stick Selenite has strong high vibrations which increase and activates the body's other energies, also good for the skeletal system, while Clear Selenite flows in strong waves throughout the body cleaning as it goes also. They help maintain clarity while being strong aids in clearing.

- Lapis Lazuli – Produces the frequencies which produce and promote multi-dimensional vision within our brains. The best is from Afghanistan.

- Sodalite – Activates and strengthens the whole brain, especially related to vision perception and production.

- Aquamarine – Thick, powerful frequencies that help energy fields or masses of similar frequencies become more solidified as a unit.

- Unakite – Unakite activates the whole brain especially the Scanner, Pineal, and all Crown Fields as well we accessing memories of other lives by accessing your Spirit on the other side of (through) the Spirit filter above your Upper Crown Field.

- Picture Jasper – The frequencies of image production and gathering. Works to produce High Definition Imagery.

- Chrysoprase – Strong relaxing healing energy for Spirit and body. Has a wonderful positive effect on your complete self, really love this stone.

- Gold – Moves energy fast but stores part of that energy.

- Crystal Quartz – Clear Quartz is Clarity in all things and can store memories and information.

- Dragon Egg Star Essenite & Star Essenite – Gaeira pulls more of your Spirit into your Spirit Core with hers and R'Ol adds his Star Essence energy to it also; Dragon Egg S.E. has more Star Matter/Energy and Crystal.

- ## UNDERSTANDING (Hypothalamus)

- Celestite – Frequencies which produce "Understanding" within the brain.

- Danburite – Strong very high vibration frequency which will run throughout your body but mostly in your brain.

- Phenacite – One of the highest vibrational frequency stones on the Planet, both strong and clean.

- Angelite – Softened frequencies which calm others and help to produce "Understanding" within the brain.

- Amethyst – This stone's frequencies of accessing knowledge and greater understanding is also beneficial to cleaning, clearing, and clarity.

- Charoite – Healing and flowing energy which helps the brain energy fields work together as well as absorb incoming data or knowledge.

- Rhodochrosite – Stimulates compassion and love with an open mindedness due to clarity from the crystal within it as the gray matter helps it be relaxing.

- Crystal Quartz – Clear Quartz is Clarity in all things and can store memories and information.

- Lapis Lazuli – Produces the frequencies which produce and promote multi-dimensional vision within our brains. The best is from Afghanistan.

- Picture Jasper – The frequencies of image production and gathering. Works to produce High Definition Imagery.

- Stick & Clear Selenite – Stick Selenite has strong high vibrations which increase and activates the body's other energies, also good for the skeletal system, while Clear Selenite flows in strong waves throughout the body cleaning as it goes also. They help maintain clarity while being strong aids in clearing.

- Chrysoprase – Strong relaxing healing energy for Spirit and body. Has a wonderful positive effect on your complete self, really love this stone.

- Aquamarine – Thick, powerful frequencies that help energy fields or masses of similar frequencies become more solidified as a unit.

- Unakite – Unakite activates the whole brain especially the Scanner, Pineal, and all Crown Fields as well we accessing memories of other lives by accessing your Spirit on the other side of (through) the Spirit filter above your Upper Crown Field.

- Silver – Moves energy super-fast, nothing in nature is faster.

- Gold – Moves energy fast but stores part of that energy.

o PITUITARY ENERGY FIELD

- Picture Jasper – The frequencies of image production and gathering. Works to produce High Definition Imagery.

- Azurite – Here lie the frequencies of mental fortitude, belief in self, and self-assurance. It you're correct about something, really feel firm about it, the stone will enhance that to help you believe in yourself. Personal Fortitude.

- Sodalite – Activates and strengthens the whole brain, especially related to vision perception and production.

- Stick & Clear Selenite – Stick Selenite has strong high vibrations which increase and activates the body's other energies, also good for the skeletal system, while Clear Selenite flows in strong waves throughout the body cleaning as it goes also. They help maintain clarity while being strong aids in clearing.

- Celestite – Frequencies which produce "Understanding" within the brain.

- Crystal Quartz – Clear Quartz is Clarity in all things and can store memories and information.

- Danburite – Strong very high vibration frequency which will run throughout your body but mostly in your brain.

- Rhodochrosite – Stimulates compassion and love with an open mindedness due to clarity from the crystal within it as the gray matter helps it be relaxing.

- Charoite – Healing and flowing energy which helps the brain energy fields work together as well as absorb incoming data or knowledge.

- Amethyst – This stone's frequencies of accessing knowledge and greater understanding is also beneficial to cleaning, clearing, and clarity.

- Amazonite – Increases vibrations while cleaning problematic frequencies.

- Unakite – Unakite activates the whole brain especially the Scanner, Pineal, and all Crown Fields as well we accessing memories of other lives by accessing your Spirit on the other side of (through) the Spirit filter above your Upper Crown Field.

- Silver – Moves energy super-fast, nothing in nature is faster.

- Gold – Moves energy fast but stores part of that energy.

  - ## HEART ENERGY FIELD

- Dragon Egg Star Essenite & Star Essenite – Gaeira pulls more of your Spirit into your Spirit Core with hers and R'Ol adds his Star Essence energy to it also; Dragon Egg S.E. has more Star Matter/Energy and Crystal.

- Ruby – The most powerful Heart Energy frequencies, with both solidity and flow.

- Rhodochrosite – Stimulates compassion and love with an open mindedness due to clarity from the crystal within it as the gray matter helps it be relaxing.

- Red Aventurine – Soft frequencies of love with soft joy and happiness which flow easily, fast, and smooth throughout your Heart Energy.

- Carnelian – Frequencies which accelerate other feelings but especially those of Heart Energy. Creates "Carnival, Party Time, and other positively aggressive heart based feelings. Actually, all feelings come from the heart anyway.

- Danburite – Strong very high vibration frequency which will run throughout your body but mostly in your brain.

- Stick & Clean Selenite – Stick Selenite has strong high vibrations which increase and activates the body's other energies, also good for the skeletal system, while Clear Selenite flows in strong waves throughout the body cleaning as it goes also. They help maintain clarity while being strong aids in clearing.

- Chrysoprase – Strong relaxing healing energy for Spirit and body. Has a wonderful positive effect on your complete self, really love this stone.

- Green Aventurine – These frequencies are those of positive purposeful Spirit Enlightening energy. They literally help all Heart Energies flow throughout the body as well as your Heart Energy leaving your body.

- Green Chalcedony – Strong solid healing energy for Spirit and body, more aggressive that Chrysoprase, a little less flowing.

- Crystal Quartz – Clear Quartz is Clarity in all things and can store memories and information.

- Celestite – Frequencies which produce "Understanding" within the brain.

  - ## Relaxed Heart Energy

- Ruby – The most powerful Heart Energy frequencies, with both solidity and flow.

- Garnet – Solidifies the energy in your Spirit Core and Heart Energy

- Clear Selenite – Very strong high frequency singular minded energy which runs hard throughout your Spirit Core and everything else it touches. It's very helpful with all bone issues as it runs along your complete skeletal network also.

- Shungite – Relaxes and flows all energies together helping them work as a unit, balances out energy focal points.

- Fuchsite – Quickly balances and fortifies the Core Energy and the energies flowing into it, gives you strong metaphysical stability.

- Chrysoprase – Strong relaxing healing energy for Spirit and body. Has a wonderful positive effect on your complete self, really love this stone.

- Green Chalcedony – Strong solid healing energy for Spirit and body, more aggressive that Chrysoprase, a little less flowing.

  - Compassion

- Pink Feldspar – Frequencies of soft but strong and stationary compassion; comfortable, relaxed compassion.

- Strawberry Quartz – Clarity of Heart Feelings with small addition of compassion/love.

- Rose Quartz – Frequencies release compassion and love from the Heart Energy field, much more suited to "letting love flow" than getting over a "broken heart". Use Rhodonite for that.

- Peach Moonstone – Frequencies which softly and slowly take us from relaxation and calm to stirred or stronger feelings. Great for just meeting someone special.

- Rhodonite – Pulls your Heart Energy together making it stronger while still flexible

- Rhodochrosite – Stimulates compassion and love with an open mindedness due to clarity from the crystal within it as the gray matter helps it be relaxing.

- Stick & Clear Selenite – Stick Selenite has strong high vibrations which increase and activates the body's other energies, also good for the skeletal system, while Clear Selenite flows in strong waves throughout the body cleaning as it goes also. They help maintain clarity while being strong aids in clearing.

- Amazonite – Increases vibrations while cleaning problematic frequencies.

- Green Aventurine – These frequencies are those of positive purposeful Spirit Enlightening energy. They literally help all Heart Energies flow throughout the body as well as your Heart Energy leaving your body.

  o Passion

- Carnelian – Frequencies which accelerate other feelings but especially those of Heart Energy. Creates "Carnival, Party Time, and other positively aggressive heart based feelings. Actually, all feelings come from the heart anyway.

- Orange Aventurine – Soft frequencies of passion, joy, and happiness which flow easily and smoothly.

- Orange Calcite – Strong frequencies of happiness, joy, and compassion.

- Clear Selenite – Very strong high frequency singular minded energy which runs hard throughout your Spirit Core and everything else it touches. It's very helpful with all bone issues as it runs along your complete skeletal network also.

- Charoite – Healing and flowing energy which helps the brain energy fields work together as well as absorb incoming data or knowledge.

- Green Aventurine – These frequencies are those of positive purposeful Spirit Enlightening energy. They literally help all Heart Energies flow throughout the body as well as your Heart Energy leaving your body.

- Love
  - Red Ruby – The most powerful Heart Energy frequencies, with both solidity and flow, the more the red flow the more the frequencies of "Love".
  - Rhodonite – Pulls your Heart Energy together making it stronger while still flexible
  - Rhodochrosite – Stimulates compassion and love with an open mindedness due to clarity from the crystal within it as the gray matter helps it be relaxing.
  - Red Aventurine – Soft frequencies of love with soft joy and happiness which flow easily, fast, and smooth throughout your Heart Energy.
  - Amazonite – Increases vibrations while cleaning problematic frequencies.
- Spiritual Healing
  - Green Aventurine – These frequencies are those of positive purposeful Spirit Enlightening energy. They literally help all Heart Energies flow throughout the body as well as your Heart Energy leaving your body.
  - Peridot – Has frequencies of "Powerful Spiritual Healing Energy" which can partially flow through your Spirit Filter above your Upper Crown Energy Field. Peridot is also found in Unakite.
  - Emerald – Strong Heart Spirit frequencies relative to healing of the Heart Energy itself.

- Chrysoprase – Strong relaxing healing energy for Spirit and body. Has a wonderful positive effect on your complete self, really love this stone.

- Rhodochrosite – Stimulates compassion and love with an open mindedness due to clarity from the crystal within it as the gray matter helps it be relaxing.

- Red Aventurine – Soft frequencies of love with soft joy and happiness which flow easily, fast, and smooth throughout your Heart Energy.

- Rhodonite – Pulls your Heart Energy together making it stronger while still flexible

- Fuchsite – Quickly balances and fortifies the Core Energy and the energies flowing into it, gives you strong metaphysical stability.

- Stick & Clear Selenite – Stick Selenite has strong high vibrations which increase and activates the body's other energies, also good for the skeletal system, while Clear Selenite flows in strong waves throughout the body cleaning as it goes also. They help maintain clarity while being strong aids in clearing.

- Unakite – Unakite activates the whole brain especially the Scanner, Pineal, and all Crown Fields as well we accessing memories of other lives by accessing your Spirit on the other side of (through) the Spirit filter above your Upper Crown Field.

- Physical Healing

- Green Chalcedony – Strong solid healing energy for Spirit and body, more aggressive that Chrysoprase, a little less flowing.

- Chrysoprase – Strong relaxing healing energy for Spirit and body. Has a wonderful positive effect on your complete self, really love this stone.

- Rhodochrosite – Stimulates compassion and love with an open mindedness due to clarity from the crystal within it as the gray matter helps it be relaxing.

- Red Aventurine – Soft frequencies of love with soft joy and happiness which flow easily, fast, and smooth throughout your Heart Energy.

- Rhodonite – Pulls your Heart Energy together making it stronger while still flexible.

- Stick & Clear Selenite – Stick Selenite has strong high vibrations which increase and activates the body's other energies, also good for the skeletal system, while Clear Selenite flows in strong waves throughout the body cleaning as it goes also. They help maintain clarity while being strong aids in clearing.

- Emerald – Strong Heart Spirit frequencies relative to healing of the Heart Energy itself.

- Amazonite – Increases vibrations while cleaning problematic frequencies.

- Fuchsite – Quickly balances and fortifies the Core Energy and the energies flowing into it, gives you strong metaphysical stability.

- Unakite – Unakite activates the whole brain especially the Scanner, Pineal, and all Crown Fields as well we accessing memories of other lives by accessing your Spirit on the other side of (through) the Spirit filter above your Upper Crown Field.

  - ## SOLAR PLEXUS ENERGY FIELD

- Dragon Egg Star Essenite & Star Essenite – Gaeira pulls more of your Spirit into your Spirit Core with hers and R'Ol adds his Star Essence energy to it also; Dragon Egg S.E. has more Star Matter/Energy and Crystal.

- Yellow Aventurine – Strong Solar Plexus and Core Energy enhancer. It has great stability and a consistent rigid flow.

- Stick Selenite – Strong high vibration increases and activates the body's other energies, helps other energies move through you, very good for the skeletal system also.

- Fuchsite – Quickly balances and fortifies the Core Energy and the energies flowing into it, gives you strong metaphysical stability.

- Garnet – Solidifies the energy in your Spirit Core and Heart Energy

- Dragon Stone Jasper – Pulls your energy together, gathers it from outside your body and pulls it in.

- Axenite & Bronzite – Solidifies all the energy inside your body but be careful, this will make an arrogant person more so

- Yellow Jade – Feeds your Solar Plexus calm natural frequencies similar to it while relaxing your body's energy, allowing you to rest for a moment

- Amazonite – Increases higher vibrations while cleaning problematic frequencies.

- Zebra Jasper – Comfortable, relaxing, and assuring frequencies.

- Yellow Jasper – Neutral, natural, relaxing energy.

- Shungite – Relaxes and flows all energies together helping them work as a unit, balances out energy focal points.

- Gold – Moves energy fast but stores part of that energy.

  - BASE ENERGY FIELD

- Nuumite – Calms all aggressive frequencies down and releases them below the knees, grounding but does not anchor you to the Earth

- Shungite – Relaxes and flows all energies together helping them work as a unit, balances out energy focal points

- Tektite – Frequencies of solid mass, no movement to speak of so it can have a calming effect on people, especially when they have excessive energy within them.

- Chrysoprase – Strong relaxing healing energy for Spirit and body. Has a wonderful positive effect on your complete self, really love this stone.

- Aquamarine – Thick, powerful frequencies that help energy fields or masses of similar frequencies become more solidified as a unit.

- Yellow Aventurine – Strong Solar Plexus and Core Energy enhancer that has great stability and a consistent rigid flow.

- Red Aventurine – Soft frequencies of love with soft joy and happiness which flow easily, fast, and smooth throughout your Heart Energy.

- Rhodonite – Pulls your Heart Energy together making it stronger while still flexible

- Fuchsite – Quickly balances and fortifies the Core Energy and the energies flowing into it, gives you strong metaphysical stability.

- Emerald – Strong Heart Spirit frequencies relative to healing of the Heart Energy itself.

- Yellow Jasper – Neutral, natural, relaxing energy.

- Pink Feldspar – Frequencies of soft but strong and stationary compassion; comfortable, relaxed compassion.

- Obsidian Family – Frequencies which slow down others allowing us to take a better, more complete look at them allowing us a better understanding of them.

- Celestite – Frequencies which produce "Understanding" within the brain.

- Citrine – A powerful focusing frequency which also cleans and clears away unwanted frequencies and physical issues from such materials as Fluoride, Calcium, and others.

- Garnet – Solidifies the energy in your Spirit Core and Heart Energy

- Jade – Calms your body's energy down, allowing your mind to rest for a moment

- Amazonite – Increases vibrations while cleaning problematic frequencies.

- Unicornite – (Bornite &/or Chalcopyrite, Peacock Ore) – Adds it's energy to your own, all through your body. It's aggressiveness towards negativity helps clear any inside your Base Focal Point.

- Stick Selenite & Black Tourmaline – Selenite vibrates your frequencies hard while Black Tourmaline makes unwanted frequencies slippery and fall away.

- Stick & Clear Selenite – Stick Selenite has strong high vibrations which increase and activates the body's other energies, also good for the skeletal system, while Clear Selenite flows in strong waves throughout the body cleaning as it goes also. They help maintain clarity while being strong aids in clearing.

- Gold – Moves energy fast but stores part of that energy.

- Dragon Egg Star Essenite & Star Essenite – Gaeira pulls more of your Spirit into your Spirit Core with hers and R'Ol adds his Star Essence energy to it also; Dragon Egg S.E. has more Star Matter/Energy and Crystal.

    o ROOT ENERGY FIELD

- Dragon Egg Star Essenite & Star Essenite – Gaeira pulls more of your Spirit into your Spirit Core with hers and R'Ol adds his Star Essence energy to it also; Dragon Egg S.E. has more Star Matter/Energy and Crystal.

- Unicornite – (Bornite &/or Chalcopyrite, Peacock Ore) – Adds it's energy to your own, all through your body. It's extremely aggressive towards negativity and acts on its own. It waits for nothing, it attacks.

- Axenite/Bronzite – Solidifies all the energy inside your body but be careful, this will make an arrogant person more so.

- Hematite – These frequencies are very strong and settle down other frequencies they come in contact with. They will help you slow down and become more attached to the Earth but be careful not to give this to more negatively centered people. It will make them more so.

- Load Stone – These relaxing frequencies are rather unique. They have a rather neutral energy that usually moves towards other frequencies to create or maintain balance between them.

- Brown Jasper – Neutral, natural, relaxing energy with a strong balanced earthy calm; relaxed, peaceful attachment to the Earth.

- Jade – Calms your body's energy down, allowing your mind to rest for a moment

- Yellow Aventurine – Strong Solar Plexus and Core Energy enhancer. It has great stability and a consistent rigid flow.

- Red Aventurine – Soft frequencies of love with soft joy and happiness which flow easily, fast, and smooth throughout your Heart Energy.

- Amazonite – Increases vibrations while cleaning problematic frequencies.

- Gold – Moves energy fast but stores part of that energy.

- Nuumite – Calms all aggressive frequencies down and releases them below the knees, grounding but does not anchor you to the Earth

- Rhodonite – Pulls your Heart Energy together making it stronger while still flexible

- Fuchsite – Quickly balances and fortifies the Core Energy and the energies flowing into it, gives you strong metaphysical stability.

- Stick Selenite – Strong high vibration increases and activates the body's other energies, helps other energies move through you, very good for the skeletal system also.

- Shungite – Relaxes and flows all energies together helping them work as a unit, balances out energy focal points.

  o EMOTIONS

Fear & Anger are emotions, not feelings. Here are some stones with energy that work against them.

  o Fear

- Helpful Categories: – Power Up / Protection / Calm / Clarity, Cleaning, & Clearing / Core / Heart / Solar Plexus / Base / Root

- Helpful Short Stone List: – Fuchsite, Snowflake Obsidian, Azurite, Axenite or Bronzite, Rhodonite, Black Tourmaline, Shungite, Dalmatian Jasper, Tektite

  o Anger

- Helpful Categories: – Calm / Clarity, Cleaning, & Clearing / Hope / Understanding / Base / Root

- Helpful Short Stone List: – *Amber, Obsidians, Fuchsite, Black Tourmaline, Jade, Shungite, Nuumite, Hematite, Smoky Quartz, Tektite, Aquamarine

The stone category listings I've given you here are not absolute. Different stones will affect different people differently. There's a lot of difference here for a reason. We are all different and each stone has its own unique character, characteristics, just as we do.

Additional Relative Stone Energy Information

Amber is Not a Stone

It's sap that came from a Plant. It can absorb your anger to help remove it from you immediately but replace it with love, compassion, and honor later. It's not bad to leave it in the sun for an hour either. Don't put it in salt.

Keep Stick Selenite Dry

Don't freak out if it gets wet, just dry in warm place, sunlight helps it dry quicker.

Cleaning Stones in Sunlight

Sunlight is Star Essence, under 2% negativity or lower frequencies. When something negative tries to hold onto a stone, the Planetary Essence Energy inside it, less than 2% negativity also, just vibrates it off. Leaving something in the sunlight as well as it being stone from the Planet pushes any unwanted frequencies off of it. It does not charge a stone, only helps it remove lower frequencies from it quicker than by itself alone.

You Can't Activate or Charge a Stone, It's Alive

Stones have Planetary Essence Energy flowing inside them. The only way to power them up is for Source Spirit to do so. Putting them in the Sun or using any other supposed method to do anything to them will do nothing. There is a danger of harming the stone if you superheat it too far.

Do Not Coat Stones with Titanium or any Other Metal

All you're doing is suffocating that stone's energy, locking it up so it can't flow. There need to be laws against this. If you like the look of Titanium put it onto glass which has no energy inside it anymore.

* Essenites, especially the Star Essenites, work with everything other than relaxing energy. I just got tired of listing them everywhere. Use your own judgment. Learn while exploring.

I've given you a general list of functions and stones relative to each function but trust yourself when you pick stones. Try different combinations and never worry about putting different stones and their energies together. None of them will every hurt you in any way. If they feel too busy or push against each other, fine, just put down what you want. There will never be any pain, only gain.

How to Feel and Talk with Stones

This might seem difficult when you first try but shortly after it's as natural as feeling a fork or spoon in your hand. It's a matter of feeling, seeing, and understanding how your body reacts to the stone as well as how the Spirit behind the stone communicates with you. You can talk with the Spirit within the material you hold in your hand. There is no Spirit inside glass or plastic but there is within most everything else.

Your particular make up of frequencies as well as your body's Primary Energy Field Focal Point will have a lot to do with how you talk with the Spirit inside stones. It's a little different for each field. This can take a little time to get used to. The thing to realize is that this is something new to you so expect nothing, wait for something to happen, and then take a moment to understand it.

If you have built in expectations you won't as easily accept the softer or quieter things that happen. Just relax, take a good full breath, and feel the stone's energy. Let it into you, accept it and let it flow. As you begin to feel it, or sometimes you see an image in your mind, just go with it. Whatever is happening is real. Look at it and believe it.

Once you're comfortable with that, it's time to talk to the particular Spirit in the stone. Almost all the stones on Earth, not asteroids that came here as meteors, will have Gaia in them. Her energy is in your body. Try holding onto a stone using the fingertips of both hands. This way the energy goes into your left hand, through your arm, into your body and right into your Spirit Core.

The right hand, arm, and body work the same way. This is the fastest way to accept energy into your body and also the most balanced as it flows equally into your core from both sides at the same time. There are stones which, especially when worn in a pocket, will want to be on the left side where your heart is, or on the right side which flows more into the Spirit Core.

You will "know" which side to use. That could also change for that same stone an hour later. Just keep trusting yourself. Remember, this is all natural and you're a natural at it. Trust yourself. If you don't think about it you'll just put it in the correct pocket without a moment's thought.

Now, holding the stone properly with fingers from both hands, relax and let the stone's energy go into you. Now take one more deep breath and in your mind, not through your mouth, ask Gaia to say hello to you. Be ready to feel, see, or understand anything that happens. Heck, you might even smell something but most of the time you will feel her touch a part of your mind or body with energy. She often touches your Heart Energy.

When you hold a piece of Essenite (stone matter from Earth and Planet Gaeira combined) you can ask Gaia to say hello and once finished there, ask Gaeira to say hello. Don't be surprised if Gaeira says hello a little stronger. She's the strongest Planetary Essence there is.

Star Essenite is the same as Essenite but stronger as there's also Male Universal Essence or Star Spirit inside it. Ask the male Star Spirit to say hello and he will. Once you get comfortable doing this, you can use it to determine whether a stone you picked up off the ground is Gaia, Essenite, or Star Essenite. Keep doing this and you'll just look at the stone and see who's in there with your Pineal and Scanner Focal Points.

That's how you talk to stone. After a while it becomes more and more natural, simply because it is. All this was so unique for me when I first started. Now it's a lot easier than typing on a keyboard. I can talk with words if necessary, usually just a few, but I prefer the "just knowing" method. It's really using all your abilities to understand each other in the Field. Just relax and do it. There is nothing to worry about. It will soon become what it already is, normal.

Informative Tidbits

Dreams, Visions, Deja-Vu, Spirit Guides (w/Ear Ringing), Ghost, Demons, & Exorcisms, Energetic Imprint Recordings, Dousing Rods, Pendulums, Kinesiology, Pictures, Dimensions & Barriers, Mirrors, Ouija Boards & Books, Darting Black Spots in the Corners of Your Eyes, Sage, Spontaneous Combustion

Dreams

A dream is usually like a vision that happens while you're in deep sleep, not consciously awake. Occasionally it's something different, more than seeing a functional or beneficial image or movie. One variation is your brain releasing frustrations or fears that have built up in your mind and unloading them from your conscious thought processes as if through a pressure relief valve. This helps you to keep going without your Base Energy Focal Point activating and hampering or even shutting down your Metabilities as well as your physical ones.

As far as the deep sleep seeing part of it, the key words here are "not conscious". A vision is sometimes the conscious version of a dream. Like a vision, it's usually either an image of something you saw by yourself, a message received from another Spirit out of body, or something another Spirit helped you see by taking you to it. It can also be a variety of other things. It can be what your mind tries to perceive while your brain is being adjusted.

Another variation of a dream is when someone on the Other Side is adjusting your brain's thought processes because you're awakening you Metabilities. This also happens after you're received an I.C.U.C. from a person with Source Spirit inside. You will be put through all your basic feelings, one after the other for 2-3 cycles. You will also see many different images, one after the other and none of them connecting in any kind of pattern that makes sense. You're just being adjusted for different through processes, simple brain adjustment.

    Brain process adjustments are even more important after Source Energy work as the brain is physically growing (the skull matches it). Your brain cells grow larger, they increase in number, and your old thought processes will no longer serve you properly. You must be adjusted to function properly again, especially with your abilities having become stronger whether you're aware of it yet or not.

Visions

    A vision can be many things so let's get started with the basics. The first understanding for a vision is that you're either conscious, or becoming conscious, when it happens. It's usually something you saw, a message from someone out of body, or another Spirit helping you see something by taking you to it. Let's cover the "becoming conscious" comment I just made.

    When you had a "dream" just before you woke up from sleep, it was really a vision. That's why you could remember it so well; your conscious mind was already functioning. Your conscious mind was functional yet calmer and quieter than normal, when it was fully engaged.

It was awake enough to store the image or video of what you were seeing into your immediate memory but you usually had to get it quick as it was likely to disappear if the Planetary Essence didn't find it important. However, as you already know, the Planetary Essence is no longer in any of you, not even one of you, so this is only relative to the past, not your present and future.

Having said that, there have been a few people whose personal Spirit got along well with the Planetary Essence Spirit inside the body with them, and when you astral-projected to get away, they were comfortable going along, as friends. I always loved seeing that. This was a live event when it happened. As it happened while asleep someone might want to call it a vision but is it a vision when you walk to the store?

This was not the most common of events but had happened on occasion. Usually the Planetary Spirit held onto the body it was in as if it was their little Planet, because for the short time they were in there, it was. As you already know, there are no longer any bodies with a Dual Spirit Core, or Kundalini. They've all been removed. Still, I need to put this here as the removal process only just happened Jan. 2018.

A vision can be active like a video or a picture, like a snap-shot taken of an action or image. You might see an explosion occur or just an artifact sitting on a table, maybe even in a room of the last house you lived in on another Planet.

Deja-Vu

Deja-Vu has two different relativities, or characteristics. There is the immediate recollection that you have seen a specific event or situation before, the very moment it happens with you. There is another which is more relative to remembering an event that you had seen earlier in a vision. Each is relative to the other.

As our true selves, we usually see each day here on Earth as part of one slightly longer continuous segment. We usually see today and about 2 to 3 days before as well as 2-3 days ahead. When we are relaxed, close to physically waking up, our conscious mind is aware yet relaxed, not very active. As Spirit we can see things that are about to happen and then barely remember them when they do.

The imagery here is so clear that we literally feel we have gone through this already as we've watched ourselves live it already. There's another way this happens, usually through the Scanner Field but sometimes through the Pineal Gland Field. When we're relaxed, in the same state of not quite consciously awake, we're seeing something that is set to happen in our near futures, sometimes up to 3 months in advance. Source can see months in advance while seeing months behind also, all as one "day" thought process.

I keep telling everyone how they're amazing beings beyond what they currently understand and soon, after a short time, they will begin to understand what I was talking about. I like that.

Spirit Guides (and Ear Ringing)

OK, here's a phrase that so many of us have heard before, that of a Spirit Guide. That word fits just right, it is the name given a Spirit that tries to help guide us through our live. Who the hell is it though? What is it? Are they like Angels, ghosts, or what? This is a legitimate question but not as prevalent as it once was. There is a ruling about which Spirit Beings (people) can be Spirit Guides for which individual field of Spirit. We'll cover that last item in just a bit.

More and more people are discovering things on their own by waking up their Metabilities. How does this *magic* happen? You know I use the word magic very loosely as there's no such thing. You simply apply your thought process to look into something and there you are, using your Metabilities. As you try to do more, usually on your own at first but it's fun to do with others, your Metabilities become stronger as you develop faith in them, in yourself.

A Spirit Guide is literally its name sake. It is any Spirit (sentient energy) out of body helping you while you're stuck in one. You have dedicated Spirit Guides before you ever get put in a body but often other friends will pop into your life at different points to help out where and when they can. You're a Spirit Guide when you're not having a body-life and want to help someone. Your Spirit Guides will never have a greater concentration of lower frequencies or negativity than you do.

You will pick out, or have picked out for you, at least a primary male and female Spirit Guide before being placed into a body. You usually have a secondary set as well, sometimes even more depending on the type of life you were about to go through.

Even the lowest frequency or most negative beings had one Spirit Guide and one powerful Original Archangel when in body. These people will never be in a body again, those few now left. It's not their fault that they were made that way. The blame for that goes to the now extinct Original First Being Male and Female.

Back to the lighter side of things, as you awaken and especially as you're being adjusted, your ears will start ringing. You might hear it in one ear, both ears, or even hear/see/feel it in between both ears. Don't worry about it. It's just our Spirit Guides working on your brain to help you, adjust your internal frequencies to function better metaphysically.

I already mentioned that any Spirit can be your guide, providing its lower frequency percentage (negativity) is no more than yours. What I haven't mentioned yet are the different types of Spirit beings (people) who can be, or will never be, your particular Spirit Guides. This is easy to list.

Angels have never been Spirit Guides for anyone and never will be. They used to control everything in our lives but those Angels have been removed from that position permanently. Almost all the Original Angels, as I've said probably too many times, were deleted. All the Original Angels left are awesome just as the new ones are, the Source Angels. Angels will come in and help us in different ways but they were never made to be constant daily Spirit Guides.

Plant Essence beings have always had many of their own family hanging around with them, and this will continue as long as Plant Essence is having lives. I would like to go into more detail regarding the lives that Plant Essence beings have but I'm left with no time now. Just know that they are Spirit, sentient beings locked into a physical body. They are intelligent, have feelings, and are more than almost all the beings on this Planet realize.

Universal Essence beings, the Female Planetary beings and the Male Star Spirit beings, have all the company they want when they desire it. They are usually in constant contact with their Universal Essence Mate but others hang around from time to time. Believe it or not, it happens a little more with the ladies (Planets) than the men, but seldom so just the same. The Stars (guys) are more in the line of loners.

Animal Essence has always had Animal Essence for guides but many others have joined them from time to time. Animal Essence beings were looked down upon by many of the Human, Fae, and Faeman Essence and Soul beings but that's no longer tolerated. This is another current change that's almost law now; it will be in a few weeks.

What we have left now is the Human, Fae, and Faeman Souls and Essence who would be Spirit Guides for anyone reading this book. However, along with them we have Animal Essence Spirit Guides doing all they can to help us deal with life's issues. I have found over the years of fighting and dealing with almost everything on the Other Side, that the most dependable Spirit Guide anyone can have is your Animal Spirit Guides. Their honor is irreproachable.

There are none with greater honor than that of Animal Essence. With all the fighting I've done, with all the lies almost every single Spirit has given me, the only beings who have never once lied to me are the Animals and a few selective others. So far as the whole singular Spirit Field is concerned, only the Field of Animal Essence has never had one member of it lie to me. That's what I was trying to say here.

The vast populations on the Other Side, all of us as Spirit, get along quite well. We aren't the same when we're not connected to these "excessive input bodies". We're much more relaxed and have access to our intelligence, remembrances of all that occurred in all our lives, our feelings about everything, and the need to do nothing other than what we desire at that exact moment.

You don't have a job but you can help others where and when you want. That's how it is now anyway. The Original First Being Male and Female had real control issues but they're gone, permanently. Often we'll merge our Spirit with another to share certain memories. We can learn from each other, go back in time and watch where and how something happened, or even go to a physical place that we enjoyed while in body, seeing old friends and family members.

Before leaving this discussion there is something that must be said. Never get upset with a Spirit Guide of any type for not telling you accurately what will happen in the future. It's your job to understand enough of what's happening to realize that the future can never be expected to be known. Source Spirit on the Other Side is running everyone's lives and they continually change their minds of how best to do so.

Even if you could read their minds, and that's not possible, they're going to modify their decisions in order to constantly improve everyone's lives. That's a whole lot of data processing going on there and, what do people do? People make decisions of their own every day all day and then change their minds when they feel it's applicable. Now Source Spirit needs to work within that frame, having to maintain certain limits but trying to make things better for everyone, all the time.

Let's add to this the fact that there is a new set of female and male Alpha Source beings running Creation who have never done this before. Only the Original First Beings did this from the first life until May of 2013. Since then it's been chaos over there.

By the time this book is published, that should have changed or is about to be. With these new alphas you will have free will, something that religions always said you had, but never did. How do you have that with one of the Original First Angels hanging on your head going into your Hypothalamus gland to take you over and make you do what it wanted you to do?

The new caretakers have had more lives than anyone ever has or will. They don't demand anything. They have all the experience to do this correctly and most beneficially for everyone and thing. Would you rather go to an auto repair service center that was run by a baker or a different one where a mechanic, who had been fixing cars all his life, was making the decisions?

These new folks are your oldest brother and sister and want nothing for themselves, only to do their job caring for everything. This is literally what they were created for in the very beginning. They are Heart Energy and Fortitude. Arae's serve and protect issues will never fade or go away. You've never had protection like this, only controlled abuse.

Things will be as never before, calm and relaxed lives with the freedom to follow your heart's desires. You'll see it in your physical lives as well as when you're your true self again, free form Spirit.

This brings us to our next discussion, ghosts.

Ghost, Demons, & Exorcisms

Here's a couple popular words that are used often and worldwide. What is a ghost? What is a demon? Can they hurt you? Do either of them even exist? Should I be afraid of them if they do? Where do they come from? Which religion is correct about them? How do you get an Exorcism if you need it? How do you know when you need one? These are all seemingly legitimate questions if you follow any religion. Religions have spread garbage everywhere concerning these topics and everything else they talk about. Here are the simple answers.

Let's look at ghosts first. What are they? The name ghost has been given to various different things, occurrences, and beings. Let's just look at the general consensus of how people think about them. The most common consensus of a ghost is a Spirit that was in a person's body that died and now for some reason is hanging around wandering the Earth.

What people are calling a ghost is just Spirit, sentient energy that's not in a body, that's all. He or she could be trying to tell you something, hanging around a place they still feel attached to and want you to see them. Sometimes, when a person was killed or had another type of tragic event in a certain location, they go back to it trying to understand how it affected them so much.

There are times that people go back the family members they used to live with, or people who were in their lives, and they try to help them or just even say hello. Because no one understands who they really are yet, it's easier to become over concerned with this type of thing. They can't hurt you unless you scare yourself and run into something trying to get away from it. Then, is it really them hurting you or yourself?

There are so many reasons that all this information must be here now. You need to understand who and what you really are, an eternal Spirit which goes into bodies from time to time. Actually it's been too much too often so that's about to be cut down. That's also how we finish releasing any leftover trauma from our previous life. It's how we relax as Spirit. That's the definition of a ghost but people are seeing other things that they're calling ghosts.

When you astral-project to someone, you often show them a very large head, like most of the height of the room you're in. You often have a straight face, looking void of any feelings. That's normal. That part of you outside your body is not attached to your feelings like it is when in you. It's a serious part of you. People have seen that and called it a ghost also.

Sometimes Angels will move something physical near you. Sometimes your Spirit Guides will condense part of their energy and make black blotches or patches of energy to move around you, especially in the corners of your eyes, just to get your attention. Then there's also the case where an extremely tragic event occurred which released so much energy that an energetic imprint recording is created in the exact location where it happened. We're going to talk about that in just a bit.

There are other things which can happen but you need to understand that none of these Spirits out of body can hurt you, unless you run away and into something physical. Try to understand who is there and why they are. If there's any problem just tell your Spirit Guides to remove them, they will. It's good to understand all this now as people are going to start seeing more of each other out of body.

Demons, here's an easy one. There is no such thing as a demon but when the religions made them up they sure made a lot of money on them. It's sad that they still do but this will change. The thought process of the existence of a demon has built the most expensive cathedrals in the world as well as all these other churches spreading lies that were made to control you.

In the beginning the Original First Being Halves went into the brains of the bodies and created religions which their Original First Angels then maintained, controlling the minds of others when they felt it proper to do so. They've been falling away for a while now and this process is about to accelerate until they become what they already are, a worthless thought that overstayed it's welcome. The only thing close to a demon was the Original First Being Halves, what everyone calls god who, with their First Original Angels, beat you up whenever they wanted to.

Our last topic here is a funny one, exorcisms. The reason for the humor here is that there are no such things as demons and the list of beings that were causing issues was a short one, almost non-existent today. The Original First Angels were doing most of the aggressive things to others. Remember that they have instantaneously created a vehicle with a human looking body inside it in the flash of an eye, and then disappear right in front of you again.

One of these idiots is screwing with me this very second as I'm trying to write this. He's handled now, only takes me a second, so much for him. Try to understand that these Angels were created only to serve the Original First Being Halves, nothing else. They were abused through constant control also. This is all part of the sadness I've always seen in Creation as well as my desire to finish this damn life so I can get to work back home.

There were also, on occasion, beings of Dark Original Source brought in, under control, to do the bidding of the Angel controlling him, not like a puppet but there as a handler telling him what to do. You can feel their negativity when they're around. There are very few Dark Original Source beings left now; almost all of them were destroyed by Arae on July 10, 2012. The Original First Begins Halves placed them in front of themselves when they attacked me, to get me (Arae) out of this body. That was a huge fight that only lasted a few seconds.

So, an exorcism is a process where a religious person (all religions are false) gets rid of a demon (which doesn't exist anyway). Whatever is bothering someone was only doing what it was told to do (forced) by the Original First Being Halves. Then, again under the command of the Original Ones, the problem leaves.

So what happened? This "god" thing created a situation, demanded special praise, and stopped what they were doing. See any issues here? How about an excessive need to be worshipped and not being worth anything more than a middle finger gesture?

Energetic Imprint Recordings

Here's another event that I've been able to experience firsthand. I was renting a house with a workshop in the basement. I had just taken a break when my roommate came downstairs. The ceiling height of the under house shop was only a bit over 7', not very tall. I could easily touch it with my hands.

Within a couple minutes we both heard someone run across the floor right above us, starting from the front door, then through the kitchen, and ending into the back bedroom. The running footprints sounded strong. Who ever made them seemed to have the sufficient weight to depress the floor boards as they ran. Nothing moved, just heard and felt it, so did she.

I knew it was male energy of some sort but couldn't see anything alive. I grabbed a large wrench and ran upstairs only to find the house empty, as it should have been. We lived alone there and she always locked the door when she came in.

I checked all the windows and doors and everything was locked shut. I checked every room but knew no one was there. They wouldn't have had enough time to get out of the house anyway. I never hesitated, just took off upstairs; only took a few seconds.

I have serious protection issues and something aggressive was in my house. The only problem was that no one was there. No one could have possibly entered the house or leave. They would have had to jump through a shut window and locked it from outside. We both heard those steps as if I was running upstairs and she was in the shop. We knew what we heard.

It took a little while but I could feel two male energy signatures and one female. They came from living beings but they weren't in the house, not recently anyway. I felt an event that occurred from physical people but it was in the past. I later found out that a young man in the Army, Special Forces, came home and killed a man that was with his wife.

So, now that we've talked about an actual event, what is it? The intensity of the energy from all the feelings expressed at that moment in time left a signature of sorts in the house. It was the energetic recording of an extremely aggressive event. Now the question is, how is it recorded?

The surge of combined frequencies from the event, embed themselves in the field. They just hang there suspended in the field. Anyone on the Other Side, as Spirit, can activate them, play the recording for you. This is why it doesn't just keep playing over and over and over again. This will be adjusted or handled accordingly as soon as Creation's new format takes place.

Dousing Rods

Dousing Rods can be fun. They're often made from metal but sometimes people use wood. They are a temporary extension of your body that is more easily manipulated by your Spirit Guides or if necessary a new Angel will pop in and manipulate them. They can move them to the sides, bend them down, or even give you a soft pushing energy to move you backwards and turn you in another direction. They can take them out of your hands and stick them 3" into the ground if they want to. That's nothing for them.

The concept here is similar to that of a pendulum. Your Spirit Guides are using their energy in your body to help guide you. It's best to talk to them directly but they will help you here too. Why not use these two together. Talk to your Spirit Guides while using the rods. Ask them where something is. Try to hear, feel, or see what they're saying. Then ask them to show you through the rods, or whatever else you're using. That's a good way to learn how to trust yourself, and them.

Pendulums

The metaphysical concept behind a pendulum is that when you hold something suspended from a chain or string, Spirit will show you what you're looking for or asking about. The thought process here that Spirit is talking to you is a good one, because they are. It's just not happening the way most everyone thinks.

You can hold a pendulum over a map and ask help in locating something. You can decide that when you ask a question and the pendulum eventually rotates clockwise the answer is yes and counter clockwise is no. You can use a straight forward and back swing as something also.

Your Spirit Guides will comply and work with you the best they can. Remember that everyone and thing everywhere is always dealing with the inconsistencies and change in life. There is no perfect anything. To attempt to achieve something that doesn't exist is to commit your life to frustration, blaming everything else for the fact that you can't do something that's not real anyway.

So, we have a pendulum in our hands, we ask a question, and the pendulum starts moving. It's a natural thought to think that the Spirit Guide is grabbing the pendulum and making it move, all by themselves. What's really happening is that your Spirit Guide is manipulating your body to make it move in the proper direction.

This is communication with your Spirit Guides. They do try to give you the best answer they can, but they're moving your body, usually your arms, to do so. If you put your arm, the one holding the pendulum, up against a wall or other stationary solid object and ask a question, it will not move. This is because you've taken away your Spirit Guides ability to give you an answer.

I've seen this, tested it out myself a long time ago. I needed to understand everything I could about everything I ran into. The harder my lessons, up to a reasonable point, the more I understood. This allowed me to explain things to others more easily and completely, later.

Kinesiology

Here's an area that has been around for a long time, much longer than the name. What is it? How does it work? Will it always work, every time? This is actually more Spirit Guide action on your behalf as well as your own self inside. Your Spirit Guides are using their energy to manipulate your muscles to tell you something just like pendulums and dousing rods. Also, there are times when it's part of you telling yourself what you need. Let's take a closer look at this.

If you use what they call applied kinesiology to see if your body needs a certain vitamin, it can have value. When your body needs a particular form nourishment you might receive an image of the food which will supply this to you, in your head either from your own self or your Spirit Guides. You can also hold a jar of vitamins in your hand. Try this.

Relax, take a full breath, and see if your hand has a tight grip on it or wants to release it. Obviously if you're holding onto it tightly you or your Spirit Guides are telling you that you need it. Your body will instinctively want it as you know inside that it needs it.

The problem with Kinesiology is twofold. The first issue here is that you're using your conscious mind too much here. If part of your thought process is the want to get something, it can easily override any message from either your Spirit Guides or Spirit inside. Remember, you are the one inside the car (human body), not the car itself.

The second issue here is that you're supposed to be talking to your Spirit Guides in your head, not walking around stores, schools, and work doing muscle testing and more. If you never learn how to trust your communication with your Spirit Guides, you'll never become the full extent of who you really are.

Pictures

I've often spoke of how I won't hesitate to look at a picture I've saved that is relative to one of my specific Animal Spirit Guides when I'm being worked on or feeling really sick. I do this for a reason. I want everyone to understand that there's nothing wrong in doing so. It will enhance you, not work against you and above all else, it's not a sign of weakness in your abilities. Don't let other people's issues become your own. Don't accept them as yours, they're not.

People who would say that either need to feel better about themselves and don't mind doing it at your expense, or they're trying to make themselves appear better than you to others. Either way you look at it, these people are worthless schmucks, worthless to whom, how about everyone? They are not helping themselves, they are not helping anyone else, and they are causing issues in changing Creation into what it needs to be.

Dimensions and Barriers

Birth of the First Dimension

Here's one of my favorite topics although I've spoken less about it than most everything else. As Arae I've made every single dimension and barrier after the Original First Being Male made the 2nd and 3rd Dimensions. I remember what I did and how I did it. If we weren't in these dumbed up physical bodies it would be easier to describe this better but what the hell, let's get at it. What is a dimension? What is a dimensional barrier? Where the hell are they? How come we can't see them?

Before we get into the barriers we need to understand what a dimension is, where they are, and a little more. First of all, a dimension is an individual field of energy containing a separated singular frequency, entirely surrounded a barrier of specific mixed frequencies, which is located either in Original Space or within another Dimension. You will always find a variety of many different frequencies inside it, Spirit people and a whole lot more, but the dimension itself is of only one separate frequency, as if it were the air which we live in.

This helps you understand how dimensions are upper and lower in relation to each other. The higher the frequency within a dimension, the higher the dimension's location will be. This is something you can count on. To do anything else there would have to be incredibly powerful barriers to maintain. That is senseless for many reasons.

There are so many frequencies which make up our area of existence, called Original Space. I don't mean the 3rd Dimension; I mean what all dimensions exist within. This part is more difficult to explain. There is a certain space or area that all of us live in, as Spirit and everything else. Before the First Dimension came together, on its own, an attraction of different energies, there was only one singular area, it was what was. I can't tell you any more about that other than the heavy particulate matter that was also floating around, little pieces spread out here and there.

As a large group of different energy fields came together, due to an energetic attraction to each other, the First Separate Dimension was born. It had no barriers; it was a group of different energy fields flowing in and out of each other as if you put 10 separate colored paints into a large container and they all started mixing themselves but never mixed together. If you looked down you could see all the colors still separate but making some seriously interesting designs.

That's exactly how the First Dimension looks. That's what it's like. Now, understand that those colors are just auric expressions of separate energy frequencies, and you can feel the different energies moving through each other sharing separate characteristics until a large metaphysical electro-magnetic field comes into it. As it moves around with the others it begins to create a sentient energy field, Spirit.

This powerful, unique, singular form of electro-magnetic energy is the bonding agent for other energy fields. Without this energy's interaction, there will be no Spirit. The Original First Being, the very first one to exist (where we came from) was made of 5 different energy fields. This was all happenstance. There has never been a god, only the happenstance of energy mixing on its own becoming sentient (Spirit) which led to the creation (separation of frequencies) of us.

Sometimes when this unique form of electro-magnetic energy comes into another field it brings with it another energy field that it's already started bonding with. This creates, again by happenstance, new beings but at a very slow rate. Once Arae had grown in size and power, he was instructed to create a barrier around the First Dimension. I remember doing so but I also remember Aramaeleous hanging around staring at me.

Aramaeleous kept growing too and eventually became the largest and second strongest of all the Source beings. He was the largest individual being of the two Clean Source Spirit couples made in the beginning by the Original First Being Halves. The more of their energy they released, the smaller and weaker the Original First Being Halves became. That caused issues for them later.

They were still very powerful, they weren't fools. They knew they needed to maintain control of everything and one. The only thing strong enough to ever take them down was the one they built to protect them and everything else, Arae. By having had so many abused, painful, and continuous lives, Arae quickly became the strongest being there was. This happened well before the release of the First Soul Wave. Aramaeleous is gone now too, just like the rest of those two Clean Source couples.

Before leaving the First Dimension, I need to say one last thing, how negativity or lower frequencies are created. What makes someone aggressively abusive towards others? Like everything else, it's a simple matter of understanding a simple concept. The energetic frequencies of heavy particulate matter are very slow. You can relate to this simply by looking at stones.

If you pick up a piece of Hematite, it's very thick, heavy, and feels solid all through it. If you pick up a piece of calcite it's solid but does not have the density of Hematite. The frequencies in calcite are not as dense yet they're heavier than those of Stick Selenite. You can see the progression here. The denser the material the heavier the frequencies, just like the weight.

These slower and lower frequencies have a slowing and lowering effect on the other frequencies as they all come together. As they start to bond they do exactly that, they mix together and become one. The lower the frequencies of the final product or new sentient being, the more aggressive and negative it will be, all from having been made from lower frequencies. There is the creation of negativity. The control of this situation has already been started. It couldn't be fully realized until the Source War was finished.

Getting back to creating dimensions; a singular frequency is separated, expanded in size (mostly width), and then barriers are set up to maintain their existence. If you think of a piece of flat Mica stone, peel off one layer and break it down into smaller sections, then expand it into 100,000 times its volume, you can get the basic idea of a dimension.

That little slice of Mica would have to be spread out thin, but that's how it's done. One singular frequency is separated from the others in a given area and then spread out covering a much larger area, about 100,000 times its normal space. It's much easier to do than explain here.

Mirrors

Mirrors have always been thought of as escape tunnels, entrance points, and even vortexes to other dimensions. The only reality here is that mirrors reflect light, images. The Fae can move through a mirror just as they can a wall.

As you can see dimensionally through the corners of your eyes, mirrors can sometimes help you see this way also. Then, last but not least, mirrors can make a good screen to put images on for you to see, more easily then when they have to create them in your head, especially if they're problematic Spirit which isn't allowed in your head anyway. Nothing can come out of a mirror to hurt you.

Ouija Boards, Books

The Original First Beings created the Ouija Board concept to offer a loop-hole for physical bodies to speak to other Spirits. What they never told anyone was that if someone used it, any Spirit nearby could come out into the 3rd Dimension and stay with you a while making your life miserable.

Your Spirit Guides were not allowed to help you here; you were on your own. The Angels that were assigned to you made sure your Spirit Guides couldn't help you. If they did, the Angels would intervene on the Original Ones' behalf. The Ouija Books worked the same way. Arae, while out of body, stopped this process. Anyone can now use them with no expected issues. It's just another way to talk with your Spirit Guides or other Spirits. They're safe now.

Darting Black Spots in the Corners of Your Eyes

Most of us have seen these events and thought nothing of them. We become aware of something, a dark gray or black something, darting usually away from us, in the corner of our eye. It will happen in both eyes. You'll see it to the right and left, but seldom both at the same time.

This is your personal Spirit Guides attempting to get your attention. They're trying to show you that there's more to life than what meets your physical eyes. Don't just dismiss them as something that's not real or something you made up in your mind; that would be silly. Feel into the energy and you will slowly be able to tell if it's one of your male or female guides.

If it's time for you to awaken your Metabilities, and you haven't taken notice of them yet, they will increase both the solidity of them (look darker) as well as show them to you more often. Some Spirit Guides are a little lazy about it though.

Sage

Sage is well known relative to thought processes involving Spirit, Indian Traditions, and metaphysical abilities such as protection. People say that it removes negativity from the area it's being used in. There's a good reason for this but it's probably not what you've been told. Here's the how and why of what actually happenings when sage is nearby.

Sage is a plant with a smell that's appeasing to most people both in its natural form, live or dry, as well as the smell of the smoke coming from it while burning. This pleasing effect relaxes the physical brain through sensory input but there's more to it than that.

As it relaxes the people in its momentary location it dissolves their aggression. On top of that, abusive or negative Spirit on the Other Side doesn't care much for its presence. The energetic frequencies released from relaxed people make them uncomfortable. It's not that they're being forced away; it's more like a bad taste in their mouth.

Spontaneous Combustion

Here's something that has perplexed people everywhere since it was first seen. Is this real? If so how does it happen, what causes it? I've seen too many pictures from long ago to just write it off as a hoax. It's a real phenomenon, depending on how you define phenomenon, which has happened more in the past than recently. There's a short, simple reason for this.

I've explained how our friends from other Planets have sensors that not only can read the frequencies coming from your body, but also have a data base they can plug that information into and find other lives that you've had in other bodies. Your past lives can be placed into the past history on different planets.

Sometimes a person's Spirit is found in a different body and someone goes after the person, killing the body they're currently in. This is not allowed and a punishable offense. The ET presence here on Earth has been changing for the better in the last 50 years. It is now been permanently changed for the better, with the removal of the 7 Annunaki Clans which previously ruled the Earth.

The Enaugk were the most common perpetuators in this form of assassination although different reptilian groups were often involved. There was a group of assassins used by the ruling Annunaki clans who were often involved in removing people that they had issues with.

The weapon used for this assault built up heat within the body as it burned from the inside outwards.

One Last Note on Spirit Guide Communication Aids

All these aids I've spoken about here are exactly that, aids. You're not meant to go through your life using tarot cards, runes, sticks, pulling your fingers apart, and what have you, to talk with your Spirit Guides. You need to literally talk to them. That's how you become a stronger person for yourself. That's how you develop into who you really are.

Don't hesitate to carry these things with you. Even after you're strong and awake, your brain might be getting worked on and you need assistance with something at that one particular moment. It happens to me from time to time. My brain gets hit real hard and sometimes I look at a picture of one of my Animal Spirit Guides because I can't see anything for myself while my head is like a lead balloon. Sometimes I get so dizzy I can barely stand up. That's another good time to help yourself.

You do want good message, don't you? Isn't that the idea of all this? Remember that you're supposed to be learning to communicate with your Spirit Guides in your head. Instant awareness of important things in your lives only comes from good communication with your guides.

They're on the Other Side right next to you. They can see exactly what's happening with great clarity although they can't tell you what will happen in the distant future, no one can. Sometimes they can't tell you about events in your near future. The future is constantly changing. Your Spirit Guides have all been instructed to help you through these messaging aids only to a point.

When you only want to use them to communicate, instead of talking too, they're to stop helping you in that manner. You also can't use them for every little thing in your life once you understand how to communicate with them. As you learn they will use them with you longer. That's a few days at most.

I've heard people say that using anything other than their intellect means that the person is weak, has no real abilities. Wow, that's not only completely incorrect but arrogant as hell. These people all consider themselves powerful and enlighten beings. Cool, a funny joke.

The first time I heard someone think that I wanted to interject that when I need to look at a picture of one of my guides, I do. I also wanted to tell him that if his role in the awakening was important he would be having pressure and dizzy issues on and off, not being able to do anything. I just smiled and told myself, why bother. He looked at me and I smiled back. He was pissed. Oh well, so what. I care about function, moving forward, not what arrogant people think of me.

When people give you a hard time about either using your abilities or that they even exist, try to remember this simple fact. People who can only use the physical part of their brain (not the major part, the metaphysical) to try to understand something they are completely clueless about, and are either afraid of it or having to make changes to their already confusing life, they are speaking from a place of ignorance, and then stupidity.

When we are unaware of something we're merely ignorant. That's all the word ignorant means, not yet aware of. Ignorance is innocent. However, if one chooses to ignore something that he's being made aware of (has no open mind and refuses to open it), then he's being stupid. This is simple. I'm ignorant of many things like how to put someone into space. I can, however, teach you how to leave your body and go there on your own.

When these people bother you, stay calm, look at them, realize what their problem is and be realistic about whether or not you can help them. Often the only way to help them is by ignoring them. They may come to you later for assistance. Either way, just let them be to themselves. Help yourselves and those willing to learn. Try to enjoy life and fulfill yourselves.

Author's Last Personal Comments

My last life (Gandhi) was devoted to helping people understand that they are all special, none of us are actually "better" than anyone else, Animals deserve our respect, and that at all time we need to respect ourselves and deny the disrespect of others. I'm still me but this life was all about bringing change everywhere, especially on the Other Side.

I also needed to awaken and power up a lot of people here, especially those of Lillian and Araean Spirit Energy. They will take all of what I've started, and everyone, forward into the 3rd Dimensions future, with a lot of help from our family in space. In my last life, as well as this my very last life, I've been myself as much as possible while being controlled in a body, just like everyone else.

I have shown by simple continuous example that I want nothing for myself, only for others. Try to keep that in mind as you move forward. I've been waiting and working a long time to finally stop having lives and perform my desired function, my original format, to serve and protect. I am your janitor, very strong with a big hammer. I will always build for you. I will always stop or destroy whatever comes at you other than within the boundaries of the strife of life.

I've added some information here about my life this time that might help you understand a little bit about the man who wrote these words. I have nothing to hide, always wore short sleeves. I've always been as true to myself as I could while in a body dealing with the Original First Being Halves and their servants, just like you.

I've left you the Creation Series with information that you've never been allowed to receive. I've given you all the tools necessary to help you develop into who you really are, to maximize your potential. I've left you with others to help you become yourselves as well as evolve your physical bodies.

Find Yourself, Be Yourself, Set Yourself Free

When I was 5 years old I was told by my parents that if I continued to say who was on the phone while it was still ringing, or what's about to happen, that I would be punched hard in the face. As a little child that scared the hell out of me, so I buried my abilities and turned away from them. My dad and mom weren't overly abusive; it just really freaked them out, especially dad. When dad finally passed he started turning radios and lights on and appearing to mom in vision during the day. Mom finally understood me better; she finally realized what I was about. Even that late in the game it felt good to see her wake up metaphysically.

The depth of our understanding grows with each step we take along our journeys in each life. This helps us develop into who we really are, how we choose to perceive things as well as act upon them, or not. As our true selves we continue to grow, to evolve into ourselves. We do the same thing while confined to these physical bodies. There is one new very big difference. There is no longer any abusive Spirit involved in running your lives. They will all soon change due to this more than anything else. In this particular life our ET family, from the vast reaches of space, are about to say hello. Not long after you will find out that they have taken away the aggressive group of beings who have been used to physically and abusively control most everything important in your lives here.

There has never been a better time or place to be in a body, the time when since the very first life, Spirits are finally free to have the lives they want. You will watch your children grow up in a new age that you couldn't have dream of, or even been brazen enough to ask for. The initial regime of control over Creation is gone. The new controlling Spirit is self-less instead of selfish. The new Alpha Female and Male Source Spirits will enable everyone to develop at a safe pace, in greater protection, and into their natural selves both individually and as a family. Isn't it about time?

This is the last time I'll ever be in a physical body. Soon now I'll be free, in weeks, not months, a lot of work to do. This book has to be written and before it's finished, everything else will be completed by that time. Now, providing they want to, it's up to others to put it to use, finding themselves where they truly reside, within their physical bodies. No one is a body, only the Spirit inside flowing throughout it.

I've been saying for years now that things will be much better in 2020 than they ever have been, relative to how all lives are run in general, how they flow, and what you'll experience. I've also said that 100 years from now a solid 40% of the Earth's population will be awake or awakening. Before the next 100 years passes everyone will find the events to come to pass close to or as I have stated here.

You'll find the value of these books yourselves. After all, they were written for your benefit. The Creation Series finally explains who you are, where you came from, why things are the way they are, and how they're going to change. This information is not available anywhere else. That's why it's important for you to have access to it, that's all.

Maybe try to take 5 minutes, twice each day, and relax, letting go of all conscious thought and just flow outward naturally. That's the real you inside. Remember, you're an incredible, powerful, intelligent sentient being of energy. You're Spirit spending a few moments of your real life inside a physical form to learn and grow. You're no longer serving anyone, you're free.

Here's a word of caution regarding the sleepers. The name Sleepers represents those who are not yet aware that they're more than a physical body. Some of these people don't want to deal with understanding anything else. Just let them be.

We're not all ready at the same time to do the same thing and we need to be shown things first, making our own initial decisions about how we feel regarding different things. Our opinions (understanding) of things change the more input we feed ourselves, hence the need for the Creation Series. Our knowledge continually evolves which does the same for our understandings. As our understandings increase in number as well as mature our wisdom grows.

Wisdom is the warehouse of understandings and data that we have developed over our lives and once out of body, from all our lives. If you just become yourself, others will see this and those who are ready and willing to awaken will start asking you questions as they begin their journey to self-awareness. Never hesitate to mention things but consider not trying to push it on them. We don't like that either. This also keeps you from becoming frustrated.

Another thing, release the frustrations thrown at you by others; they do not belong to you! Every once in a while you will have someone tell you that you're crazy. Because all my information is new, because I have said things that no one has ever heard of, because I have offered information about myself and what I've done as myself, Arae, not Jay, I had to prove to the status quo that I'm not mentally ill. I went to an extreme in doing so. I had to give you physical proof that I was not mentally deranged.

I placed myself in jeopardy by creating the circumstances to be put into a hospital where after about a week they sent me directly to a rehab center. I did this for out of necessity to prove I wasn't imaging what I see. I had to prove the reality behind my words. You do not. "NEVER DO THIS YOURSELF, YOU ARE NOT ME INSIDE."

If this board of psychiatrists found me to have mental issues, they had the expressed right, and by law would be required to, send me to an institution for at least a year, with no hope of being freed before then. The 5,500 mg of phenobarbital I took would knock down three large adult male elephants. I came out unscathed. They didn't even put me on drugs or schedule future visits. They didn't quite know what to make of me but everyone appreciated how I helped them while there.

This place is locked down 24/7, definitely a high security facility. While there I taught others how to feel their energy, see more of themselves, and tried to convince them to stay away from putting garbage into their systems. One might think me a hypocrite for speaking like that but I had to do what I did to get there. The amazing thing is how almost 40% of the people locked up with me began to realize they were more, and could do more, than they ever realized. Simple meditation techniques helped them also.

I was only there for 8 days. The minimum is 5 days but I was lucky enough to be stuck there through the New Year holiday. All the doctors take a 3 day holiday for it. I arrived in a wheel chair as I had polluted my body so much that some of it was actually absorbed in my bones and took a while to come out.

Three days later I was walking on my own. I have degenerative joint disease so I couldn't walk far or well anyway. Heck, I have COPD, CLLI (Chronic Lower Lung Infections), Cirrhosis, and serious heart issues, two strong heart attacks at the end of 2017. I'm not whining, I'm offering data. I was in a work accident 4/20/2000 when I was almost covered with 10 gallons of gas and burned by a stray spark. I was making bad jokes in the ambulance on the way down to Grady Hospital and its burn center.

The staff at this institution came to know me almost immediately. They didn't know just what to think of me at first. The night before I left, the head shift nurse asked if she could see the QEEG data sheets that Diana had printed out and brought to me during my stay. I handed them to her a she took a few minutes to read them. You should have seen the doctors and psychiatrists reading them.

They would look at the first page, then second, then first, then third, fourth, and back to the first again before setting them down. They didn't just glance at them, they were analyzing the date and graphs on them. This was their field. A psychiatrist is a doctor, they can write prescriptions. These folk are doctors, not nurses. By the way, I was never put on any hard drugs while there, just my lung medications and stuff which are bad enough.

They looked at me like I was an alien sitting in the chair next to them. They realized what the data meant, that I was able to reach across the Atlantic Ocean and do what no one has ever done before; access a brain with my own energy and not only massively increase the amount of energy flowing through it but alter its frequencies also.

I'm only feeding you this much information so you can, if you so desire, research it for yourself. I am what I say I am. I do what I say I do. I prove who I am through my actions, have all my life, and I open myself to the scrutiny of others.

Getting back to the staff nurse to end this conversation, while she was looking at the QEEG data and graph sheets I said, (Kinda funny that an old man in overalls could do that, huh?" She handed me the papers back and smiled saying "The whole stuff in this building is talking about the man in overalls, about what you're doing." I quoted her as best I could. That really made me feel good, a little embarrassed, but nice. That's all I ever want to do, here lies my feelings of accomplishment, helping others.

I was also helping the staff there as much as the patients. They let me get out of my room early and go to a separate room with a lot of windows to meditate. Cameras were everywhere and sometimes a new person would freak out when they saw me there. I was still supposed to be locked down. Their cameras saw me doing "energy exercises". What I was actually doing is deleting a large male Source being. It only looked like making the energy spheres that I taught everyone else how to make with their own energy.

There's just one last thing I need to say before leaving this unfortunate journey. Part of this rehab process is to see a psychiatrist about 2 weeks after you're freed from the institution. Of course, I did. When I sat down with the psychiatrist I grabbed the seat closest to her and relaxed, waiting for her to initiate the conversation. As we began to talk, my Spirit Energy started to fire up. I knew where that was going.

As we started talking I immediately told her what I did and that I was a little different. She already had a file on me from the institution. She stopped talking abruptly and looked at me with a confused yet shocked face and said, "I can feel your energy!" That was funny, I smiled back at her. We talked for about an hour and she said, just like the rehab center, that neither further care nor prescriptions were applicable to me. So we parted on a happy note with me and a somewhat excited yet confusing note for her. Diana and I went home.

Many of the psychiatrists, psychologists, and even medical doctors were aware that there were events occurring in the brain that they didn't understand yet, couldn't explain. That's because the brain actually uses about 85% of its capacity, not 10%. This additional 75% uses metaphysical energy that they can't even see yet let alone understand.

There are many doctors, scientists, and professional people today who refuse to accept anything metaphysical despite the fact they use their Metabilities every day all day. These are some of the ones who need to be left alone. If they ever wake up they will have to want to and the vast majority of them never will. Their children however are another story.

As we finally leave this late chapter in my life I want you to know it was necessary that I put myself through this so you would be left with some sort of physical proof that I was not a nut job, mentally disturbed. I also needed to introduce this information (QEEG) to expose them to the reality of the metaphysical part of our existence. I have also brought my abilities, a brief understanding of Metabilities, and what exists metaphysically into the courts of law here in the U.S.A.

There is one last thing I want you to be aware of as you and those you care for awaken; a warning for you about critics. There is no shortage of people out there, especially on the internet, calling themselves critics or analysts. The proper working title here is analyst as they are self-absorbed and assist themselves only by spreading their opinions in search of personal attention. If there is nothing to learn, only how they feel about something, where's the benefit for others?

When someone can't do something themselves, when they have no personal information to offer you, they might become one of these. They can't do anything worthwhile so they try to put others down that are already doing something worthwhile, how sad they are. They are only seeking attention and praise for themselves. It's best to speak your peace once and then just leave them to their own pitiful existence of sorrows.

If you engage them in their endless shortcomings, how will you do anything beneficial for anyone else, including yourself? When I deemed it necessary, and that seldom ever occurred, I would reply to one of these selfish children with an explanation of what they were, what they were doing, why they were acting that way, and something personal in their life that I couldn't have known about. They almost always shut up but some don't at first.

One of these people, actually two, wanted to keep making up trash and throwing it around on the internet. Both of them initially said that I couldn't do what I said. Eventually they both said, "OK, so he can do that." Take that quote loosely in terms of the exact words spoken. The meaning is exactly that. One of them wound up putting a gun to his head and ending his body's life.

Just state your feelings, your understanding, and let these self-serving idiots go. Things are changing now and you will become known by what you do, not what some schmuck says you are. We're a unique community, the family from the First Original Being who is gone now.

Try to welcome our physical friends from all reaches of space. You were likely once having a life in one of those bodies, try to remember that. We're about to join a new family, one of many different peoples from thousands of other Planets. Creation has already completely changed in the 2nd Dimension. It's coming here now. There has never been a better time for you to be in a body having a life.

Don't be afraid to be who you already are anyway. Be who you are inside more than outside. Do what feels right. Open up and let yourself loose, evolve. Be the change, some will follow, some will leave. Become who you were always meant to be.

Awakening:

Becoming Aware of Your Full Self and All That Surrounds You

Seeing the Fullness of Reality Using All Your Natural Abilities

Everything Starts Happening Now.

Live a Full Life, as Yourself.

Made in the USA
Columbia, SC
02 June 2018